D1083066

THE MAN
AND THE BOOK
NOBODY KNOWS

THE MAN
AND THE BOOK
NOBODY KNOWS

BRUCE BARTON

THE BOBBS-MERRILL COMPANY, INC.

Indianapolis   New York

Author's Note

The Man Nobody Knows and *The Book Nobody Knows* were the work of a young man who did not realize that he might be rushing in where angels fear to tread. Yet when I finished the manuscript of *The Man Nobody Knows*, I did send it to my mother, a saintly and deeply orthodox Christian, and said to her: "I wish you and Father would read this. If in any way it disturbs you or makes you think it might do harm, then I won't submit it. If you tell me that you think it will do good and should be published, then I'll send it to a publisher. . . ."

After a couple of weeks the manuscript came back with a note from Father, saying he and Mother had read it and agreed that it should be published.

I thought it might sell a thousand or perhaps three thousand copies. No one was more amazed when it got on the best-seller lists here and in England, and continued there for a long time. Though I was better prepared for its acceptance, I was equally pleased that *The Book Nobody Knows* also seemed to fill a need.

Nor has the interest in either book ever died. The books have gone on in edition after edition. As I read what I had written long before, I did see ways in which the essential meanings of both books might be made more immediate. This is what I have tried to do. The revised edition of the two books is offered in the hope that whatever service they have accomplished may be a little extended.

Bruce Barton

March 1956

About a week before the death of Sir Walter Scott, he said to his son-in-law, Lockhart, "Read to me from the Book."

"And when I asked him from what book, he said, 'Need you ask? There is but one.'"

—*The Bible in Scots Literature*
JAMES MOFFATT

CONTENTS

THE MAN NOBODY KNOWS

THE BOOK NOBODY KNOWS

THE MAN
NOBODY KNOWS

How It Came to Be Written

THE little boy sat bolt upright and still in the rough wooden chair, but his mind was very busy.

This was his weekly hour of revolt.

The kindly lady who could never seem to find her glasses would have been terribly shocked if she had known what was going on inside the little boy's mind.

"You must love Jesus," she said every Sunday, "and God."

The little boy did not say anything. He was afraid to say anything; he was almost afraid that something would happen to him because of the things he thought.

Love God! Who was always picking on people for having a good time and sending little boys to hell because they couldn't do better in a world which He had made so hard! Why didn't God pick on someone His own size?

Love Jesus! The little boy looked up at the picture which hung on the Sunday-school wall. It showed a pale young man with no muscle and a sad expression. The young man had red whiskers.

Then the little boy looked across to the other wall. There was Daniel, good old Daniel, standing off the lions. The little boy liked Daniel. He liked David, too, with the trusty sling that landed a stone square on the forehead of Goliath. And Moses, with his rod and his big brass snake. They were fighters—those three. He wondered if David could whip the champ. Samson could! That would have been a fight!

But Jesus! Jesus was the "Lamb of God." The little boy did not know what that meant, but it sounded like Mary's little lamb, something for girls—sissified. Jesus was also "meek and lowly," a "man of sorrows and acquainted with grief." He went around for three years telling people not to do things.

Sunday was Jesus' day; it was wrong to feel comfortable or laugh on Sunday.

The little boy was glad when the superintendent rang the bell and announced, "We will now sing the closing hymn." One more bad hour was over. For one more week the little boy had left Jesus behind.

Years went by and the boy grew up.

He began to wonder about Jesus.

He said to himself: "Only strong men inspire greatly and build greatly. Yet Jesus has inspired millions; what he founded changed the world. It is extraordinary."

The more sermons the man heard and the more books he read the more mystified he became.

One day he decided to wipe his mind clean of books and sermons.

He said, "I will read what the men who knew Jesus personally said about Him. I will read about Him as though He were a character in history, new to me, about whom I had never heard anything at all."

The man was amazed.

A physical weakling! Where did they get that idea? Jesus pushed a plane and swung an adz; He was a good carpenter. He slept outdoors and spent His days walking around His favorite lake. His muscles were so strong that when He drove the moneychangers out, nobody dared to oppose Him!

A kill-joy! He was the most popular dinner guest in Jerusalem! The criticism which proper people made was that He spent too much time with publicans and sinners (very good fellows, on the whole, the man thought) and enjoyed society too much. They called Him a "wine bibber and a gluttonous man."

A failure! He picked up twelve humble men and created an organization that won the world.

When the man had finished his reading, he exclaimed, "This is a man nobody knows!

"Someday," said he, "someone will write a book about Jesus. He will describe the same discovery I have made about Him, that many other people are waiting to make." For, as the man's little-boy notions and prejudices vanished, he saw the day-to-day life of Him who lived the greatest life and was alive and knowable beyond the mists of tradition.

So the man waited for someone to write the book, but no one did. Instead, more books were published that showed the vital Christ as one who was weak and unhappy, passive and resigned.

The man became impatient. One day he said, "I believe I will try to write that book myself."

And he did.

chapter I

The Leader

IT WAS very late in the afternoon.

If you would like to learn the measure of a man, that is the time of day to watch him. We are all half an inch taller in the morning than at night; it is fairly easy to take a large view of things when the mind is rested and the nerves are calm. But the day is a steady drain of small annoyances, and the difference in the size of men becomes hourly more apparent. The little man loses his temper; the big man takes a firmer hold.

It was very late in the afternoon in Galilee.

The dozen men who had walked all day over the dusty roads were hot and tired, and the sight of a village was very cheering as they looked down on it from the top of a little hill. Their leader, deciding that they had gone far enough, sent two members of the party ahead to arrange for accommodations, while He and the others sat down by the roadside to wait.

After a bit the messengers were seen returning, and even at a distance it was apparent that something unpleasant had occurred. Their cheeks were flushed, their voices angry, and as they came nearer they quickened their pace, each wanting to be the first to explode the bad news. Breathlessly they told it— the people in the village had refused to receive them, had given them blunt notice to seek shelter somewhere else.

The indignation of the messengers communicated itself to

15

the others, who at first could hardly believe their ears. This backwoods village refuse to entertain their master—it was unthinkable. He was a famous public figure in that part of the world. He had healed sick people and given freely to the poor. In the capital city crowds had followed Him enthusiastically, so that even His disciples had become men of importance, looked up to and talked about. And now to have this country village deny them admittance as its guests——

"Lord, these people are insufferable," one of them cried. "Let us call down fire from Heaven and consume them."

The others joined in with enthusiasm. Fire from Heaven—that was the idea! Make them smart for their boorishness! Show them that they can't affront *us* with impunity! Come, Lord, the fire——

There are times when nothing a man can say is nearly so powerful as saying nothing. A business executive can understand that. To argue brings him down to the level of those with whom he argues; silence convicts them of their folly; they wish they had not spoken so quickly; they wonder what he thinks. The lips of Jesus tightened; His fine features showed the strain of the preceding weeks, and in His eyes there was a foreshadowing of the more bitter weeks to come. He needed that night's rest, but He said not a word. Quietly He gathered up His garments and started on, His outraged companions following. It is easy to imagine His keen disappointment. He had been working with them for three years . . . would they never catch a true vision of what He was about! He had so little time, and they were constantly wasting His time. . . . He had come to save mankind, and they wanted Him to gratify His personal resentment by burning up a village!

Down the hot road they trailed after Him, awed by His silence, vaguely conscious that they had failed again to measure up. "And they went to another village," says the narrative—nothing more. No debate; no bitterness; no futile conversation. In the mind of Jesus the thing was too small for comment. In a world where so much must be done, and done quickly, memory could not afford to be burdened with a petty slight.

"And they went to another village."

Eighteen hundred years later an important man left the White House in Washington for the War Office, with a letter from the President to the Secretary of War. In a very few minutes he was back in the White House again, bursting with indignation.

The President looked up in mild surprise. "Did you give the message to Stanton?" he asked.

The other man nodded, too angry for words.

"What did he do?"

"He tore it up," exclaimed the outraged citizen, "and what's more, sir, he said you are a fool."

The President rose slowly from the desk, stretching his long frame to its full height, and regarding the wrath of the other with a quizzical glance.

"Did Stanton call me that?" he asked.

"He did, sir, and repeated it."

"Well," said the President with a dry laugh, "I reckon it must be true then, because Stanton is generally right."

The angry gentleman waited for the storm to break, but nothing happened. Abraham Lincoln turned quietly to his desk and went on with his work. It was not the first time that he had been rebuffed. In the early months of the war when every messenger brought bad news, and no one in Washington knew at what hour the soldiers of Lee might appear at the outskirts, he had gone to call on General McClellan, taking a member of the Cabinet with him. Official etiquette prescribes that the President shall not visit a citizen, but the times were too tense for etiquette; he wanted first-hand news from the only man who could give it.

The general was out, and for an hour they waited in the deserted parlor. They heard his voice at last in the hall and supposed of course that he would come in at once. But the "Young Napoleon" was too filled with his own importance; without so much as a word of greeting he brushed by, and proceeded on his haughty way upstairs. Ten minutes passed, fifteen, half an hour—they sent a servant to remind him that the President was still waiting. Obviously shocked and embarrassed, the man returned. The general was too tired for a conference, he said; he had undressed and gone to bed!

Not to make a scene before the servants, the Cabinet member restrained himself until they were on the sidewalk. Then he burst forth, demanding that this conceited upstart be removed instantly from command. Lincoln laid a soothing hand on the other's shoulder. "There, there," he said with his deep, sad smile, "I will hold McClellan's horse if only he will bring us victories."

Other leaders in history have had that superiority to personal resentment and small annoyances which is one of the surest signs of greatness, but Jesus infinitely surpasses all. He knew that pettiness brings its own punishment. The law of compensation operates inexorably to reward and afflict us by and through ourselves. The man who is mean is mean only to himself. The village that had refused to admit Him required no fire; it was already dealt with. No miracles were performed in that village. No sick were healed; no hungry were fed; no poor received the message of encouragement and inspiration—that was the penalty for its boorishness. As for Him, He forgot the incident immediately. He had work to do.

For some, formal theology has diminished the thrill to be

found in His life by assuming that He knew everything from the beginning—that His three years of public work were a kind of dress rehearsal, with no real problems or crises. What interest would there be in such a life? What inspiration? You who read these pages have your own creed concerning Him; I have mine. Let us forget all creed for the time being, and take the story just as the simple narratives give it—a poor boy, growing up in a peasant family, working in a carpenter shop; gradually feeling His powers expanding, beginning to have an influence over His neighbors, recruiting a few followers, suffering disappointments, reverses and finally death. Yet building so solidly and well that death was only the beginning of His influence! Stripped of all dogma, this is the grandest achievement story of all! In the pages of this book let us treat it as such. If, in so doing, we are criticized for overemphasizing the human side of His character, we shall have the satisfaction of knowing that our overemphasis tends a little to offset the very great overemphasis which has been exerted on the other side. Books and books and books have been written about Him as the Son of God; surely we have a reverent right to remember that His favorite title for Himself was the Son of Man.

Nazareth, where He grew up, was a little town in an outlying province. In the fashionable circles of Jerusalem it was quite the thing to make fun of Nazareth—its crudities of custom and speech, its simplicity of manner. "Can any good thing come out of Nazareth?" they asked derisively when the report spread that a new prophet had arisen in that country town. The question was regarded as a complete rebuttal of His pretensions.

The Galileans were quite conscious of the city folks' contempt, but they bore it lightly. Life was a cheerful and easy-going affair with them. The sun shone almost every day; the land was fruitful; making a living was nothing much to worry about. There was plenty of time to visit. Families went on picnics in Nazareth as elsewhere in the world; young people walked together in the moonlight and fell in love in the spring. Boys laughed boisterously at their games and got into trouble with their pranks. And Jesus, the boy who worked in the carpenter shop, must have been a leader among them.

Later on we shall refer again to those boyhood experiences, noting how they contributed to the vigorous physique which carried Him triumphantly through His work. We are quite unmindful of chronology in writing this book. We are not bound by the familiar outline which begins with the song of the angels at Bethlehem and ends with the weeping of the women at the cross. We shall thread our way back and forth through the rich variety of His life, picking up this incident and that bit of conversation, this dramatic contact and that audacious decision. We shall bring them together to illustrate our purpose as well as we can. For that purpose is not to write a biography but to paint a portrait. So in this first chapter we pass quickly over thirty years of His life, noting only that somehow, somewhere, there occurred in those years the eternal miracle—the awakening of the inner consciousness of power.

The eternal miracle! In New York one day a luncheon was tendered by a gathering of distinguished gentlemen. There were perhaps two hundred at the tables. The food was good and the speeches were impressive. But what stirred one's imagination was a study of the men at the speakers' table. There they were—some of the most influential citizens of the present-day world; and *who* were they? At one end an international financier—the son of a poor country parson. Beside him a great newspaper proprietor—he came from a tiny town in Maine and landed in New York with less than a hundred dollars. A little farther along the president of a world-wide press association—a copy boy in a country newspaper office.

And, in the center, a boy who grew up in the poverty of an obscure village and became a commanding statesman.

When and how and where did the eternal miracle occur in the lives of those men? At what hour, in the morning, in the afternoon, in the long quiet evenings, did the audacious thought enter the mind of each of them that he was larger than the limits of a country town, that his life might be bigger than his father's? When did the thought come to Jesus? Was it one morning when He stood at the carpenter's bench, the sun streaming in across the hills? Was it late in the night, after the family had retired, and He had slipped out to walk and wonder under the stars? Nobody knows. All we can be sure of is this—that the consciousness of His divinity must have come to Him in a time of solitude, of awe in the presence of Nature. The Western Hemisphere has been fertile in material progress, but the great religions have all come out of the East. The deserts are a symbol of the infinite; the vast spaces that divide men from the stars fill the human soul with wonder. Somewhere, at some unforgettable hour, the daring filled His heart. He knew that He was bigger than Nazareth.

Another young man had grown up near by and was beginning to be heard from in the larger world. His name was John. How much the two boys may have seen of each other we do not know; but certainly the younger, Jesus, looked up to and admired His handsome, fearless cousin. We can imagine with what eager interest He must have listened to the reports of John's impressive reception at the capital. He was the sensation of that season. The fashionable folk of the city were flocking out to the river to hear his denunciations; some of them even accepted his demand for repentance and were baptized. His fame grew; his uncompromising speeches were quoted far and wide. The businessmen of Nazareth who had been up to Jerusalem brought back stories and quotations. There was considerable head wagging as there always is; these folk had known of John as a boy; they could hardly believe that he was as much of a man as the world seemed to think. But there was one who had no doubts. A day came when He was missing from the carpenter shop; the sensational news spread through the streets that He had gone to Jerusalem, to John, to be baptized.

John's reception of Him was flattering. During the ceremony of baptism and for the rest of that day Jesus was in a state of splendid exultation. No shadow of a doubt darkened His enthusiasm. He was going to do the big things which John had done; He felt the power stirring in Him; He was all eager to begin. Then the day closed and the night descended, and with it came the doubts. The narrative describes them as a threefold temptation and introduces Satan to add to the dramatic quality of the event. In our simple story we need not spend much time with the description of Satan. We do not know whether he is to be regarded as a personality or as a personification of an inner experience. The temptation is more real without him, more akin to our own trials and doubts. With him or without him, however, the meaning of the experience is clear.

This is its meaning: the day of supreme assurance had passed; the days of fearful misgiving had come. What man of outstanding genius has ever been allowed to escape them? For how many days and weeks do you think the soul of Lincoln must have been tortured? Inside himself he felt his power, but where and when would opportunity come? Must he forever ride the country circuit, and sit in a dingy office settling a community's petty disputes? Had he perhaps mistaken the inner message? Was he, after all, only a common fellow—a fair country lawyer and a good teller of jokes? Those who rode with him on the circuit testify to his terrifying moods of silence. What solemn thoughts besieged him in those silences? What fear of failure? What futile rebellion at the narrow limits of his life?

The days of Jesus' doubt are set down as forty in number. It is easy to imagine that lonely struggle. He had left a good trade among people who knew and trusted Him—and for what? To become a wandering preacher, talking to folks who never heard of Him? And what was He to talk about? How, with His lack of experience, should He find words for His message? Where should He begin? Who would listen? *Would* they listen? Hadn't He perhaps made a mistake? Satan, says the narrative, tempted Him, saying: "You are hungry; here are stones. Make them into bread." The temptation of material success. It was entirely unnecessary for Him to be hungry *ever*. He had a good trade; He knew well enough that His organizing ability was better than Joseph's. He could build up a far more prosperous business and acquire comfort and wealth. Why not?

Satan comes in again, according to the narrative, taking Him up into a high mountain and showing Him the kingdoms of the world. "All these can be yours, if you will only compromise." He could go to Jerusalem and enter the priesthood; that was a sure road to distinction. He could do good in that way, and have the satisfaction of success as well. Or He might enter the public service and seek political leadership. There was plenty of discontent on which He could have capitalized, and He knew the farmer and the laborer. He was one of them; they would listen to Him.

For forty days and nights the incessant fight went on, but, once settled, it was settled forever. In the calm of that wilderness there came the majestic conviction which is the very soul of leadership—the faith that His spirit was linked with the Eternal, that God had sent Him into the world to do a work which no one else could do, which—if He neglected it—

would never be done. Magnify this temptation scene as greatly as you will; say that God spoke more clearly to Him than
to anyone else who has ever lived. It is true. But to *every*
man of vision the clear Voice speaks; there is no great leadership where there is not a mystic. Nothing splendid has ever
been achieved except by those who dared believe that something inside themselves was superior to circumstance. To
choose the sure thing is treason to the soul. . . .

If this was not the meaning of the forty days in the wilderness, if Jesus did not have a *real* temptation which might have
ended in His going back to the bench at Nazareth, then the
forty days' struggle has no real significance to us. The youth
who had been a carpenter stayed in the wilderness; a man
came out. Not the full-fledged Master who within the
shadow of the cross could cry, "I have overcome the world."
He had still much growth to make, much progress in vision
and self-confidence. But the beginnings were there. Men
who looked on Him from that hour felt the authority of one
who has put his spiritual house in order and knows clearly
what he is about.

The mastery of ideas, the achievement of ideals—what we
call success is always exciting; we never grow tired of asking
what and how. What, then, were the principal elements in
His power over men? How was it that the boy from a country village became the greatest leader?

First of all, He must have had the voice and manner of the
leader—the personal magnetism which begets loyalty and
commands respect. The beginnings of it were present in Him
even as a boy. John felt them. On the day when John looked
up from the river where he was baptizing converts and saw
Jesus standing on the bank, he drew back in protest. "I have
need to be baptized of thee," he exclaimed, "and comest thou
to me?" The lesser man recognized the greater instinctively.
We speak of personal magnetism as though there were some-

thing mysterious about it—a magic quality bestowed on one in a thousand and denied to all the rest. This is not true. The essential element in personal magnetism is a consuming sincerity—an overwhelming faith in the importance of the work one has to do. Emerson said, "What you *are* thunders so loud I can't hear what you say." The hardened French captain, Robert de Baudricourt, could hardly be expected to believe a peasant girl's story about heavenly voices promising she would do what the Dauphin's armies couldn't. Yet he gave Joan of Arc her first sword.

Most of us go through the world mentally divided against ourselves. We wonder whether we are in the right jobs, whether we are making the right investments, whether, after all, anything is as important as it seems to be. Our enemies are those of our own being and creation. Instinctively we wait for a commanding voice, for one who shall say authoritatively, "I have the truth. This way lies happiness and salvation." There was in Jesus supremely that quality of conviction.

Even very prominent people were moved by it. Jesus had been in Jerusalem only a day or two when there came a knock at His door at night. He opened it to find Nicodemus, one of the principal men of the city, a member of the Sanhedrin, a supreme court judge. One feels the dramatic quality of the meeting—the young, almost unknown teacher and the great man, half curious, half convinced. It would have been easy to make a mistake. Jesus might very naturally have expressed His sense of honor at the visit, might have said: "I appreciate your coming, sir. You are an older man and successful. I am just starting on my work. I should like to have you advise me as to how I may best proceed." But there was no such note in the interview—no effort to make it easy for this notable visitor to become a convert. One catches his breath involuntarily at the audacity of the speech:

"Verily, verily, I say to you, Nicodemus, except you are born again you can not see the kingdom of Heaven." And a few moments later, "If I have told you earthly things and you have not believed, how shall you believe if I tell you heavenly things?"

The famous visitor did not enroll as a disciple, was not invited to enroll; but he never forgot the impression made by the young man's amazing self-assurance. In a few weeks the crowds along the shores of the Sea of Galilee were to feel the same power and respond to it. They were quite accustomed to the discourses of the Scribes and Pharisees—long, involved arguments backed up by many citations from the law. But this teacher was different. He quoted nobody; His own word was offered as sufficient. He taught as "one having authority and not as the scribes."

Still later we have yet more striking proof of the power that supreme conviction can carry. At this date He had become so large a public influence as to threaten the peace of the rulers, and they sent a detachment of soldiers to arrest Him. They were stern men, presumably immune to sentiment. They returned, after a while, empty-handed.

"What's the matter?" their commander demanded angrily. "Why didn't you bring Him in?"

And they, smarting under their failure and hardly knowing how to explain it, could make only a surly excuse.

"You'll have to send someone else," they said. "We don't want to go against Him. *Never man so spake.*"

They were armed; He had no defense but His manner and tone, but these were enough. In any crowd and in any circumstances the leader stands out. By the power of his faith in himself he commands, and men instinctively obey.

This blazing conviction was the first and greatest element in the success of Jesus. The second was His powerful gift of picking men and recognizing hidden capacities in them. It

must have amazed Nicodemus when he learned the names of
the twelve whom the young teacher had chosen to be His
associates. What a list! Not a single well-known person on
it. Nobody who had ever accomplished anything. A hap-
hazard collection of fishermen and small-town businessmen,
and one tax collector—a member of the most hated element
in the community. What a crowd!

Nowhere is there such a startling example of success in
leadership as the way in which that organization was brought
together. Take the tax collector, Matthew, as the most striking instance. His occupation carried a heavy weight of social
ostracism, but it was profitable. He was probably well-to-do
according to the simple standards of the neighborhood; certainly he was a busy man and not subject to impulsive action.
His addition to the group of disciples is told in a single sentence:

"And *as Jesus passed by*, he called Matthew."

Amazing. No argument; no pleading. A small leader
would have been compelled to set up the advantages of the
opportunity. "Of course you are doing well where you are
and making money," He might have said. "I can't offer you
as much as you are getting; in fact you may have some difficulty in making ends meet. But I think we are going to have
an interesting time and shall probably accomplish a big work."
Such a conversation would have been met with Matthew's
reply that he would "have to think it over," and the world
would never have heard his name.

There was no such trifling with Jesus. *As He passed by*
He called Matthew. No leader in the world can read that
sentence without acknowledging that here indeed is the
Master.

He had the born leader's gift for seeing powers in men of
which they themselves were often almost unconscious. One
day as He was coming into a certain town a tremendous

crowd pressed around Him. There was a rich man named Zacchaeus in the town, small in stature, but with such keen business ability that he had got himself generally disliked. Being curious to see the distinguished visitor, he had climbed up into a tree. Imagine his surprise when Jesus stopped under the tree and commanded him to come down, saying, "Today I intend to eat at your house." The crowd was stunned. Some of the bolder spirits took it on themselves to tell Jesus of His social blunder. He couldn't afford to make the mistake of visiting Zacchaeus, they said. Their protests were without avail. They saw in Zacchaeus merely a dishonest and greedy little man; He saw in him a person of unusual generosity and a fine sense of justice, who needed only to have those qualities revealed by someone who understood. So with Matthew—the crowd saw only a despised taxgatherer. Jesus saw the potential writer of a book which will live forever.

So also with that "certain Centurion," who is one of the anonymous characters in history that every businessman would like to meet. The disciples brought him to Jesus with some misgivings and apology. They said, "Of course this man is a Roman employee, and you may reprove us for introducing him. But really he is a very good fellow, a generous man and a respecter of our faith." Jesus and the Centurion looking at each other found an immediate bond of union— each responding to the other's strength.

Said the Centurion: "Master, my servant is ill; but it is unnecessary for you to visit my house. I understand how such things are done, for I, too, am a man of authority; I say to this man 'Go' and he goeth; and to another 'Come,' and he cometh; and to my servant, 'Do this,' and he doeth it. Therefore, speak the word only, and I know my servant will be healed."

Jesus' face kindled with admiration. "I have not found anywhere such faith as this," He exclaimed. This man understood Him. The Centurion knew from his own experience that authority depends on faith, and that faith may depend on authority. Every businessman, every leader in any field today, knows—or should know—what the Centurion knew.

Having gathered together His organization, there remained for Jesus the tremendous task of training it. And herein lay the third great element of His success—His vast unending patience. The Church has attached to each of the disciples the title of Saint, and it may be that thinking of them exclusively as Saints robs us of an essential reality. They were very far from sainthood when He picked them up. For three years He had them with Him day and night, His whole energy and resources poured out in an effort to create an understanding in them. Yet through it all they never fully understood. We have seen, at the beginning of this chapter, an example of their petulance. The narratives are full of similar discouragements.

In spite of all He could do or say, they were persuaded that He planned to overthrow the Roman power and set Himself up as ruler in Jerusalem. Hence they never tired of wrangling as to how the offices should be divided. Two of them, James and John, got their mother to come to Him and ask that her sons might sit, one on His right hand and one on His left. When the other ten heard of it, they were angry with James and John; but Jesus never lost His patience. He believed that the way to get faith out of men is to show that you have faith in them.

Of all the disciples Simon was most noisy and aggressive. It was he who was always volunteering advice, forever proclaiming the stanchness of his own courage and faith. One day Jesus said to him, "Before the cock crows tomorrow you will deny me thrice." Simon was indignant. Though they killed him, he cried, he would never deny! Jesus merely smiled—and that night it happened. . . . A lesser leader would have dropped Simon. "You have had your chance," he would have said, "I am sorry, but I must have men around me on whom I can depend." Jesus had the rare understanding that the same man will usually not make the same mistake twice. To this frail, very human, very likable former fisherman He spoke no work of rebuke. Instead He kept His faith that Peter would carry on bravely. It was daring, but He knew His man. The shame of the denial had tempered the iron of that nature like fire; from that time on there was no faltering in Peter even at the death.

The Bible presents an interesting collection of contrasts in this matter of executive ability. Samson had almost all the attributes of leadership. He was physically powerful and handsome; he had the great courage to which men always respond. No man was ever given a finer opportunity to free his countrymen from the oppressors and build up a great place of power for himself. Yet Samson failed miserably. He could do wonders singlehanded, but he could not organize.

Moses started out under the same handicap. He tried to be everything and do everything—and was almost on the verge of failure. It was his father-in-law, Jethro, who saved him from calamity. Said that shrewd old man: "The thing that thou doest is not good. Thou wilt surely wear away, both thou and this people that is with thee, for this thing is too heavy for thee, for thou art not able to perform it thyself alone."

Moses took the advice and associated with himself a partner, Aaron, who was strong where he was weak. They supplemented each other and together achieved what neither of them could have done alone.

John the Baptist had the same lack. He could denounce, but he could not construct. He drew crowds who were willing to repent at his command, but he had no program for them after their repentance. They waited for him to organize them for some sort of effective service, but he was no organizer. So his followers drifted away and his movement gradually collapsed. The same thing might have happened to the work of Jesus. He started with much less than John and a much smaller group of followers. He had only twelve, and they were untrained, simple men, with elementary weakness and passions. Yet because of the fire of His personal conviction, because of His marvelous instinct for discovering their latent powers, and because of His unwavering faith and patience, He molded them into an organization which carried on victoriously. Within a very few years after His death, it was reported in a far-off corner of the Roman Empire that "these who have turned the world upside down have come hither also." A few decades later the proud Emperor himself bowed his head to the teachings of this Nazareth carpenter, transmitted through common men.

chapter 2

The Outdoor Man

To MOST of the crowd there was nothing unusual in the scene. That is the tragedy of it.

The air was filthy with the smell of animals and human beings herded together. Men and women trampled one another, crying aloud their imprecations. At one side of the court were the pens of the cattle; the dove cages at the other. In the foreground, hard-faced priests and money-changers sat behind long tables, exacting the utmost farthing from those who came to buy. One would never imagine that this was a place of worship. Yet it was the Temple—the center of the religious life of the nation. And to the crowds who jammed its courts the spectacle seemed perfectly normal.

That was the tragedy of it.

Standing a little apart from the rest, the young man from Nazareth watched in amazement which deepened gradually into anger. It was no familiar sight to Him. He had not been in the Temple since His twelfth year, when Joseph and Mary took Him up to be legally enrolled as a son of the law. His chief memory of that previous visit was of a long conversation with certain old men in a quiet room. He had not witnessed the turmoil in the outer courts, or, if He had, it made small impression on His youthful mind.

But this day was different. For weeks He had looked forward to the visit, planning the journey with a company of

Galilean pilgrims who tramped all day and spent the nights in their tents under the open sky. To be sure some of the older ones muttered about the extortions of the money-changers. A woman told how the lamb, which she had raised with so much devotion the previous year, had been scornfully rejected by the priests, who directed her to buy from the dealers. An old man related his experience. He had brought down the savings of months to purchase his gift, and the money-changers converted his provincial currency into the Temple coin at a robber's rate. Other pilgrims had similar stories, but after all they were old people, prone to complain. The journey and the sacrifice were worth the cost. One must expect to pay for so great a privilege.

So the young man may have thought the night before; but today He faced the sordid reality, and His cheeks flushed. A woman's shrill tones pierced His reverie like a knife; He turned to see a peasant mother protesting vainly against a ruthless exaction. An unruly animal threatened to break through the bars, and a part of the crowd fell back with cries of terror. A money-changer with the face of a pig leaned gloatingly over his hoard. . . . The young man had picked up a handful of cords from the pavement and half unconsciously now was braiding them into a whip, watching the whole scene silently.

And suddenly, without a word of warning, He strode to the table where the fat money-changer sat, and hurled it violently across the court. The startled robber lurched forward, grasping at his gains, lost his balance and fell sprawling on the ground. Another step and a second table was overturned, and another and another. The crowd, which had melted back at the start, began to catch a glimmering of what was up and surged forward around the young man. He strode on, looking neither to right nor left. He reached the counters where the dove cages stood; with quick sure movements the cages were opened and the occupants released. Brushing aside the group of dealers who had taken their stand in front of the cattle pens, He threw down the bars and drove the bellowing animals out through the crowd and into the streets, striking vigorous blows with His little whip.

The whole thing happened so quickly that the priests were swept off their feet. Now, however, they collected themselves and bore down on Him in a body. Who was He that dared this act of defiance? Where had He come from? By what authority did He presume to interrupt their business? The crowds gave way again at the onslaught; they enjoyed the tumult as a crowd always does, and they hated the priests and robbers, but when it came to answering for the consequences, they were perfectly willing to leave it to Him.

And He was willing they should. He stood flushed and panting, the little whip still in His hands. His glance swept scornfully over the faces distorted by anger and greed.

"*This* is my authority," He cried. "It is written, 'My house shall be called a house of prayer for all the nations,' but ye have made it a den of robbers."

Stung by His taunt, His accusers hesitated and in their moment of hesitation were lost. The soldiers turned their backs; it was nothing that they cared about. But the crowd burst forth in a mighty cheer and rushing forward bore Him out of the Temple, the priests and the money-changers scurrying before Him. That night His action was the talk of the town.

"Did you hear what happened in the Temple today?"

"Not a man of them dared stand up to Him."

"Dirty thieves—it was coming to them."

"What's His name?"

"Jesus. . . . Used to be a carpenter up in Nazareth."

It was a very familiar story, much preached upon and pictured. But almost invariably the pictures show Him with a halo around His head, as though *that* was the explanation of His triumph. The truth is so much simpler and more impressive. There was in His eyes a flaming moral purpose, and greed and oppression have always shriveled before such fire. But with the majesty of His glance there was something else which counted powerfully in His favor. As His right arm rose and fell, striking its blows with that little whip, the sleeve dropped back to reveal muscles hard as iron. No one who watched Him in action had any doubt that He was fully capable of taking care of Himself. The evidence is clear that no angry priest or money-changer cared to try conclusions with that arm.

There are those to whom it will seem almost irreverent to suggest that Jesus was physically strong. They think of Him as a voice, a presence, a spirit; they never feel the rich contagion of His laughter, nor remember how heartily He enjoyed good food, nor think of what His years of hard toil must have done to His arms and back and legs. Look for a minute at those first thirty years.

There was no soft bed for His mother on the night He entered the world. He was brought forth in a stable amid animals and the animallike men who tended them. He was wrapped in rough garments and expected, almost from the beginning, to look after Himself. When He was still an infant, the family hurried away into Egypt. On the long trip back some years later, He was judged old enough to walk, for there were younger children; and so, day after day, He trudged beside the little donkey or scurried into the woods by the roadside to find fuel. It was a hard school for babyhood, but it gave Him a hardness that was an enormous asset later on.

Early in His boyhood Jesus, as the eldest son, went into the family carpenter shop. The practice of carpentry was no easy business in those simpler days. Doubtless the man who took a contract for a house assumed responsibilities for digging into the rough hillside for its foundations, for felling trees in the forest and shaping them with an adz. In after years those who listened to the talk of Jesus by the Sea of Galilee and heard Him speak of the "man who built his house upon a rock" had no doubt that He knew what He was talking about. Some of them had seen Him bending His strong clean shoulders to deliver heavy blows; or watched Him trudge away into the woods, His ax over His shoulder, and return at nightfall with a rough-hewn beam.

So He "waxed strong," as the narrative tells us—a phrase which has rather been buried under the too-frequent repetition of "the meek and lowly" and "the Lamb." As He grew in stature and experience, He developed with His personal skill an unusual capacity for directing the work of other men, so that Joseph allowed Him an increasing responsibility in the management of the shop. And this was fortunate, for the day came when Joseph stood at the bench no longer—having sawed his last board, and planed it smooth—and the management of the business descended on the shoulders of the boy who had learned it so thoroughly at his side.

Is it not high time for a larger reverence to be given to that quiet unassuming Joseph? To Mary, his wife, the church has assigned a place of eternal glory, and no thoughtful man can fail to be thankful for that. It is impossible to estimate how great an influence has been exerted for the betterment of woman's life by the fact that millions of human beings have been taught from infancy to venerate a woman. But with the glorification of Mary, there has been an almost complete neglect of Joseph. The same theology which has painted the son as soft and gentle to the point of weakness has exalted the feminine influence in its worship, and denied any large place to the masculine. This is partly because Mary lived to be known and remembered by the disciples, while nobody remembered Joseph. Was he just an untutored peasant, married to a superior woman and baffled by the genius of a son whom he could never understand? Or was there, underneath his self-effacement, a vigor and faith that molded the boy's plastic years? Was he a happy companion to the youngsters? Did he carry the youngest, laughing and crowing on his shoulders, from the shop? Was he full of jokes at dinnertime? Was he ever tired and short-tempered? Did he ever punish? To all these questions the narrative gives no answer. And since this is so—since there is none who can refute us—we have a right to form our own conception of the character of this vastly significant and wholly unknown man, and to be guided by the one momentous fact which we do know. It is this. He *must* have been friendly and patient and fine; he *must* have seemed to his children an almost ideal parent—for when Jesus sought to give mankind a new conception of the character of God, He could find no more exalted term for His meaning than the one word "Father."

Thirty years went by. Jesus had discharged His duty; the younger children were big enough for self-support. The strange stirrings that had gone on inside Him for years, setting Him off more and more from His associates, were crystallized by the reports of John's success. The hour of the great decision arrived; He hung up His tools and walked out of town.

What did He look like that day when He appeared on the bank of the Jordan and applied to John for baptism? What had the thirty years of physical toil given Him in stature and physique? Unfortunately the Gospel narratives supply no satisfying answer to these questions, and the only passage in ancient literature which purports to be a contemporary description of Him has been proved a forgery. Nevertheless, it requires only a little reading between the lines to be sure that almost all the painters have misled us. They have shown us a frail man, undermuscled, with a soft face—a woman's face covered by a beard—and a benign but baffled look, as though the problems of living were so grievous that death would be a welcome release.

This is not the Jesus at whose word the disciples left their work to enlist in an unknown cause.

And for proof of that assertion consider only four aspects of His experience: the health that flowed out of Him to create health in others; the appeal of His personality to women— weakness does not appeal to them; His lifetime of outdoor living; and the steellike hardness of His nerves.

First, then, His power of healing.

He was teaching one day in Capernaum, in a house crowded to the doors, when a commotion occurred in the courtyard. A man sick in bed for years had heard reports of His marvelous power and persuaded four friends to carry him to the house. Now at the very entrance their way was blocked. The eager listeners inside would not give way even to a sick man; they refused to sacrifice a single word. Sorrowfully the four friends started to carry the invalid back to his house again.

But the poor fellow's will was strong even if his body was weak. Rising on his elbow he insisted that they take him up the stairway on the outside of the house and lower him through the roof. They protested, but he was inflexible. It was his only chance for health, and he would not give up until everything had been tried. So at length they consented, and in the midst of a sentence the Teacher was interrupted dramatically; the sick man lay helpless at His feet.

Jesus stopped and bent down, taking the limp hand in His firm grasp; His face was lighted with a wonderful smile.

"Son, thy sins are forgiven thee," He said. "Rise, take up thy bed and walk."

The sick man was stupefied. "Walk!" He had never expected to walk again. Didn't this stranger understand that he had been bedridden for years? Was this some sort of cruel jest to make him the laughingstock of the crowd? A bitter protest rushed to his lips; he started to speak and then, halting himself, he looked up—up to the calm assurance of those blue eyes, the supple strength of those muscles, the ruddy skin that testified to the rich red blood beneath—and the healing occurred! It was as though health poured out of that strong body into the weak one like electric current from a dynamo. The invalid felt the blood quicken in his palsied limbs; a faint flush crept into his thin drawn cheeks; almost involuntarily he tried to rise and found to his joy that he could!

"Walk!" Do you suppose for one minute that a weakling, uttering that syllable, would have produced any result? If the Jesus who looked down on that pitiful wreck had been the Jesus of the painters, the sick man would have dropped back with a scornful sneer and motioned his friends to carry him out. But the health of the Teacher was irresistible; it seemed to cry out, "Nothing is impossible if only your will power is strong enough." And the man who so long ago had surrendered to despair, rose and gathered up his bed and went away, healed—like hundreds of others in Galilee—by strength from an overflowing fountain of strength.

One day later, as Jesus walked in a crowd, a woman pushed forward and touched His garment, and by that single touch was cured. The witnesses acclaimed it a miracle and so it was, but we need some definition of that word. He Himself was very reticent about His "miracles." It is perfectly clear that He did not interpret them in the same way that His followers did, nor attach the same importance to them. He was often reluctant to perform them, and frequently insisted that the individual who had been healed should "go and tell no man." And on one celebrated occasion—His visit to His home town, Nazareth—the narrative tells us clearly that the miraculous power failed, and for a very interesting and impressive reason. The people of Nazareth were His boyhood acquaintances and they were skeptical. They had heard with cynical scorn the stories of the wonders He had performed in other towns; they were determined not to be fooled. He might deceive the world, which knew Him only as a teacher, but they knew Him better—He was just Jesus, their old neighbor, the son of the local carpenter. So of that visit the gospel writers set down one of the most tragic sentences in literature. "He could do there no mighty work," they tell us, "*because of their unbelief*." Whatever the explanation of His miraculous power, it is clear that something big was required of the recipient as well as the giver. Without a belief in health on the part of the sick man, no health was forthcoming. And no man could have inspired that belief unless his own health and strength were so perfect as to make even the impossible seem easy.

Men followed Him, and the leaders of men have very often been physically strong. But women worshiped Him. This is significant. The names of women constitute a very large proportion of the list of His close friends. They were women from widely varying stations in life, headed by His mother. Perhaps she never fully appreciated His genius; certainly she was not without her periods of serious doubt, as we shall discover later on. Yet her loyalty to His best interests, as she conceived them, remained true, and she stood tearful but unwavering at the foot of the cross. There were Mary and Martha, two gentle maiden ladies who lived outside Jerusalem and in whose home with Lazarus, their brother, He enjoyed frequent hospitality. There was Joanna, a rich woman, the wife of one of Herod's stewards. These, and many others of the type which we are accustomed to designate as "good" women, followed Him with a devotion which knew no weariness or fear.

The important, and too often forgotten, fact in these relationships is this—that women are *not* drawn by weakness. The sallow-faced, thin-lipped, so-called spiritual type of man may awaken maternal instinct, stirring an emotion which is half regard, half pity. But since the world began, no power has fastened the affection of women upon a man like manliness. Men who have been women's men in the finest sense have been vital figures of history.

The other sort of women came into contact with Him, too—women of less fortunate experience and reputation, whose illusions regarding men were gone, whose eyes saw piercingly and whose lips were well versed in phrases of contempt. As He taught in the Temple, one of them was hurried into His presence by a vulgar crowd of self-righteous Scribes and Pharisees. She had been taken in the act of infidelity, and according to the Mosaic law she could be stoned to death. Shrinking, embarrassed, yet with a look in which defiance and scorn were mingled too, she stood in His presence and listened while their unclean lips played with the story of her shame. What thoughts must have raced through her mind —she who knew men and despised them all and now was brought to judgment before a man! They were all alike, in her philosophy; what would this one do and say?

To her amazement and the discomfiture of her critics, He said nothing. He "stooped down, and with his finger wrote on the ground, as though he heard them not." They craned their necks to see what He wrote and continued to taunt Him with their questions:

"Moses says stone her; what do you say?"

"Come now, if you are a prophet, here's a matter for you to decide."

"We found her in the house of So and So. She is guilty; what's *your* answer?"

All this time He had not once looked at the woman's face, and He did not look at her now. Slowly He "lifted himself up," faced the evil-minded pack and said quietly:

"He that is without sin among you let him first cast a stone at her."

And again, says the narrative, He stooped down and wrote on the ground.

A painful silence fell on the crowd; He continued writing. Writing what? Some have ventured the conjecture that He traced names of people and places that brought a blush of shame to men in that crowd. That may be so, but it is more impressive to think that He wrote nothing of significance; that He merely busied His finger in the sand, so as not to add to her discomfiture by looking in her eyes. He wrote—and one by one the thick-lipped champions of morality drew their garments around them and slipped away, until the court was empty except for Him and her. Then, and only then, His glance was lifted.

"Woman, where are those thine accusers? Hath no man condemned thee?" He inquired, as if in surprise.

Amazed at the sudden turn of affairs, she could hardly find her voice. "No man, Lord," she murmured.

"Neither do I condemn thee," He answered simply. "Go, and sin no more."

From the moment when the noisy vulgar throng had broken in on Him, He was complete master of the situation. Those were men not easily abashed, but they slunk out of His presence without waiting for His command. And she, who knew men so much more truly than men ever know one another, felt His mastery, responded to His power and spoke to Him reverently as "Lord."

All His days were spent in the open air—this is the third outstanding testimony to His strength. On the Sabbath He was in the synagogue because that was where the people were gathered, but by far the greater part of His teaching was done on the shores of His lake, or in the cool recesses of the hills. He walked constantly from village to village; His face was tanned by the sun and wind. Even at night He slept outdoors when He could—turning His back on the hot walls of the city and slipping away into the healthful freshness of the Mount of Olives. He was an energetic outdoor man. The vigorous activities of His days gave His nerves the strength of steel. As much as any nation ever, Americans understand and respect this kind of man.

He stepped into a sailboat with His disciples late one afternoon and, being very tired, lay down in the stern and was almost immediately asleep. The clouds grew thicker and the surface of the lake, which had been quiet a few minutes before, was broken into sudden waves. The little boat dived and tossed, and still He slept. His disciples had grown up on the shores of that lake; they were fishermen, accustomed to its moods and not easily frightened. But they had never been out in such a storm as this. It grew fiercer; water began to come in over the side and every moment seemed to threaten destruction. At last they could stand the strain no longer; they went to the stern and woke Him.

He rose without the slightest suggestion of hurry or alarm. A quick glance was enough to give Him a full understanding of the situation. He issued a few quiet orders, and presently the menaced boat swung round into the smoother waters of safety. Call it a miracle or not—the fact remains that it is one of the finest examples of self-control in all human history. Napoleon said that he had met few men with courage of the "two o'clock in the morning variety." Many men can be brave in the warmth of the sun and amid the heartening plaudits of the crowd; but to be wakened suddenly out of sound sleep and then to exhibit instant mastery—that is a type of courage which is rare indeed.

Jesus had that courage, and no man ever needed it more. In the last year of His public work the forces of opposition took on a form and coherency whose significance was perfectly clear. If He refused to retreat or to compromise, there could be but one end to His career. He knew they would kill Him, and He knew *how* they would kill Him. More than once in His journeys He had passed the victims of the justice of that day, writhing, tortured beings nailed to crosses and waiting piteously for release. Sometimes they wilted for days before the end. The memory of such sights must have been constantly with Him; at every sunset He was conscious that He had walked just one day nearer His own ordeal.

Yet He never faltered. Calmly, cheerfully, He went forward, cheering the spirits of His disciples, and striking those fiery blows against hypocrisy and oppression which were to be echoed by the hammer blows upon His cross. And when the soldiers came to arrest Him, they found Him ready and still calm.

The week of His trial and crucifixion takes up a large portion of the Gospels. For that week alone we can follow Him almost hour by hour; we know where He ate and slept, what He said and to whom; we can trace the gathering storm of fury which finally bore Him down. And this is the magnificent thing to remember—that through all that long torture of imprisonment, court trials, midnight hearings, scourgings, loss of food and loss of sleep, He never once ceased to be the Master. His accusers were determined. They thronged the courtyard before the palace, clamoring for His blood, yet even they felt a momentary awe when He appeared before them on the balcony.

Even Pilate felt it. The two men offered a strange contrast standing there—the Roman governor whose lips were so soon to speak the sentence of death, and the silent, self-possessed former carpenter—accused and doomed—yet bearing Himself with so much majesty, as though He were somehow beyond the reach of man-made law, and safe from the hurt of its penalties. In the face of the Roman were deep unpleasant lines; his cheeks were fatty with self-indulgence; he had the colorless look of indoor living. The straight young man stood inches above him, bronzed and hard and clean as the air of His loved mountain and lake.

Pilate raised his hand; the tumult died; a stillness descended on the crowd. He turned and faced Jesus, and from his coarse lips there burst a sentence which is a truer portrait than any painter has ever given us. The involuntary testimony of the dissipated cynical Roman in the presence of perfect strength, perfect assurance, perfect calm:

"Behold," he cried, "the man!"

chapter 3

The Sociable Man

A WICKED falsehood has come down through the ages.

It reappears every once in a while, usually in works by reputable and well-meaning writers, and usually in some such form as this: The author will, in his reading and research, have come onto the supposed description of Jesus by the Roman Lentulus, who succeeded Pilate as Governor of Jerusalem. Lentulus' description was detailed, and it concluded with the unfortunate statement: "Nobody has ever seen him laugh."

We want to be reverent. But to worship a Lord who never laughed—it is a strain.

The quotation from Lentulus is a forgery, penned by an unknown impostor in a later century; yet how persistently it has lived, and with what tragic thoroughness it has done its work. How many millions of happy-minded folk, when they have thought of Jesus at all, have had a feeling of uneasiness! "Suppose," they have said, "He were to enter the room and find us laughing and enjoying ourselves! When there is so much suffering and sin in the world, is it right to be happy? What would Jesus say?"

With such compunctions cheerful folk have had their brighter moments tinctured. The friendliest man who ever

46

lived has been shut off by a black wall of tradition from those whose friendship He would most enjoy. Theology has reared a graven image and robbed the world of the joy and laughter of the Great Companion.

It is not hard to understand when you remember the character of the early theologians. They lived in sad days; they were men of introspection to whom every simple thing was symbolic of some hidden mystery and life itself was a tangle of philosophic formulas.

Baffled by the death of Jesus, they rejected the splendid truth and fashioned a creed instead. Lambs were put to death in the Temple as a sacrifice for the sins of the worshipers; ergo, Jesus was the Lamb of God. His death had been planned from the beginning of the world. The human race was hopelessly wayward; God knew that it would be, and nothing would turn Him from His vindictive purpose to destroy it but the sacrifice of an innocent Son. . . . Thomas Paine remarked truly that no religion can be really divine which has in it any doctrine that offends the sensibilities of a little child. Is there any reader of this page whose childish sensibilities were not shocked when the traditional explanation of the death of Jesus was first poured into his ears? Would any human father, loving his children, have sentenced all of them to death, and been persuaded to commute the sentence only by the suffering of his best beloved?

Small wonder that the Jesus of such a doctrine was supposed never to have laughed!

The Gospels tell a different story. But the writers were men of simple minds, and naturally gave greatest emphasis to the events which impressed them most. Since death is the most dramatic of all the phenomena of life, the crucifixion and the events immediately preceding it are set forth in complete detail. The denunciation of the Pharisees (as startling to the disciples as the denunciation of the United States Sen-

ate by a barefooted philosopher would be to us); the arrest
by the soldiers at night; the trial before the Sanhedrin; the
hushed moment of the appearance on the balcony of Herod's
palace; the long sad struggle out to Calvary, and the hours of
agony on the cross—these were the scenes that burned themselves indelibly into their memories, and all the sunny days
preceding faded into less importance. The life of Jesus, as we
read it, is what the life of Lincoln would be if we were given
nothing of his boyhood and young manhood, very little of
his work in the White House and every detail of his assassina-
tion.

All of the four Gospels contain very full accounts of the
weeping which attended the crucifixion—the final miracle;
John alone remembered the laughter amid which the first one
was performed. It was in the little town of Cana, not far
from Nazareth. Jesus and His mother had been invited to a
wedding feast. Often such a celebration continued for several
days. Everybody was expected to enjoy himself to the utmost as long as the food and drink lasted—and it was a point
of pride with the bride's mother that both food and drink
should last a long time.

Enthusiasm was at a high pitch on this occasion when a
servant entered nervously and whispered a distressing message
to the hostess. The wine had given out. Picture if you will
the poor woman's chagrin! This was her daughter's wedding
—the one social event in the life of the family. For it they
had made every sort of sacrifice, cutting a little from their
living expenses, going without a new garment, neglecting a
needed repair in the house. After it was over they could
count the cost and find some way to even up; but until the
last guest had gone, no effort should be spared to uphold the
family's dignity in the neighborhood. To this end the poor
woman had planned it all in her proud sensitive fashion,
and now, at the very height of success, the whole structure of

her dreams came tumbling down. The wine had given out.

Most of the guests were too busy to note the entrance of the servant or the quick flush that mounted to the hostess's cheek. But one woman's sight and sympathy were keener. The mother of Jesus saw every move in the little tragedy, and with that instinct which is quicker than reason she understood its meaning.

She leaned over to her son and confided the message which her friendly eyes had read: "Son, the wine is gone."

Well, what of it? He was only one of a score of guests, perhaps a hundred. There had been wine enough as it was; the party was noisy and none too restrained. Let them quiet themselves, say good-by to their hostess and get off to bed. They would feel much better for it in the morning. . . . Or, if they persisted in carrying on, let the relatives of the hostess make up the deficiency. He was only a guest from another town. Doubtless the woman's brothers were present, or, if not, then some of her neighbors. They could easily slip out and bring back wine from their own stores before the shortage was commented on. . . . Why should He be worried with what was none of His affair?

Besides, there was a precedent in the matter. Only a few weeks before when He was tortured by hunger in the wilderness, He had refused to use His miraculous power to transform stones into bread. If the recruiting of His own strength was beneath the dignity of a miracle, surely He could hardly be expected to intervene to prolong a party like this. . . . "My friends, we have had a very pleasant evening and I am surely indebted to our hostess for it. I think we have trespassed as far as we should upon her generosity. I suggest that we wish the happy couple a long and prosperous life, and take our way home." Surely this is the solemn fashion in which a teacher ought to talk.

Did any such thoughts cross His mind? If they did, we

have no record of it. He glanced across at the wistful face of the hostess—already tears sparkled under her lids—He remembered that the event was the one social triumph of her self-sacrificing life, and instantly His decision was formed. He sent for six pots and ordered them filled with water. When the contents of the first one was drawn, the ruler of the feast lifted his glass to the bridegroom and the bewildered but happy hostess: "Every man setteth on first the good wine," he cried, "and when men have drunk freely, then that which is worse; but thou hast kept the good wine until now."

The mother of Jesus looked on in wonder. She had never fully understood her son; she did not ask to understand. He had somehow saved the situation; she did not question how. And what was sufficient for her is sufficient for us. The whole problem of His "miracles" is beyond our arguments at this distance. We either accept them or reject them according to the make-up of our minds. But if they are to be accepted at all, then surely this first one ought not to be omitted. It often is omitted from the comments on His life or at least passed over hastily. But to us who think first of His friendliness, it seems gloriously characteristic, setting the pattern for all the three years that were to follow. "I came that ye might have life," He exclaimed, "and have it more abundantly." So, at the very outset, He makes use of His mighty power, not to point a solemn moral, not to relieve a sufferer's pain, but to keep a happy party from breaking up too soon, to save a hostess from embarrassment. . . . See, the ruler of the feast rises to propose a toast . . . hark to the discordant strains of the neighborhood orchestra. Look, a tall broad-shouldered man towers above the crowd . . . listen, hear His laugh!

The Jewish prophets were stern-faced men; there are few if any gleams of humor in the Old Testament from beginning to end. It was the business of a prophet to denounce folks for their sins. Go to the Boston Public Library and look at their portraits. You are moved by their moral grandeur but rather glad to get away. They are not the kind of men whom you would choose as companions on a fishing trip.

John the Baptist was the last of this majestic succession of thunderers. He forsook the cities as being wicked beyond any hope, and pitched his camp in a wilderness beside the banks of the Jordan. For clothes he wore the skins of animals; his food was locusts and wild honey. He indulged in long fasts and vigils, from which he emerged with flaming eyes to deliver his uncompromising challenge. "Repent," he cried, stretching out his gaunt arm toward the thoughtless capital, "repent while you still have time. God has given up hope. His patience is exhausted; He is about to wind up the affairs of the world." Many people flocked out to his camp, and his fiery language burned through to consciences that were overgrown with a very thick crust.

Fresh from the carpenter shop came Jesus to stand and listen with the rest. To what degree was He influenced? Did He, too, believe that the world was almost at an end? Did He see Himself cast in a role like John's, a Voice in the Wilderness, crying destruction? There is some evidence to make us think so. He went away from John's camp and hid Himself in the woods, and there for forty days and nights He fought the thing through. But at the end His mind was made up. His place was among His fellows. For a time His preaching bore a decided resemblance to John's. He, too, talked of the imminence of the Kingdom of Heaven and warned His hearers that time was short. But little by little the note of warning diminished; the appeal to righteousness as a happier, more satisfying way of living increased. God ceased to be the stern, unforgiving judge and became the loving, friendly Father. He Himself was less and less the prophet, more and more the companion. So much so that John—imprisoned and depressed—began to be tortured by doubt. Was this Jesus really the man whom he had hoped would carry on his work? Had he, John, made a mistake? What were these rumors that came to him of Jesus' conduct—His presence at parties, His failure to keep the stipulated fasts, the unconventional habits of His followers? What did such unprophetic conduct mean?

John sent two of his disciples to watch and to ask. And Jesus, knowing how wide was the difference between their attitudes and His, refused to argue or defend. "Go and tell your master what you have seen and heard," He said. "The sick are healed, the blind receive their sight and the poor have the gospel preached to them. . . . It is true that I do not fast, nor forgo the everyday pleasures of life. John did his work and it was fine; but I cannot work in his way. I must be myself . . . and these results which you have seen . . . these are my evidence."

He loved to be in the crowd. Apparently He attended all the feasts at Jerusalem not merely as religious festivals but because all the folks were there and He had an all-embracing fondness for folks. We err if we think of Him as a social outsider. To be sure it was the "poor" who "heard him gladly," and most of His close disciples were men and women of the lower classes. But there was a time when He was quite the favorite in Jerusalem. The story of His days is dotted with these phrases: "A certain ruler desired him that he should eat with him." . . . "They desired him greatly to remain and he abode two days." Even after He had denounced the Pharisees as "hypocrites" and "children of the devil," even when the clouds of disapproval were gathering for the final storm, they still could not resist the charm of His presence, nor the stimulation of His talk. Close up to the end of the story we read that a "certain chief of the Pharisees desired him that he would dine at his house."

No other public figure ever had a more interesting list of friends. It ran from the top of the social ladder to the bottom. Nicodemus, the member of the supreme court, had too big a stake in the social order to dare to be a disciple, but he was friendly all the way through and notably at the end. Some unknown rich man, the owner of an estate on the Mount of Olives, threw it open to Jesus gladly as a place of retirement and rest. When He needed a room for the Last Supper with His friends, He had only to send a messenger ahead and ask for it. The request was enough. A Roman centurion was glad to be counted among His acquaintances; the wife of the steward of Herod, and probably the steward himself, contributed to His comfort. And in the last sad hours, when the hatred of His enemies had completed its work and His body hung lifeless from the cross, it was a rich man named Joseph—a rich man who would have sunk into oblivion like the other rich men of all the ages except for this one great act of friendship—who begged the authorities for His body and, having prepared it for burial, laid it in a private tomb.

Such were His associates among the socially elect. What sort of people made up the rest of His circle? All sorts. Pharisees, fishermen; merchants and tax collectors; cultivated women and outcast women; soldiers, lawyers, beggars, lepers, publicans and sinners. What a spectacle they must have presented trailing after Him through the streets, or covering the side of the green slopes of the mountain where He delivered His one long discourse! How they reveled in the keen thrust of His answers when some smart member of the company tried to trip Him up! What heated arguments carried back and forth; what shrewd retorts, what pointed jokes! He loved it all—the pressure of the crowd, the clash of wits, the eating and the after-dinner talk. When He was criticized because He enjoyed it so much and because His disciples did not fast and go about with gloomy looks, He gave an answer that throws a wonderful light on His own conception of His mission.

"Do the friends of the bridegroom fast while the bridegroom is still with them?" He demanded. "Not a bit of it; they enjoy every moment of his stay. I am the bridegroom; these are my hours of celebration. Let my friends be happy with me for the little while that we are together. There will be plenty of time for solemn thoughts after I am gone."

This was His own picture of Himself—a bridegroom! The center and soul of a glorious existence; a bringer of news so wonderful that those who received it should be marked by their radiance as by a badge. Of course, He disregarded the narrow Code of the Pharisees.

"You shall walk only so far on the Sabbath," said the Code. He walked as far as He liked.

"These things you may eat and these you shall not," said the Code.

"You're not defiled by what goes into your mouth," He answered, "but by what comes out."

"All prayers must be submitted according to the forms provided," said the Code. "None other are acceptable."

It was blasphemy to Him. His God was no Bureau, no Rule Maker, no Accountant. "God is a spirit," He cried. "Between the great Spirit and the spirits of men—which are a tiny part of His—no one has the right to intervene with formulas and rules."

He told a story which must have outraged the self-righteous members of His audience. He said that a certain man had two sons. The elder, a perfectly proper and perfectly uninteresting young man, worked hard, saved his money and conducted himself generally as a respectable member of society. But people were gloomier rather than happier when he came around. He never once gave way to a generous impulse.

The younger son was a reckless ne'er-do-well, who took his portion of the estate and went into a far country where he led a wild life and presently was penniless and repentant. In that mood he proceeded to work his way back to his father's house. The father had never ceased to watch and hope; he saw the boy coming a long way down the road, ran to him, threw his arms around his son's dusty shoulders, kissed the boy's forehead and bore him in triumph to the front door.

"Bring a fatted calf," the father cried. "Make a feast; call the neighbors in to celebrate. For this my son which was gone has come back; he was dead to decency and idealism. Now he has cleaned up his thinking and is alive again."

There were high doings in that house that day, and everyone enjoyed them except the older son. He was sullen and self-pitying. "Where do I come in?" he exclaimed. "Here I work and save and have never had a good time. This irresponsible youngster has had nothing but good times and now, when he comes home after having run through his money, they give him a party. It's wrong."

The father did not defend the younger son, but he rebuked the elder. That was what hurt the smugly complacent members of the audience to whom Jesus told the story. The implication was too plain. "There are two ways in which a man may waste his life," the story said in effect. "One is to run away from his responsibilities, causing sorrow to his parents and hurt to his associates, killing his finer nature. That is wrong, and a man must repent of such conduct and change his life if he is to be received again into his Father's house.

"But the other is equally wrong. God is a generous Giver, and selfish getting is sin. God laughs in the sunshine and sings through the throats of birds. They who neither laugh nor sing are out of tune with the Infinite. God has exercised all His ingenuity in making a world a pleasant place. Those who find no pleasure and give none offer Him a constant affront. However precise their conduct, their spirits are an offense. . . .

Woe to you, Scribes and Pharisees. You are painfully carefully careful to give exactly one-tenth of your incomes to the Temple, figuring down to fractions of pennies. But you neglect the weightier matters of the law—the supreme obligation to leave the world a little more cheerful because you have passed through."

This was His message—a happy God, wanting His sons and daughters to be happy.

Jesus grew tremendously sure of Himself as His ministry progressed. No passages in all literature are more scathing than His denunciations of the cheerless, self-righteous Pharisees. They smarted under the sting, and the crowds laughed at their discomfiture and cheered the young man who dared to call Himself the greatest of the prophets and who proclaimed that life is a gift to be enjoyed, not a penance to be served. All persons who achieve something have a sublime disregard of criticism. "Never explain; never retract; never apologize; get it done and let them howl," said a great Englishman. Jesus too ignored personal criticism. "No man can expect to accomplish anything if he stands in terror of public opinion," He said in substance. "People will talk against you no matter how you live or what you do. Look at John the Baptist. He came neither eating nor drinking and they said he had a devil. I come both eating and drinking, and what do they call me? A wine bibber and a gluttonous man!"

He must have told it as a joke on Himself and on John, though the Gospels do not say so. Indeed, we must often wonder how much of His humor has been lost to us by the literal-mindedness of His chroniclers. How about that incident, for example, at the pool of Bethesda? The pool was in Jerusalem near the sheep market and was supposed to have magic properties. Hundreds of sick people were left along the edges to wait for the moment when the waters would be stirred by the visit of an angel from Heaven; whoever managed to get into the water first, after the stirring, was healed. Passing by it one afternoon, Jesus heard the whining voice of an old fellow who had been lying there for thirty-eight years. Every time the pool stirred, he made a half-hearted effort to jump in; but there was always someone with more determination or more helpful friends. So the old chap would drop back onto his couch and bemoan his hard luck. He was bemoaning it on this day when Jesus stopped and looked at him with a whimsical smile.

"Wilt thou be made whole?" Jesus demanded.

The old man was instantly resentful. What an absurd question! Of course he wanted to be made whole! Hadn't he been trying for thirty-eight years? Why annoy him with such an impertinence?

The smile on the face of Jesus broadened. He knew better. Enjoying poor health was the old fellow's profession. He was a marked man in those parts; in the daily grumblings when the sufferers aired their complaints he was the principal speaker. Nobody had so many pains as he; no other symptoms were so distressing. Let these newcomers take a back seat. His was the only original hard-luck story. He had been there for thirty-eight years.

The keen eyes of Jesus saw deep into the souls of men. There was a twinkle in them now.

"Get up," He said briskly, "and walk."

The old chap spluttered and grumbled, but there was no resisting the command of that presence. He rose, discovered to his own amazement that he could stand, rolled up his bed and walked off. A reverent hush fell on the assembled crowd, but before they could find their voices Jesus, too, was gone. The disciples were too deeply impressed for comment; they dropped back a respectful distance and Jesus walked on alone. Suppose they had followed closer? Wouldn't their ears have been startled by something suspiciously like a chuckle? It was a good joke on the old chap. He imagined that he'd had hard luck, but his real hard luck was just beginning. . . . No more of the pleasure of self-pity for him. . . . What would his folks say that night when he came walking in? What a shock to him in the morning when they told him that he'd have to go to work!

The shortest verse in the New Testament is "Jesus wept." That tragic note in His story the Gospel record has carefully preserved. How we wish it might also have told us what occurred on the night after the chronic old grumbler was healed! Did Jesus stop suddenly in the middle of the supper, and set down His cup, while a broad smile spread across His wonderful face? If He did, the disciples were probably puzzled—they were so often puzzled—but surely we have the right to guess, with reverence, what was in His mind as He pictured the home-coming of that cured old man. On that evening surely Jesus must have laughed.

Someone has said that genius is the ability to become a boy again at will. Lincoln had that type of genius. Around his table in Washington sat the members of his Cabinet, silenced by their overwhelming sense of responsibility. It was one of the most momentous meetings in our history. To their amazement, instead of addressing himself directly to the business in hand, Lincoln picked up a volume and began to read aloud a delightful chapter of nonsense from Artemus Ward.

Frequent chuckles interrupted the reading, but they came only from the President. The Secretaries were too shocked for expression! Humor at such an hour—it was well nigh sacrilegious! Heedless of their protesting looks, Lincoln finished the chapter, closed the book and scanned their gloomy faces with a sigh.

"Gentlemen, why don't you laugh?" he exclaimed. "With the fearful strain that is upon me night and day, if I did not laugh I should die; and you need this medicine as much as I."

With that remark he turned to his tall hat which was on the table and drew forth what Secretary Stanton described as a "little white paper."

The "little white paper" was the Emancipation Proclamation.

Stanton could scarcely restrain his impulse to stalk out of the room. No one of his Cabinet really understood Lincoln. He was constantly scandalizing them by his calm disregard of convention and his seemingly prodigal waste of time. The friends and advisers of Jesus were similarly shocked. How could anyone with such important business allow himself to be so casually interrupted! One of the surest marks of greatness, of course, is accessibility and the appearance of having an unstinted allowance of time. The man who appears too busy is not always getting much done. The disciples were extremely busy, Judas most of all. He was the treasurer of the group, harassed because expenses ran high and there was no certainty of tomorrow's income. Jesus brushed away such petty worries with a smile.

"Consider the lilies of the field," He exclaimed; "they toil not, neither do they spin, yet Solomon in all his glory was not arrayed like one of these." That was all very poetic, very nice, but it did not fool Judas. He knew that you cannot get anywhere in the world without money, and it was his job to find the money. The other disciples had similar worries. They wanted to get it clear as to their relative positions in the new Kingdom; they were concerned because outsiders, not properly initiated into the organization, were claiming to be followers of Jesus and doing miracles in His name. They fretted because there was so much work to be done and the days were too short for doing it.

But He towered magnificently above it all. Wherever He went the children flocked. Pomp and circumstances mean nothing to them. They are neither attracted by prominence

nor awed in its presence. Their instinct cuts through all outward semblance with a keen swift edge; unfailingly they comprehend who are real and who are not. With a knowledge
which is the accumulated wisdom of all the ages they recognize their friends.

So they swarmed around, climbing on His knees, tugging
at His garments, smiling up into His eyes, begging to hear
more of His stories. It was all highly improper and wasteful
in the disciples' eyes. With bustling efficiency they hastened
to remind Him that He had important appointments; they
tried to push eager mothers back.

But Jesus would have none of it. "Suffer the little children
to come unto me!" He commanded. And He added one of
those sayings which should make so clear the message of His
Gospel: "They are the very essence of the Kingdom of
Heaven," He said; "unless you become like them you shall in
no wise enter in." Like them . . . like little children, laughing,
joyous, unaffected, trusting implicitly . . . with time to be
kind.

To be sure He was not always in the crowd. He had His
long hours of withdrawal when, in communion with His
Father, He refilled the deep reservoirs of His strength and
love. Toward the end He was more preoccupied. He knew
months in advance that if He made another journey to Jerusalem His fate would be sealed; yet He never wavered in His
decision to make that journey. Starting out on it, His mind
filled with the approaching conflict, His shoulders burdened
with the whole world's need, He heard His name called out
from the roadside in shrill unfamiliar tones: "Jesus . . . Jesus,
thou son of David, have mercy on me."

It was the voice of a useless blind beggar. At once the
disciples were on him, commanding silence. Couldn't he see
the Master was deep in thought? Who was he to interrupt? . . .
Keep still, blind man . . . get back where you belong.

But frantic hope knows no reserve. It was the poor fellow's one possible chance. He cared no more for their rebuke than they for his need. Again the shrill insistent voice: "Jesus, thou son of David, have mercy on me."

Jesus stopped.

"Who called my name!"

"Nobody, Master . . . only a blind beggar, a worthless fellow. . . . Bartimaeus, nobody at all . . . we'll tend to him."

"Bring him here."

Trembling with hope, he was guided forward. The deep rich eyes of the Master looked into those sightless eyes. The mind which had been buried in the greatest problem with which a mind ever wrestled gave itself unreservedly to the problem of one forlorn human life. Here was need, and He had time. . . .

A long time ago a sermon was preached in St. John's Church, New York, which dealt very severely with the frailties of poor human nature, and put forth, with unctuous assurance, the promise of eternal punishment for a large proportion of the race. Among the worshipers was a gentleman of unfortunate reputation but keen mind, whose name lingers unforgettably in our history.

As he left the church a lady spoke to him: "What did you think of the sermon, Mr. Burr?" she asked.

"I think," responded Aaron Burr, "that God is better than most people suppose."

That was the message of Jesus—that God is supremely better than anybody had ever dared to believe. Not a petulant Creator, who had lost control of His creation and, in wrath, was determined to destroy it all. Not a stern Judge dispensing impersonal justice. Not a vain King who must be flattered and bribed into concessions of mercy. Not a rigid Accountant, checking up the sins against the penances and striking a cold hard balance. Not any of these . . . nothing like these;

but a great Companion, a wonderful Friend, a kindly indul-
gent, joy-loving Father. . . .

For three years Jesus walked up and down the shores of
His lake and through the streets of towns and cities, trying to
make them understand. Then came the end and, almost before His fine firm flesh was cold, the distortion began. He
who cared nothing for ceremonies and forms was made the
idol of formalism. Men hid themselves in monasteries; they
lashed themselves with whips; they tortured their skins with
harsh garments and cried out that they were followers of
Him—of Him who loved the crowd, who gathered children
about Him wherever He went, who celebrated the calling of a
new disciple with a feast in which all the neighborhood
joined! "Hold your heads high," He had exclaimed; "you
are lords of the universe . . . only a little lower than the
angels . . . children of God." But the hymn writers knew
better. They wrote:

"Oh to be *nothing, nothing*"

and

"For such a *worm* as I."

His last supper with His disciples was an hour of solemn
memories. Their minds were heavy with foreboding. He
talked earnestly, but the whole purpose of His talk was to lift
up their hearts, to make them think nobly of themselves, to
fill their spirits with a conquering faith.

"My joy I leave with you," He exclaimed.

"Be of good cheer," He exclaimed.

Joy, cheer—these are the words by which He wished to be
remembered. But down through the ages has come the
wicked falsehood that He never laughed.

chapter 4

His Method

MANY leaders have dared to lay out ambitious programs, but this is the most daring of all:

Matthew and Mark report in different words that they and nine of their fellows were commanded to preach the Gospel *to the whole creation.*

Consider the sublime audacity of that command. To carry Roman civilization across the then known world had cost millions of lives and billions in treasure. To create any sort of reception for a new idea today involves a vast expense and well-organized machinery of propaganda. Jesus had no funds and no machinery. His organization was a tiny group of uneducated men, one of whom had abandoned the cause as hopeless, deserting to the enemy before the command was given. He had come proclaiming a Kingdom and was to end on a cross; He knew He would not be physically present much longer; yet He dared to talk of His Gospel conquering all creation. What was the source of His faith in that handful of followers? By what methods had He trained them? What had they learned from Him of persuading men?

We speak of the law of "supply and demand," but the words have got turned around. With anything which is not a basic necessity the supply always precedes the demand. Elias Howe invented the sewing machine, but it nearly rusted away before American women could be persuaded to use it. With their sewing finished so quickly what would they ever do with their spare time? Howe had vision and had made his vision come true, but he could not sell! So his biographer paints a tragic picture—the man who had done more than any other in his generation to lighten the labor of women is forced to attend—in a borrowed suit of clothes!—the funeral of the woman he loved.

Nor are men less stubborn than women in opposition to the new idea. The typewriter had been a demonstrated success for years before businessmen could be persuaded to buy it. How could anyone have letters enough to justify the investment of one hundred dollars in a writing machine? Only when the Remingtons sold the Caligraph Company the right to manufacture machines under the Remington patent, and two groups of salesmen set forth in competition, was the resistance broken down.

Almost every invention has had a similar battle. Said Robert Fulton of the *Clermont:*

"As I had occasion daily to pass to and from the shipyard where my boat was in progress, I often loitered near the groups of strangers and heard various inquiries as to the object of this new vehicle. The language was uniformly that of scorn, sneer or ridicule. The loud laugh often rose at my expense; the dry jest; the wise calculations of losses or expenditures; the dull repetition of 'Fulton's Folly.' Never did a single encouraging remark, a bright hope, a warm wish cross my path."

That is the kind of human beings we are—wise in our own conceit, impervious to suggestions, perfectly sure that what has never been done never will be done. Nineteen and a half centuries ago we were even more impenetrable, for modern science has frequently shot through the hard shell of our complacency. . . . *To the whole creation.* . . . Assuredly there was no demand for a new religion; the world was already over-supplied. And Jesus proposed to send forth eleven men and expected them to substitute a new kind of thinking for all existing religious thought!

In this great act of courage He was the successor, and the surpasser, of all the prophets who had gone before. We spoke a moment ago of the prophets as deficient in humor, but what they lacked in the amenities of life they made up richly in vision. Each one of them brought to the world a revolutionary idea, and we cannot understand truly the significance of the work of Jesus unless we remember that He began where they left off, building on the firm foundations they had laid. Let us glance at them a moment, starting with Moses. What a miracle he wrought in the thinking of his race! The world was full of gods in his day—male gods, female gods, wooden and iron gods—it was a poverty-stricken tribe which could not boast of at least a hundred gods. The human mind had never been able to leap beyond the idea that every natural phenomenon was the expression of a different deity. Along came Moses, one of the majestic intellects of history. His understanding transformed humanity. His great truth can be contained in one short sentence: *There is one God.*

What an overwhelming idea and how magnificent its consequences! Taking his disorganized people who had been slaves in Egypt for generations—their spirits broken by rule and rod—Moses persuaded them that God, this one all-powerful God, was their special friend and protector, fired them with faith in that conviction and transformed them from slaves to men who could know freedom and have the courage to win it.

Moses died and his nation carried on under the momentum which he had given it until there arose Amos, a worthy successor.

"There is one God," Moses had said.

"God is a God of justice," added Amos.

That assertion is such an elementary part of our conscious-ness that we are almost shocked by the suggestion that it could ever have been new. But if you would have a true measure of the importance of Amos' contribution, remember the gods that were current in his day—the gods of the Greeks, for example. Zeus was chief of them, a philandering old repro-bate who visited his wrath upon such mortals as were unlucky enough to interfere in his love affairs and threw his influence to whichever side offered the largest bribes. His wife and sons and daughters were no better; nor was the moral standard of the God of the Israelites very much superior until Amos came. He was a trading God, ready to offer so much victory for so many sacrifices, and insistent on prerogatives. It was the high privilege of Amos to proclaim a God who could not be bought, whose ears were deaf to pleadings if the cause was unfair, who would show no discrimination in judgment be-tween the strong and weak, the rich and poor. It was a stu-pendous conception, but Amos persuaded men to accept it, and it has remained a part of our spiritual heritage.

Years passed and Hosea spoke. His had not been a happy life. His wife deserted him; heartbroken and vengeful, he was determined to cast her off forever. Yet his love would not let him do it. He went to her, forgave her and took her back. Then in his hours of lonely brooding a great thought came to him! If he, a mere man, could love so unselfishly one who had broken faith with him, must not God be capable of as great, or greater forgiveness toward erring human beings? The thought fired his imagination. He stood up before the nation and with burning zeal proclaimed a God so strong that He could destroy, yet so tender that He would not!

One God.

A just God.

A good God.

These were the three steps in the development of the greatest of all ideas. Hundreds of generations have died since the days of Moses, of Amos and Hosea. The thought of the world on almost every other subject has changed, but the conception of God which these three achieved has dominated the religious thinking of much of the world down to this very hour.

What was there for Jesus to add? Only one thought. But it was so much more splendid than all previous ideas that it altered again and even more surely the current of history. He invited frail bewildered humanity to stand upright and look at God face to face! He called on men to throw away fear, disregard the limitations of their mortality and claim the Lord of Creation as Father. It is the basis of all revolt against injustice and repression, all democracy. For if God is the Father of all men, then *all* are His children and hence the commonest is equally as precious as the king. No wonder the authorities trembled. They were not fools; they recognized the implications of the teaching. Either Jesus' life or their power must go. No wonder succeeding generations of authorities have embroidered His idea and corrupted it, so that the simplest faith in the world has become a complex thing of form and ritual, of enforced observances and "thou shall nots." It was too dangerous a Power to be allowed to wander the world unleashed and uncontrolled.

This then was what Jesus wished to send to all creation through the instrumentality of His eleven men. What were His methods of training? How did He meet prospective believers? How did He deal with objections? By what sort of strategy did He interest and persuade?

He was making the journey back from Jerusalem after His spectacular triumph in cleansing the Temple when He came to Jacob's Well and, being tired, sat down. His disciples had stopped at one of the villages to purchase food, so He was alone. The well furnished the water supply for the neighboring city of the Samaritans, and after a little time a woman came out to it, carrying her pitcher on her shoulder. Between her people, the Samaritans, and His people, the Jews, there was a feud of centuries. To be touched by even the shadow of a Samaritan was defilement, according to the strict Code of the Pharisees; to speak to one was a crime. The woman made no concealment of her resentment at finding Him there. Almost any remark from His lips would have kindled her anger. She would at least have turned away in scorn; she might have summoned her relatives and driven Him away.

A difficult, perhaps dangerous situation. How could He meet it? How give a message to one who was forbidden by everything holy to listen? The incident is very revealing: there are times when any word is the wrong word, when only silence can prevail. Jesus knew well this precious principle. As the woman drew closer, He made no move to indicate that He was conscious of her approach. His gaze was on the ground. When He spoke, He spoke quietly, musingly, as if to Himself.

"If you knew who I am," He said, "you would not need to come out here for water. I would give you living water."

The woman stopped short, her interest challenged in spite of herself; she set down the pitcher and looked at the stranger. It was a burning hot day; the well was far from the city; she was tired. What did He mean by such a remark? She started to speak, checked herself and burst out impulsively, her curiosity overleaping her caution:

"What are you talking about? Do you mean to say you are greater than our father Jacob who gave us this well? Have you some magic that will save us this long walk in the sun?"

Dramatic, isn't it—a single sentence achieving triumph, arousing interest and creating desire? With sure instinct He followed up His initial advantage. He began to talk to her in terms of her own life, her ambitions, her hopes, knowing so well that each of us is interested first of all and most of all in himself. When the disciples came up a few minutes later, they found the unbelievable—a Samaritan listening with rapt attention to the teaching of a Jew.

He prepared to go but she would not allow it. She ran back to the city to summon her brothers and relatives. "Come," she cried, "and see a man who told me all things ever I did."

They followed her out to the well—these prejudiced, reluctant men and women who, an hour before, would have thought it incredible that they should ever hold conversation with one of their traditional enemies. Suspiciously at first but with steadily ascending interest, they listened to His talk. It is said that great leaders are born, not made. The saying is true to this degree—that no man can persuade people to do what he wants them to do unless he genuinely likes people and believes that what he wants them to do is to their own advantage. One of the reasons for Jesus' success was an affection for people which so shone in His eyes and rang in His tones that even the commonest man in a crowd felt instinctively that here was a friend. . . .

The afternoon shadows lengthened while He talked. Other citizens, attracted by the gathering, made their way out to the well and swelled the audience. Before the evening meal He prepared to go. They would not hear of it. He must be their guest, meet their neighbors, tell them more, persuade them further!

"They besought him to abide with them; and he abode there two days."

Some years later a tired pilgrim arrived in the modern and perfectly self-satisfied city of Athens. He arrived on foot because he had no money for riding. His shoes were sadly worn and his clothing frayed and covered with dust. One would say that these disadvantages were enough to disqualify him for success in a town so smart and critical, but he had other handicaps more fundamental. He was too short and thickset to be impressive; his eyes had a decided squint; in fact, he was not at all the kind of man who commands respect before a crowd. That he should come to the most sophisticated center of the ancient world and expect to make an impression was extraordinary. The principal business of the clever gentlemen of that city was standing around the market place, there to "hear or to tell some new thing." They were the joke makers and fashion setters of their era. They originated new ideas; they did not buy them from the provinces. And as for investing in a new religion—they had hundreds of religions, some new, some fairly new, some old, but all entirely unused.

A fine appreciative atmosphere for the foreign visitor named Paul! See him trudging along through the suburbs and up toward the center of the town. Poor little chap! Wait until the wise ones catch sight of him; they will certainly have a fine afternoon's sport!

Straight on he marched until he reached Mars Hill, the Broadway and Forty-second Street corner of town. A few of the clever ones gathered about, moved by the same cynical curiosity which would have prompted them to look at a sword swallower or a three-legged calf. The critical moment had come. Paul must say something, and no matter what he said, it would be wrong. Suppose he had begun in the usual way: "Good morning, gentlemen. I have something new in the way of a religion which I'd like to explain, if you'll give me just a minute of your time." A boisterous laugh would have ended his talk. A new religion—what did they care about that?

But Paul knew the psychology of the crowd.

"Men of Athens, I congratulate you on having so many

fine religions." Nothing in that to which anyone could take offense. The sophisticated pressed up a little closer; what was the chap driving at, anyhow? "I've traveled about quite a bit and your assortment is larger and better than I have seen anywhere else. For as I passed up your main street I noticed that you not only have altars erected to all the regular gods and goddesses; you even have one dedicated to the UNKNOWN GOD.

"Let me tell you an interesting coincidence, gentlemen. This God whom you worship without knowing His name is the very God whom I represent."

Can you see the crowd? Cynical but curious, eager to turn the whole thing into a joke, yet unwilling to miss a chance to hear the latest. Paul stopped short for a moment, and voices called out demanding that he go on. It appears later in the narrative that after his talk was over "some mocked, and others said, 'We will hear thee again of this matter.'" It was not a complete victory such as his Master had achieved at Jacob's Well; but the audience which confronted Paul was hostile, and his initial success was so cleverly won that this story deserves a place beside the one which we have just related. Together they help us to understand the great mystery—how a religion, originating in a despised province of a petty country, could so quickly carry around the world. It conquered not because there was any *demand* for another religion but because Jesus knew how, and taught His followers how, to catch the attention of the indifferent, and translate a great spiritual conception into terms of practical self-concern.

This aspect of Jesus' universal genius may perhaps be best understood by the psychologist and the businessman. From everyday experience they will understand that—except for the infinitely greater value of His work—Jesus was using a method not unlike those used now as the most modern technique of overcoming unreasoning resistance to a helpful idea, service or product. A wise and good man who was also a splendid salesman explained it like this:

When you want to get aboard a train which is already in motion, you don't run at it from right angles and try to make the platform in one wild leap. If you do, you're likely to find yourself on the ground. No. You run along beside the car, increasing your pace until you are moving just as rapidly as it is moving and in the same direction. Then you step aboard easily, without danger or jolt.

"The minds of busy men are in motion," he would continue. "They are engaged with something very different from the thought you have to present. You can't jump directly at them and expect to make an effective landing. You must put yourself in the other man's place; try to imagine what he is thinking; let your first remark be sincere and honest but in line with his thoughts; follow it by another such with which you know he will not disagree. Thus, gradually, your two minds reach a point at which small differences are lost in common understanding of a truth. Then with perfect sincerity he will say 'yes' and 'yes' and 'that's right' and 'I've noticed that myself.'"

Jesus taught all this without ever teaching it. Every one of His conversations, every contact between His mind and others, is worthy of the attentive study of any sales manager. Passing along the shores of a lake one day, He saw two of the men whom He wanted as disciples. Their minds were in motion; their hands were busy with their nets; their conversation was about conditions in the fishing trade and the prospects of a good market for the day's catch. To have broken in on such thinking with the offer of employment as preachers of a new religion would have been to confuse them and invite a sure rebuff. What was Jesus' approach?

"Come with me," He said, "and I will make you fishers of men."

Fishers—that was a word they could understand. . . . Fishers of men—that was a new idea. . . . What was He driving at? Fishers of men—it sounded interesting . . . well, what is it, anyway?

He sat on a hillside overlooking a fertile country. Many of the crowd who gathered around Him were farmers with their wives and sons and daughters. He wanted their interest and attention; it was important to make them understand, at the very outset, that what He had to say was nothing vague or theoretical but of direct and immediate application to their daily lives.

"A sower went forth to sow," He began, "and when he sowed some seeds fell by the wayside and the fowls came and devoured them up. . . ." Were they interested . . . *were* they? Every man of them had gone through that experience! The thievish crows—many a good day's work they had spoiled. . . . So this Teacher knew something about the troubles that farmers had to put up with, did He? Fair enough . . . let's hear what He has to say. . . .

It would be easy to multiply examples, taking each of His parables and pointing out the keen knowledge of human motives on which it is based. The examples already given are enough for this chapter. They show how instantly He won His audiences. With His very first sentence He identified Himself with them; it invariably expressed a thought they readily understood, a truth easy for even the dullest to comprehend. And the first sentence awakened an appetite for more.

Jesus knew very well the value of being able to sense an objection and meet it before it was advanced. He went one night to dine with a prominent Pharisee. His presence in any house attracted strangers who found it easy under the far from rigid conventions of those days to make their way into the room, where they could watch Him and listen. Thus, while the Pharisee's dinner was in progress, a woman generally considered immoral came into the room and, kneeling down by

Jesus, began to bathe His feet with precious ointment and wipe them with her hair. Jesus knew what that outburst of unselfishness meant to an overburdened spirit, and He accepted the tribute with gracious dignity, even though its emotional warmth must have been embarrassing. But all the time He was perfectly well aware of the thoughts that were passing through the self-satisfied mind of His host.

"Ah," that cynical gentleman was saying to himself, "if He were a prophet, He would have known that this woman is a sinner and would have refused to let her touch Him."

He might have been tempted to put his thought into words, but he never had a chance.

Quick as a flash Jesus turned on him: "Simon, I have somewhat to say to thee."

"Teacher, say on." It was a half-concealed sneer.

"There was a man who had two debtors," said Jesus. "One owed him five hundred shillings and the other fifty. Neither could pay and he forgave them both. Which of them, do you think, will love him most?"

Simon sensed a trap and moved cautiously.

"I imagine the one who owed him the most," he said, and wondered what was coming next.

"Right," said Jesus. "Simon, seest thou this woman?"

Simon nodded. He began to wish the conversation had not started.

"When I came into your house, you gave me no water for my feet," Jesus continued with that extraordinary frankness which cut straight to the heart of things. "But she has washed my feet with her tears and dried them with her hair. You gave me no kiss, but she has not ceased to kiss my feet. You poured none of your expensive oil on my head, but she has taken her precious ointment, which she could ill afford, and anointed me."

Simon squirmed in his seat. It was not comfortable to be

reminded before a crowd of his delinquencies as a host. He had invited this "interesting" former carpenter because it was quite the fad to invite Him. But the whole atmosphere had been one of condescension—the unspoken intimation was "Here's a good dinner; now go on and amuse us with your ideas." There had been none of the niceties; the rich are so well accustomed to being inconsiderate!

The dining room was silent; every eye was turned to the Teacher; the poor woman still knelt at His feet, embarrassed that her action should have caused so much comment, wondering if the incident was to end in a rebuke. Jesus did not look down at her; He was not yet through with Simon.

"She is like the debtor who owed the five hundred shillings," He said. "Her sins which are many are forgiven, for she loved much. To whom little is forgiven, the same loves little." And then with a glance of infinite tenderness:

"Thy sins are forgiven," He said to her simply. "Thy faith has saved thee; go in peace."

It is easy to imagine that the conversation rather dragged during the remainder of the meal. Even very supercilious and self-assured gentlemen hesitated to expose themselves to the thrusts of a mind which could anticipate criticisms before they were uttered and deal with them so crisply.

On other occasions He won His case with a single question —one of the best weapons in the whole armory of persuasion and all too infrequently employed. How often a blundering advocate allows himself to be dragged into futile argument, when by throwing the burden back onto his opponent's shoulders he could attain an easy mastery. Jesus seldom argued. The record of His questions is a fruitful study for all of us who, in our everyday affairs, must deal with other minds. Let us recall two of those questions.

The Pharisees set a trap for Him. One Sabbath day they hunted up a man with a withered hand and deposited him in the Temple where Jesus would be sure to pass. Then they waited. If Jesus healed him, it would be a breach of the Code, which forbade any activity on the Sabbath. They would have that to recall when the crisis came. Jesus sensed the test and met it without hesitation.

"Stand forth," He said to the poor chap.

The bigoted formalists pushed in close. This was their moment. They had dug the pit cleverly, and now He was about to fall in. The soft light went out of Jesus' eyes, the muscles of His jaw grew tense, He looked "round on them with anger," as He demanded:

"Is it lawful on the Sabbath day to do good or to do harm? To save a life or to kill?"

He waited for an answer but none came. What could they say? If they replied that the law forbade a good deed, their answer would be repeated all over town. The crowd of common men who followed Him were His friends, not theirs—only too glad to spread a story which would cast discredit on the proud defenders of the law. The Pharisees had sense enough to recognize that fact, at least. They "held their peace" and sullenly slipped away.

On another day it was His own disciples who learned how He could compress a whole philosophy into a well-directed question. They were by no means free from the frailties of ordinary human nature. They fussed about little things—arguing among themselves as to who should have pre-eminence; wondering how their bills were to be met, and just where the whole enterprise was coming out.

He brought them up short with a question.

"Which of you by being anixous can add a single day to his life?" He demanded. "And if you can't do this simple thing, why worry about the rest? Consider the ravens; they don't sow or reap; they have no storehouses or barns, and yet

God takes care of them. Don't you suppose that you are of more value in His sight than a flock of birds?"

How trivial seemed their concern and controversy after a question like that!

In all the three years of His public work there was not one moment when He failed to be complete master of the situation. He was accessible to anybody—in the market place, in the Temple and on the main streets—fair game for the keen and clever. It became quite a recognized sport to match wits with Him. Pharisees tried it; Scribes tried it; "a certain lawyer" tried it. Always they came off second-best. At length the very chiefs of the priests came one afternoon. Lesser antagonists had gone down; now the leaders themselves would take the matter in hand. They would demolish this presumptuous upstart; by the splendor of their presence and their offices, they would awe Him into line.

"By what authority do you do these things," they demanded briskly, "and who gave you this authority?"

If they expected Him to yield an inch, they received the surprise of their lives. His retort was instantaneous.

"I'll ask you a question," he exclaimed, "and if you answer it, then I'll tell you by what authority I work. Answer me now, what about John; was his work in baptizing inspired by Heaven or by men?"

They caught their breath. Their heads came together; excited and disturbing whispers were exchanged. What shall we say? If we answer that John had come from Heaven, He will say, "Well, why then didn't you believe him?" If we say that he came from men, this crowd of fools will tear us to pieces, because every last one of them believes that John was a prophet. What shall we do? Better tell Him we don't know; better get out of here as quickly as we can. . . .

"We don't know," they muttered.

"All right," said Jesus serenely. "You don't answer my question. Neither will I answer yours."

It was a perfect triumph. Amid the jeers of the delighted crowd the chiefs gathered up their fine robes and went away.

You would think as you read the narratives that the wise ones would have been wise enough to let Him alone. Even a child, having burned its fingers once, knows enough to avoid the fire. But their jealousy and anger drove them back again and again; and every time He was too much for them. In the very last week the "Pharisees and Herodians" gathered together a picked delegation of sharp wits and sent them to Jesus with what looked like an absolutely foolproof bomb. They started in with flattery; after all, He was a simple fellow from the provinces—a few kind words and His head would be turned. Then they would catch Him off guard.

"Teacher, we know that you speak the truth," they said, "and that you don't care anything about the authority or office which a man holds. You treat them all alike, and speak your mind bluntly because you get your thoughts direct from God.

"Now, tell us, is it lawful to give tribute unto Caesar or not?"

Very clever, gentlemen, very clever indeed. If He answers that it isn't lawful, you will have the record of His reply in Herod's hands in an hour and instantly He will be under arrest for propagating rebellion against the Roman power. If He answers that it is lawful, He will lose His popular following—because the people hate the Romans and dodge the taxes at every turn . . . very, very clever.

He looked at them with frank contempt as if to say, "Do you really think I am quite as simple as all that?"

"Somebody lend me a coin," He exclaimed. An eager listener dug into his purse and produced it. Jesus held it up where all could see.

"Whose picture is here?" He demanded. "Whose name?"

They began to be uneasy. The shrewdest suspected that the path was leading toward the precipice, yet there was no escape. They must answer. "Caesar's," they replied.

"Very good," He said. "Render unto Caesar the things that are Caesar's and unto God the things that are God's."

Another repulse for the best legal talent in the city, another good laugh for the crowd, another story to tell in the taverns, in the Temple court, in the market place . . . wherever the common folk crowded together. In describing the defeated questioners three of the Gospels say: "they marveled at him" and a little later we read, "and no man after that durst ask him any question." Every objection had been turned back on the objectors; every trap had been sprung on the fingers of those who had set it. No argument was left for them except the final one which is always a confession of failure. They had brute force on their side. They could not stand against His thinking but they could, and did, nail Him on the cross.

Not in time, however. Not until His work was finished. Not until He had trained and equipped a force which would carry on with double power because of the very fact of His death. . . . Every year in our country there are thousands of conventions—political, charitable, business. Most of them are a waste. They are conducted on the false assumption that overselling and exaggeration are potent forces—that the energies of men respond most powerfully to promises of easy victory and soft rewards. The great leaders of the world have known better.

Gideon, for example. When he called for volunteers to fight the Midianites, thirty-two thousand responded. Gideon looked them over critically. He knew the conflicting motives that had brought them there—some had come from mere love of adventure, some because they were afraid to be taunted with cowardice, some for plunder, some to get away from their wives. He determined to weed them out immediately.

"Whosoever is fearful and afraid, let him go home tonight," he proclaimed.

The next morning twenty-two thousand had vanished. Only ten thousand remained.

Still Gideon was unsatisfied. He hit on a stratagem. Down the hillside and across a little brook he led the whole band. It was a hot morning; the men were thirsty and tired. Gideon, standing on the bank and watching, had a shrewd idea that character would show itself under the strain. Sure enough, of the ten thousand, a vast majority knelt down and pushed their faces into the cool clear water, taking long refreshing draughts. But a few were too much in earnest to loiter. They caught up the water in their hands, dashed it into their faces and hurried across to the other bank, restless to go on!

Only a handful; only three hundred. But Gideon kept them and sent the rest home. Better three hundred who could not be held back from the battle than ten thousand who were halfheartedly ready to go.

With the three hundred he won.

It is a higher type of leadership that calls forth men's greatest energies by the promise of obstacles rather than the picture of rewards. In our time we heard Churchill's "blood, sweat and tears" address to his countrymen, and we saw their response.

Jesus was the great master of this kind of leadership. By it He tempered the soft metal of His disciples' nature into keen hard steel. The final conference by which He prepared them for their work is thrilling in its majestic appeal to courage. Listen to the calm recital of the deprivations and dangers:

> Provide neither gold, nor silver, nor brass in your purses,
> Nor scrip for your journey, neither two coats, neither shoes, nor yet staves . . . (Matt. 10:9-10)

Behold, I send you forth as sheep in the midst of
wolves . . .

But beware of men: for they will deliver you up to the
councils, and they will scourge you in their synagogues;

And ye shall be brought before governors and kings
for my sake . . . (Matt. 10:16-18)

He that loveth father or mother more than me: and he
that loveth son or daughter more than me is not worthy
of me.

And he that taketh not his cross, and followeth after
me, is not worthy of me.

He that findeth his life shall lose it: and he that loseth
his life for my sake shall find it. (Matt. 10:37-39)

Watch the faces and the figures. See the shoulders straight-
en, the muscles of the lips grow hard. There is power in those
faces that will not be withstood—power born of the most
transforming appeal which ever fell on human ears. The voice
of the speaker was stilled at the cross, but the power carried
on. It withstood prisons and scourging; shipwreck and weariness; public condemnation and the loss of personal friends;
chains, and the roar of lions and the flames. James was the
first to die—Herod Agrippa killed him. His brother John,
imprisoned for years on the stony island of Patmos, suffered
martyrdom in frightful torture. Andrew died on a cross
whose pattern bears his name to this day. Simon Peter insisted that he be crucified head downward, deeming himself
unworthy to suffer in the manner of his Lord. Nero stilled
the voice of Paul by beheading him; but the spirit of Paul
which had proclaimed that "we are in all things more than
conquerors," began at that moment to have its larger influence.

Just a few brief years and every member of the original
organization was gone, but the "blood of the martyrs was the
seed of the church." The Master's training had done its work.

The great Idea prevailed.

chapter 5

His Work and Words

JESUS WAS, as we say, many-sided, and every man sees the side of His nature which appeals most to himself.

The doctor thinks of the great Physician whose touch never failed, who by the genius that remains a mystery to man preceded modern science in a knowledge of the relation of the spirit to health, a knowledge still incomplete. The preacher studies the Sermon on the Mount and marvels that truths so profound should be expressed in words so clear and simple. The politically active man remembers best His courage in opposing the most powerful elements in His community and is awed by His capacity to speak honestly without loss of loyalty. Lawyers have written in praise of His pleading at His trial; and the literary critics of every age have cheerfully acknowledged His mastery as a storyteller.

Each man, it is plain, understands that part of His universal genius which with his own abilities and skills he can most nearly approach. I am not a doctor or lawyer or critic but an advertising man. That means that I am and have been concerned with the ways in which words, design and color may carry conviction to people, with the art-science of bringing others to your point of view. It is perhaps not unnatural that I can think of the brilliant plumage of the bird as color advertising addressed to the emotions of its mate. This is, you may grant, a view not unsupported by observable fact.

It has been remarked that "no astronomer can be an atheist," which is only another way of saying that the scientist knows God because he has seen an order so vast and perfect that the idea of purposeful creation must be part of any thought about it.

My view is less exalted, but my purpose deeply sincere. I propose in this chapter to consider some words and deeds of Jesus which persuaded and still persuade men of the wisdom and justice in His teaching. So I have, I hope, seen Jesus as a man who lived and worked, and not as the symbol conventionally displayed.

Let us begin by asking why He could command public attention and why, in contrast, His churches have not done so well. The answer is twofold. His mission was to teach men. But before even He could teach, He must get men to listen. He was never trite; He had no single method. The Gospels show clearly that no one could predict what He would say or do; His actions and words were always new, arresting, challenging and meaningful to the men among whom He lived.

Take one day as an example. The four Gospel narratives are not chronological. They are personal records written after His death, not diaries in which entries were made every night. Thus we cannot say of most of the incidents: "This happened on such and such a day." The four stories repeat, conflict and overlap. In one place, however—the ninth chapter of Matthew—we have a detailed account of just one day's work. One of the events was the calling of Matthew himself to discipleship; hence we have every reason to suppose that the writer's memory of this particular day must have been more than usually reliable. Let us look at these twenty-four hours.

The activity begins at sunrise. Jesus was an early riser; He knew that the simplest way to live *more* than an average life is to add an hour to the fresh end of the day. At sunrise, therefore, we discover a little boat pushing out from the shore of the lake. It makes its way steadily across and deposits Jesus and His disciples in Capernaum, His favorite city. He proceeds at once to the house of a friend, but not without being discovered. The report spreads instantly that He is in town, and before He can finish breakfast a crowd of townsmen has collected outside the gate—a poor palsied chap among them.

The day's work begins.

Having slept soundly in the open air, Jesus meets the call quietly. The smile that carried confidence into even the most hopeless heart spreads over His features; He stoops down toward the sufferer.

"Be of good cheer, my son," He says; "your sins are all forgiven."

Sins forgiven! Indeed! The respectable members of the audience draw back with sharp disapproval. "What a blasphemous phrase!" "Who authorized this man to exercise the functions of God? What right has He to decide whose sins shall be forgiven?"

Jesus sensed rather than heard their protest. He never courted controversy; He never dodged it, and much of His fame arose out of the reports of His verbal victories. Men have been elected to office—even such high office as the Presidency —by being so good-natured that they never made enemies. But the leaders who are remembered are those who had plenty of critics and dealt with them vigorously.

"What's the objection?" He exclaimed, turning on the dissenters. "Why do you stand there and criticize? Is it easier to say, 'Thy sins be forgiven thee,' or to say, 'Arise, take up thy bed and walk'? The results are the same."

Bending over the sick man again, He said, "Arise, take up thy bed and go unto thine house."

The man stirred and was amazed to find that his muscles responded. Slowly, doubtingly, he struggled to his feet, and with a great shout of happiness started off, surrounded by his jubilant friends. The critics had received their answer, but they refused to give up. For an hour or more they persisted in angry argument, until the meeting ended in a tumult.

It's hardly necessary to say that Jesus did not heal merely to stir, awe and anger doubters. Yet His honest directness had a startling, far-reaching effect. One of those who had been attracted by the excitement was a tax collector named Matthew. Being a man of business he could not stay through the argument, but slipped away early and was hard at work when Jesus passed by a few minutes before noon.

"Matthew, I want you," said Jesus.

That was all. No argument; no offer of inducements; no promise of rewards. Merely "I want you"; and the prosperous tax collector closed his office, prepared a feast for the brilliant young teacher and forthwith announced himself a disciple. Once again we can be sure Jesus' purpose was single. But we can easily believe also that His instant winning of Matthew shook Capernaum for the second time that day.

A feast provided by Matthew furnished a third sensation. It was not at all the kind of affair which a religious teacher would be expected to approve. Decidedly, it was good-natured and noisy.

No theological test was applied in limiting the invitation. No one stood at the entrance to demand, "What is your belief regarding Jesus?" or, "Have you or have you not been baptized?" The doors were flung wide, and, along with the disciples and the respectable folks, a swarm of publicans and sinners trooped in.

"Outrageous," grumbled the worthy folk. "Surely if this Teacher had any moral standards He never would eat with such rabble."

They were shocked, but He was not. That He had condemned Himself according to their formula worried Him not a whit. His liking for people overran all social boundaries; He just could not seem to remember that some people are nice people, proper people, and some are not.

"Come, come," He exclaimed to the Pharisees, "won't you ever stop nagging at me because I eat with these outsiders? Who needs the doctor most—they that are well or they that are sick?

"And here's another thing to think about," He added. "You lay so much stress on forms and creeds and occasions—do you suppose God cares about all that? What do you think He meant when He said: 'I will have mercy and not sacrifice'? Take that home and puzzle over it."

A fourth event to rouse the town. You may be sure it was carried into hundreds of homes during the next few weeks, and formed the basis for many a long evening's discussion. Jesus had been intent only on His ministry. Though He had not sought attention, the streets rang with His name. Indifference to such a manner was impossible.

As the meal drew to its close there came a dramatic interruption—a ruler of the city made his way slowly to the head of the table and stood silent, bowed by a terrible weight of grief. That morning he had sat at his daughter's bedside, clasping her frail hand in his, watching the flutter of the pulse, trying by the force of his longing to hold that little life back from the precipice. And at last the doctors had told him that it was useless to hope any more. So he had come, this ruler, to the strange young man whose deeds of healing were the sensation of the day.

Was it too late? The ruler had thought so when he entered the door, but as he stood in that splendid presence a new thrilling conviction gripped him:

"Master, my daughter is even now dead," he exclaimed; "but come and lay your hand on her and she will live."

Jesus rose from His seat, drawn by that splendid outburst

of faith, and without hesitation or questioning He started for the door. All His life He seemed to feel that there was no limit at all to what He could do if only those who beseeched Him believed enough. He grasped the ruler's arm and led the way up the street. His disciples and motley crowd walked behind.

They had several blocks to travel, and before their journey was completed another interruption occurred.

A woman who had been sick for twelve years edged through the crowd, eluded the sharp eyes of the disciples and touched the hem of His garment. "For she said within herself, if I may but touch His garment, I shall be whole." What an idea! What a personality His must have been to provoke such ideas! "My daughter is dead, but lay your hands on her and she will live." . . . "I've been sick for twelve years; the doctors can do nothing, but if I only touch His coat I'll be all right."

The woman won her victory. By that touch, by His smile, by the few words He spoke, her faith rose triumphant over disease. She "was made whole from that hour."

Again He moved forward, the crowd pressing hard. The ruler's residence was now in sight. The paid mourners, hired by the hour, were busy about the doorway; they increased their activities as their employer came in sight—hideous wails and the dull sounding of cymbals, a horrible pretense of grief. Jesus quickened His stride.

"Give place," He called out to them with a commanding gesture. "The maid is not dead but sleepeth."

They laughed Him to scorn. He brushed them aside, strode into the house and took the little girl by the hand. The crowd looked on dumfounded, for at the magic of His Touch she opened her eyes and sat up.

Now every citizen must have been thinking of this man. Every citizen had to answer questions about Him. Had these things really happened? A woman sick twelve years and healed! A child whom the doctors had abandoned for dead sits up and smiles! No wonder a thousand tongues were busy that night discussing His name and work. "The fame thereof went abroad into all that land," says the narrative. Nothing could keep it from going abroad. It was irresistible news!

He was known by His service, not by His sermons; this is the noteworthy fact. His preaching seems in the light of such events almost incidental. On only one occasion did He deliver a long discourse, and that was probably interrupted often by questions and debates. He did not come to establish a theology but to lead a good life. Living more healthfully than any of His contemporaries, He spread health wherever He went. Thinking more daringly, more divinely, than anyone before Him, He expressed Himself in words of great beauty. His sermons, if they may be called sermons, were chiefly explanatory of His service. He healed a lame man, gave sight to a blind man, fed the hungry, cheered the poor; and by these works He was known.

The church, which hopes to spread widely the news of good work, often receives little attention. Yet it is much more fruitful in such good works than the uninformed suspect. Most of our colleges were founded under its inspiration; most of our hospitals grew out of, and are supported by, its membership; the ideals that animate all civic enterprises are its ideals; and its members furnish to such movements the most dependable support. More than this, the day-by-day life of any genuine pastor is a constant succession of healings and helpings, as anyone who has been privileged to grow up in a minister's family very well knows. The doorbell or telephone rings at breakfast time; it rings at dinner time; it rings late at night—and every ring means that someone has come to cast his burden on the parsonage. A man comes blinded by his greed or hatred or fear—he opens his heart to the pastor and goes away having received his sight. A parent whose child is dead in selfishness comes leading the child by the hand. And sometimes the preacher is able to touch the withered veins of conscience, and life becomes normal and wholesome again. A man out of work, whose family is hungry, knocks timidly at the parsonage door. And somehow, from the parson's few loaves and fishes, the other family is fed.

These are Jesus' works, done in Jesus' name. If He lived again now, He would be known by His service, not merely by His sermons. One thing is certain; He would not neglect the market place. Few of His sermons were delivered in synagogues. For the most part He was in the crowded places, the Temple court, the city squares, the centers where goods were bought and sold. I emphasized this fact once to a group of preachers.

"You mean that we ought to do street preaching," one of them exclaimed.

But street preaching is not at all analogous to what Jesus did. The cities in which He worked were both small and leisurely; the market was a gathering place where everybody came at some time—the place of exchange for all merchandise and for ideas. The world is no longer so small. Where will you find such a market place in modern days? A corner of Fifth Avenue? A block on Broadway? Only a tiny fraction of the city's people pass any given point in the downtown district on any given day. A man might stand and preach for years at Fifth Avenue and Thirtieth Street, and only one in a hundred thousand would ever know that he lived.

No. Few ideas gain currency unless they may be presented simultaneously to hundreds of thousands. Magazines, newspapers, radio and television networks are now the street in Capernaum. Here our goods are sold; here voices are raised to win our loyalty to ideas, to causes—to faiths. That the voice of Jesus should be still in our market place is an omission which He could soon find a way to correct. The minds He challenged in Capernaum cannot be so different from ours. We are not stirred because we do not hear. If it came to us so directly as it came to the townsmen of Capernaum, could we refuse to heed His call:

> For what shall it profit a man, if he shall gain the whole world, and lose his own soul?
> Or what shall a man give in exchange for his soul? (Mark 8:36-37)

Suppose His challenge were in every newspaper and magazine; and with it an invitation to share in the joyous enterprise of His work.

One eminent publisher has a rule that no photograph shall ever be printed in his newspapers unless it contains human beings. You and I are interested most of all in ourselves; next to that we are interested in other people. What do they look like? How old are they? What have they done and said? Jesus recognized this trait of human nature. One of the most revealing of all verses to those who would understand the secret of His power is this: "All these things spake Jesus unto the multitude in parables; and without a parable spake he not unto them." A parable is a story. He told them stories, stories about people, and let the stories carry His message.

He might have adopted very different methods—many teachers and would-be leaders do. He might have dealt in generalities, saying: "When you are going about your business, be as kind as you can. Be thoughtful of the other travelers on the highways of life. Take time to look for those who have fared less fortunately; lend them a helping hand whenever you can."

I say He might have uttered such generalities. But if He had, do you suppose that they would ever have been remembered? Would the disciples have recorded them? Would our age ever have heard His name? He was far wiser in the laws and habits of the human mind. Instead of such commonplace phrases, He painted this striking picture: "A certain man went down from Jerusalem to Jericho and fell among thieves." There's your illustration! If you had lived near Jerusalem or Jericho, if you often had occasion to use that very road, wouldn't you want to know what happened to that unfortunate traveler?

"They stripped off his raiment," the parable continues, "and wounded him, and departed, leaving him half dead." Soon a priest came by and seeing the victim said to himself, "That's a shameful thing. The police ought to do something about these outrages." But he crossed the road carefully and passed by on the other side. A certain respectable Levite also appeared. "His own fault," he sniffed; "ought to be more careful." And he too passed by. Then a third traveler drew near and stopped—and the whole world knows what happened. . . . Generalities would have been soon forgotten. But the story that had its roots in everyday human experience and need lives and will live forever. The parable of the Good Samaritan condenses the philosophy of Christianity into a half dozen unforgettable paragraphs.

Take any one of the parables, no matter which—you will find that it is a perfect example of the way in which a new idea may be presented. Always a picture in the very first sentence; crisp, graphic language and a message so clear that even the least interested cannot escape it. "Ten virgins . . . went forth to meet the bridegroom."

A striking picture, and the story which follows has not a single wasted word:

And five of them were wise, and five were foolish.
They that were foolish took their lamps, and took no oil with them:

But the wise took oil in their vessels with their lamps.

While the bridegroom tarried, they all slumbered and slept.

And at midnight there was a cry made, Behold, the bridegroom cometh; go ye out to meet him.

Then all those virgins arose, and trimmed their lamps.

And the foolish said unto the wise, Give us of your oil; for our lamps are gone out.

But the wise answered, saying, Not so; lest there be not enough for us and you: but go ye rather to them that sell, and buy for yourselves.

And while they went to buy, the bridegroom came; and they that were ready went in with him to the marriage: and the door was shut.

Afterward came also the other virgins, saying, Lord, Lord, open to us.

But he answered and said, Verily I say unto you, I know you not.

Watch therefore, for ye know neither the day nor the hour wherein the Son of man cometh. (Matt. 25:2-13)

And another:

What man of you, having an hundred sheep, if he lose one of them, doth not leave the ninety and nine in the wilderness, and go after that which is lost, until he find it?

And when he hath found it, he layeth it on his shoulders, rejoicing.

And when he cometh home, he calleth together his friends and neighbours, saying unto them, Rejoice with me; for I have found my sheep which was lost.

I say unto you, that likewise joy shall be in heaven over one sinner that repenteth, more than over ninety and nine just persons, which need no repentance. (Luke 15:4-7)

If you were given the task of making known to the world that God cares enormously for one human life—no matter how wayward and wrong the life may be—how could you phrase a message more memorably than that? Yet how simple, how sincere, how splendidly crisp and direct! Benjamin Franklin in his autobiography tells the process which he went through in acquiring an effective style. He would read a passage from some great master of English, then lay the book aside and attempt to reproduce the thought in his own words. Comparing his version with the original, he discovered wherein he had obscured the thought or wasted words or failed to drive straight to the point. Every man who wishes to know a little more of Jesus should study the parables in the same fashion, schooling himself in their language and learning the elements of their power.

1. First of all they are marvelously condensed. Charles A. Dana, it is reported, once issued an assignment to a new reporter on the *New York Sun*, directing him to confine his article to a column. The reporter protested that the story was too big to be compressed into so small a space.

"Get a copy of the Bible and read the first chapter of Genesis," said Dana. "You'll be surprised to find that the whole story of the creation of the world can be told in six hundred words."

Jesus had no introductions. A single sentence grips attention; three or four more tell the story; one or two more and both the thought and its application are clear. And this is true of ideas that reformed the moral structure of the world! When He wanted a new disciple, He said simply, "Follow me." When He sought to explain the deepest philosophic mystery—the personality and character of God—He said, "A king made a banquet and invited many guests. God is that king and you are the guests; the Kingdom of Heaven is happiness—a banquet to be enjoyed."

Two men spoke on the battleground of Gettysburg more than ninety years ago. The first delivered an oration of more than two hours in length; not one person in ten who reads this page can even recall his name; certainly not one in a hundred can quote a single sentence from his masterly effort. The second speaker uttered two hundred and fifty words, and those words, Lincoln's Gettysburg Address, are a part of the mental endowment of almost every American.

Many noble prayers have been sent up to the Throne of Grace—long impressive utterances. The prayer which Jesus taught His disciples consists of sixty-eight words and can be written on the back of a post card. Many poems and essays have been penned by writers who hoped that they were making a permanent place for themselves in literature, but one of the greatest poems ever written consists of one hundred and eighty-eight words. It is the Twenty-third Psalm.

Jesus hated prosy dullness. He praised the Centurion who was anxious not to waste His time; the only prayer which He publicly commended was uttered by a poor publican who merely cried out, "God, be merciful to me a sinner." A seven-word prayer, and Jesus called it a good one. A sixty-eight-word prayer, He said, contained all that men needed to say or God to hear. What would be His verdict on most of our prayers and our speeches and our writing?

2. His language was marvelously simple—a second great essential. There is hardly a sentence in His teaching which a child cannot understand. His illustrations were all drawn from the commonest experiences of life: "a sower went forth to sow"; "a certain man had two sons"; "a man built his house on the sands"; "the kingdom of heaven is like a grain of mustard seed."

The absence of adjectives is striking. Henry Ward Beecher said once that "to a large extent adjectives are like leaves on a switch; they may make it look pretty, as a branch, but they prevent it striking tinglingly when you use it.

"I recollect a case in which my father at a public meeting

was appointed to draw up an article," Beecher continued. "He had written one sentence: 'It is wrong.' Someone in the meeting got up and moved in his enthusiasm that this be corrected, and that the sentence read: 'It is exceedingly wrong.' My father got up and said, in his mild way, 'When I was writing out this resolution in its original shape that was the way I wrote it, but to make it stronger, I took out the "exceedingly." ' "

Jesus used few qualifying words and no long ones. We referred a minute ago to those three literary masterpieces. The Lord's Prayer, The Twenty-third Psalm, The Gettysburg Address. Recall their phraseology:

Our Father which art in Heaven, hallowed be thy name

The Lord is my shepherd; I shall not want

Four score and seven years ago

Not a single three-syllable word; hardly any two-syllable words. All the greatest things in human life are one-syllable things—love, joy, hope, home, child, wife, trust, faith, God—and the great pieces of writing, generally speaking, use the small word in place of the large if meaning permits.

3. Sincerity illuminates strongly every word, every sentence He uttered; sincerity is the third essential. Many wealthy men have purchased newspapers with the idea of advancing their personal fortunes or bringing about some political action in which they have a private interest. Such newspapers almost invariably fail. No matter how much money is spent on them, no matter how zealously the secret of their ownership is guarded, readers eventually become conscious that something is wrong. They come to feel that the voice of the editor is not his own.

It was the way Jesus looked at men, and the life He led among them, that gave His words transforming power. What He was and what He said were one and the same thing. Nobody could stand at His side for even a minute without being persuaded that here was a man who loved people and considered even the humblest of them worthy of the best He had to give. There is no presupposition more deadening to a writer than the idea that he can "write down" to his readers. No man was ever big enough to build enduringly on the basis of insincerity; but many like Peter the Hermit, fired with conviction, have been able to create and sustain a very considerable influence.

Jesus was notably tolerant of almost all kinds of sinners. He liked the companionship of the rough-and-ready folk who were entirely outside the churches; He was tender toward unfortunate women; He had a special fondness for James and John, whose ungovernable tempers had given them the title of "Sons of Thunder"; He forgave the weakness of Peter who denied Him; and He was not resentful at the unbelief of His near relatives and His native town. But for one sin He had no mercy. He denounced the insincerity of the Pharisees in phrases which sting like the lash of a whip. They thought they had a first mortgage on the Kingdom of Heaven, and He told them scornfully that only those who become like little children have any chance of entering in.

Little children know no pretense. They are startlingly frank. They look at the world through clear eyes and say only what they think. No writer, no orator, no salesman, exercises any large dominion in the world unless he can humble himself and partake of their nature.

"Though I speak with the tongues of men and of angels and have not charity, I am become as sounding brass or a tinkling cymbal," wrote Saint Paul.

Much brass has been sounded and many cymbals have

tinkled in the presentation of ideas infinitely less complex and true. Persuasion depends on respect for the listeners, and in Jesus great respect coupled with great love.

4. Finally Jesus knew that any idea may have to be repeated.

One of the sons of President Garfield was traveling with his father through Ohio when the President was addressing county fairs. At the close of the day he asked the boy what he thought of his speeches.

The boy was embarrassed by the question. "Why . . . why they were fine, Dad," he stammered, "but I felt uncomfortable part of the time. You repeated yourself so often; once you said the very same thing in different words four times over."

With a hearty laugh, Garfield slapped the boy's shoulder.

"So you thought your old dad was running out of ideas, did you?" he cried. "Well, I don't blame you; but there's a method in my madness. Tomorrow when I reach that passage in my talk, you watch the audience. The first time I make the point, you'll see by the faces that a few folks near the platform get it. But further back there will be noise and commotion; people will be turning their heads to find out who has just driven up, or what sort of hat Mrs. Jones has on, and they won't hear me at all. When I repeat it the first time a few faces in the middle of the crowd will show a response; on the third go, I'll make still more converts and on the fourth trial they'll all have a notion of what I am talking about. But it takes four shots to land them all; experience with all sorts of audiences has made me sure of that."

It has been said that "reputation is repetition." No important truth can be impressed on the minds of any large number of people by being said only once. The thoughts which Jesus had to give the world were revolutionary, but they were few in number. "God is your father," He said, "caring more for the welfare of every one of you than any human father can possibly care for his children. His Kingdom is happiness! His rule is love." This is what He had to teach, and He knew the necessity of driving it home from every possible angle. So in one of His stories God is the Shepherd searching the wilds for one wandering sheep; in another the Father welcoming home a prodigal boy; in another a King who forgives his debtors large amounts and expects them to be forgiving in turn—many stories but the same big Idea.

Because the stories were unforgettable, the idea lived and is today one of the most powerful influences on human action and thought. To be sure the work is far from complete. The idea that God is the Father of all men—not merely of a specially selected few—has still to reach some areas and to establish its dominance in society. More or less unconsciously a lot of us share the feeling of the French nobleman in Saint Simon's immortal story, who was sure that God would "think twice before damning a person of his quality."

Said the Duchess of Buckingham to the Countess of Huntingdon, in a delicious letter:

> I thank your Ladyship for the information concerning the Methodist preachers; their doctrines are most repulsive and strongly tinctured with impertinence and disrespect toward their superiors. . . . It is monstrous to be told you have a heart as sinful as the common wretches that crawl on the earth. This is highly offensive and insulting, and I cannot but wonder that your Ladyship should relish any sentiments so much at variance with high rank and good breeding.

In spite of all the Duchesses of Buckingham, however, the great parables continue to advance. Monarchies are succeeded by democracies, building their governments on the firm foundation that men are free and equally entitled to a chance at the good things of life. The privileged protest and the agitators denounce, but slowly the world is learning.

And whoever feels an impulse to make his own life count in the grand process of human betterment can have no surer guide for his activities than Jesus. Let him learn the lesson of the parables: that in teaching people you first capture their interest; that your service rather than your sermons must be your claim on their attention; that what you say must be simple and brief and above all *sincere*—the unmistakable voice of true regard and affection.

"Ye," said He, "are my *friends*."

chapter 6

His Way in Our World

When Jesus was twelve years old, His father and mother took Him to the feast at Jerusalem.

It was the big national vacation; even peasant families saved their pennies and looked forward to it through the year. Towns like Nazareth were emptied of their inhabitants except for the few old people who were left behind to look after the very young ones. Crowds of cheerful pilgrims filled the highways, laughing on their way across the hills and under the stars at night.

In such a mass of people it was not surprising that a boy of twelve should be lost. When Mary and Joseph missed Him on the homeward trip, they took it calmly and began a search among the relatives.

The inquiry produced no result. Some remembered having seen Him in the Temple, but no one had seen Him since. Mary grew frightened; where could He be? Back there in the city alone? Wandering hungry and tired through the friendless streets? Carried away by other travelers into a distant country? She pictured a hundred calamities. Nervously she and Joseph hurried back over the hot roads, through the suburbs, up through the narrow city streets, up to the courts of the Temple itself.

And there He was.

Not lost; not a bit worried. Apparently unconscious that the feast was over, He sat in the midst of a group of old men, who were questioning Him and applauding the common sense of His replies. Involuntarily His parents halted—they were simple folk, uneasy among strangers and disheveled by their haste. But after all they were His parents, and a very human feeling of irritation quickly overcame their diffidence.

Mary stepped forward and grasped His arm. "Son, why hast thou thus dealt with us?" she demanded. "Behold, thy father and I have sought thee sorrowing."

I wonder what answer she expected to receive. Did she ever know exactly what He was going to say? Did anyone in Nazareth quite understand this keen eager lad who had such curious moments of abstraction and was forever breaking out with remarks that seemed far beyond His years?

He spoke to her now, with deference as always, but in words that did not dispel but rather added to her uncertainty.

"How is it that ye sought me?" He asked. "Wist ye not that I must be about my Father's business?"

Of course the anxious parents did not fully understand. Even if we consider they understood the boy's words as Luke is translated in the Revised Standard Version—"Did you not know I must be in my Father's house?"—we can imagine nothing but puzzlement. A prosperous carpenter shop was exactly the place for the boy.

Yet Mary said nothing more. Something in His look and tone silenced her. She and Joseph turned and started out, and Jesus followed them—away from the Temple and the city back to little Nazareth. Luke tells it with a grave and beautiful simplicity. "And he went down with them, and came to Nazareth, and was subject unto them; but his mother kept all these sayings in her heart."

His hour of boyish triumph had not turned His head. He knew how thorough must be His preparation. A building can rise high into the air only as it has sunk its foundations deep into the earth; the part of a man's life which the world sees is effective in proportion as it rests on solid foundations never seen. He knew this. For eighteen years more He was content to remain in the little town—until His strength was mature; until He had done His full duty by His mother and the younger children. Until His hour had come. "And Jesus increased in wisdom and stature, and in favour with God and man."

But what interests us most in this one recorded incident of His boyhood is that He defined here and at this age the purpose of His career. He did not say, "Wist ye not that I must show men the range of my understanding?" or "Wist ye not that I must get ready to meet the arguments of men like these?" The language and intent were quite different. However we translate, the essential remains the same. Here He announced to men His dedication. We know what followed. Thus we understand that those who first heard could not. He was saying that, obedient to God's will, He offered His life to men. To what extent is this principle by which He conducted His life applicable to ours? And if He were among us again in a time again tormented by selfishness, ambition, pride and misunderstanding, would His philosophy work?

Before we consider that let's turn to another occasion when, you recall, He stated more fully the great principle.

It was on the afternoon when James and John came to ask Him what promotion they might expect. They were two of the most energetic of the lot, called "the sons of thunder" by the rest, being noisy and always in the middle of some sort of storm. They had joined the ranks because they liked Him, but they had no very definite idea of what it was all about. Now they wanted to know where the enterprise was heading and just what there would be in it for them.

"Master," they said, "we want to ask what plans you have

in mind for us. You're going to need strong men around you when you establish your kingdom; our ambition is to sit on either side of you, one on your right hand and the other on your left."

Can we really object to that attitude? Each of us has asked or hoped for advancement. If we want a better place, we usually ask for it.

Jesus answered with a sentence of great poetry. But wouldn't it have sounded absurd to the sons of thunder?

"Whosoever will be great among you, shall be your minister," He said, "and whosoever of you will be the chiefest, shall be servant of all." And He added that He had come "not to be ministered unto but to minister . . ."

Grand sounding, yes. But isn't it contradictory? Be a good servant and you will be great; be the best possible servant and you will occupy the highest possible place. A splendid speech but utterly impractical; nothing to take seriously in a common-sense world. That is just what most men thought century after century; and then, quite suddenly, great enterprises—science, industry, business services—woke up to a great discovery. For several decades now that discovery has been proclaimed more and more widely and frequently as something distinctly modern.

Free men, acting independently of government, pool their skills and money to aid other men in other countries who have been enslaved. The wealth of a family or a corporation is put to work in the service of science, the arts, education.

The principle that he who serves best accomplishes most spreads to every area. I observe most closely what is closest to me, and I know that business and industry have learned that a real understanding of and regard for the individual and the social or business community, large or small, must be part of every aspect of work. The huge plants and financial strength of, say, an automobile manufacturer rest on the willingness and ability not only to provide for your safety, comfort and convenience but to feel—and convince you of it—a genuine concern for your pleasure in the product, your benefit from it.

Of course the manufacturer has a profit motive. But to say that as if it made the service a mere sales trick is to misread the record and miss the point entirely. Some self-interest (not selfishness) can be shown in almost any human enterprise, and it may well be a vital worthy part of most. The important fact is that we seem to be increasing our awareness that worthiness is related to any advancement or gain.

The evidence of this new attitude is overwhelming. Manufacturers of building equipment, of clothes, of food; presidents of railroads and steamship companies; the heads of banks and investment houses—*all* of them tell the same story. They call it the "spirit of modern business"; they suppose, most of them, that it is something very new. Jesus preached it more than nineteen hundred years ago.

One afternoon in a Pullman car I listened to a wise man who certainly understood what Jesus was saying to James and John.

"I am amazed by some of the young men who ask me to use my influence to get them better positions or increases in salary," he said. "Such an attitude on their part shows an absolute failure to understand fundamentals. I spent many years in one business, with one company. I never once asked what my salary or title was to be. None of the men who made that company ever wasted time over such questions. We had a vision of extending our company's service throughout the world, of making it the finest, most useful institution of its kind." True, the company made this gentleman rich. My own conviction is that he thought of service, not of gain if he served.

"If you're forever thinking about saving your life," Jesus said, "you'll lose it; but the man who loses his life shall find it."

Because He said it and He was a religious teacher, because it's printed in the Bible, does it fail to apply in any way to a man's work? What did the man on the Pullman mean if it wasn't that he and his friends buried themselves in a great undertaking, literally lost their lives in it? And when they found their lives again, they were all of them bigger and richer in all ways than they had ever supposed they could be. Would they have achieved so much if they had been careful and calculating about themselves? "We mustn't overdo this thing," they might have said. "This is a good company and deserves to grow, but every man must look out for his own interests. Just what is there going to be in it for us?" Instead they worked selflessly to build something they considered good and useful. Does the financial reward make worthless the dedication that never had this profit in view?

One spring morning the founder of a great manufacturing company tipped a kitchen chair back against the wall and asked me: "Have you ever noticed that the man who starts out in life with a determination to make money never makes very much?"

It was rather a startling question, and without waiting for my comment he went on to answer it. "When we were building our original model, do you suppose that it was money we were thinking about? Of course we expected that it would be profitable if it succeeded, but that wasn't in the front of our minds. We wanted to make our product so inexpensive that every family in the United States could afford to have one. So we worked morning, noon and night, until our muscles ached and our nerves were ragged. One night when we were almost at the breaking point I said to the boys, 'Well, there's one consolation. Nobody can deliver more for less if he's not willing to work harder than we've worked.' And so far," he concluded with a whimsical smile, "nobody has been willing to do that."

Though it happened long ago I'll never forget one trip from Chicago to New York on the Twentieth Century Limited. We were due at Grand Central Station at nine-forty, a nice leisurely hour, and three of us who were traveling together decided to make a comfortable morning of it. We got out of our berths at a quarter after eight, shaved and dressed and half an hour later were making our way back to the dining car.

A door to one of the drawing rooms was open, and as we walked by we could hardly keep from looking in. The bed in the room had been made up long since; a table stood between the windows, and at the table, buried in work, was a man whose face the newspapers have made familiar to everyone. He had been Governor of New York, a Justice of the Supreme Court, a candidate for the Presidency of the United States.

My companions and I were young men; he was well along in middle life. We were unknown; he was famous. We were doing all that was required of us. We were up and dressed and would be ready for work when the train pulled in at a little before ten. But this man, of whom nothing was actually required, was doing far more. I thought to myself as we passed on to our leisurely breakfast, "That explains him; now I understand how he has done what he has done."

"And whosoever shall compel thee to go a mile," Jesus said, "go with him twain."

Which, as I understand it, means, "Do more than is required of you, do twice as much." Another startling bit of advice. Where will a man ever get if he delivers twice as much as he is expected or paid to do? The answer is that he will probably succeed in whatever he is doing.

Here is another principle, seemingly equally impracticable.

Remember the words of Jesus when He said, "It is more blessed to give than to receive."

We came perilously near to losing those words. They are not recorded in any one of the four Gospels. Matthew, Mark, Luke and John did not set them down. Of course we don't know why. Yet it's possible to believe that even to these devoted men the words must have seemed to contradict all experience. At any rate they all passed over the saying. But Paul did not. He who had abandoned a social position and an assured career for the service of the Galilean, he who had already given so much and would later give his life, *he* heard the words and remembered. He understood.

Are they empty words? Is a man a fool to let them be a guiding influence in his life? I talked one day with a great historian. I said:

"You have stood upon a mountain and viewed the whole panorama of human progress. You have seen the captains and kings, the princes and the prophets, the scientists and the adventurers, the millionaires and the dreamers. What heads rise above the common level? Among all those who have fought for fame, *who* have actually achieved it? What half dozen men among them all deserve to be called great?"

He turned the question over in his mind for a day or two, and then gave a list of six names, with his reasons for each. An extraordinary list!

Jesus of Nazareth

Buddha

Asoka

Aristotle

Roger Bacon

Abraham Lincoln

Think of the thousands of emperors who have battled for fame, who have decreed themselves immortal and fashioned their immortality into monuments of brick and stone. Yet Asoka, who ruled in India centuries before Christ, is the only emperor on the list, and he is there not because of his victories but because he voluntarily abandoned war and devoted himself to the betterment of his millions of subjects. Think of the hosts who have struggled for wealth, fretting over figures, denying their generous instincts, cheating and grasping and worrying. But no millionaire is on the list, with the exception again of Asoka. Who sat on the throne in Rome when Jesus of Nazareth hung on the cross? Who ruled the hosts of Persia when Aristotle thought and taught? Who was King of England when Roger Bacon laid the foundations of modern scientific research?

And when the historian, looking over the field where they contended for the prize, seeks for something which has endured, he finds the message of a teacher, the dream of a scientist, the vision of a seer. "These six men stood on the corners of history," the historian said. "Events hinged on them. The current of human thought was freer and clearer because they had lived and worked. They took little from the world and left it much. They did not get; they gave and, in the giving, gained eternal influence."

In our own country, in Monticello, Virginia, an American statesman lies buried. He was Secretary of State, Minister to France, President of the United States. His epitaph makes reference to none of these honors. It reads:

Here was buried
Thomas Jefferson
Author
of the Declaration of American Independence
of the Statute of Virginia
for Religious Freedom
and Father of the
University of Virginia

The offices that he held are forgotten on the stone. He desired to be remembered only by what he gave. And he has his wish.

Somewhere in his *Essays* Emerson has a sentence to this effect: "See how the mass of men worry themselves into nameless graves, while here and there a great unselfish soul forgets himself into immortality." It is a fine thought, finely phrased, but Jesus thought it first.

So we have the main points of His philosophy:

1. Whoever will be great must render great service.

2. Whoever will find himself at the top must be willing to lose himself at the bottom.

3. The rewards come to those who travel the second, undemanded mile.

Judas would have sneered at all this. Not really a bad fellow at heart, he had the virtues and the weaknesses of the small-bore businessman. He was hard-boiled, and proud of it; he "looked out for Number One." It was no easy job being treasurer for a lot of idealists, Judas would have you know. He held the bag and gave every cent a good tight squeeze before he let it pass. When the grateful woman broke her box of costly ointment over Jesus' feet, the other disciples thought it was fine, but Judas knew better. "Pretty wasteful business," he grumbled to himself. The big talk of the others about "thrones" and "kingdoms" and "victory" did not fool him; he could read a balance sheet, and he knew that the jig was up. So he made his private little deal with the priests, probably supposing that Jesus would be arrested, reproved and warned not to preach in Jerusalem again. "I will get mine and retire," he said to himself.

But Jesus said, "I, if I be lifted up [on the cross; that is to say, if I lose my life] will draw all men to me." Each made his decision and received his reward.

We have spoken of a few men and a few pursuits, but the same sound principles apply to every walk of life. Great progress will be made in the world when we rid ourselves of the idea that there is a difference between work and religious work. We have been taught that a man's daily business activities are selfish, and that only the time which he devotes to church meetings and social service activities can be sincerely dedicated to accomplishing good. Ask any ten people what Jesus meant by His "Father's business," and nine of them will answer "preaching." To interpret the words in this narrow sense is to lose the real significance of His life. It was not to preach that He came into the world—nor to teach nor to heal. These are all aspects of His Father's business, but the business itself is far larger, more inclusive. For if human life has any significance, it is this—that God has set going here an experiment to which all His resources are committed. He seeks to develop perfect human beings, superior to circumstance, victorious over fate. No single kind of human talent or effort can be spared if the experiment is to succeed. The race must be fed and clothed and housed and transported, as well as preached to and taught and healed. All work *can* be worship; all useful service prayer. And whoever works wholeheartedly at any worthy calling associates himself with the Almighty in the great enterprise which He has initiated but which can never be finished until men do their full part.

How does a man achieve? What constitutes "success"? Jesus spoke of crowns and died on a cross. He talked of His kingdom, and ended His days amid the jeers and taunts of His enemies. "He was in all points tempted like as we are," says the Epistle to the Hebrews. We have read it often, heard it read oftener, but we have never believed it, of course. . . . The conception of His character which some theologians have given us makes any such idea impossible. He was born differently from the rest of us, they insist. He did not belong among us at all, but came down from Heaven on a brief visit, spent a few years in reproving men for their mistakes, died and went back to Heaven again. A hollow bit of stage play. What chance for temptation in such a career? How can an actor go wrong when his whole part is written and learned in advance?

It is frightfully hard to free the mind from the numbing grip of long-established attitudes. But let us make the effort. Let us touch once more the great episodes in this finest, most exalted story, considering now the perils and crises of success in its truest sense.

Jesus was not at all sure where He was going when He laid down His tools and turned His back on the carpenter shop—unless we can believe this, His struggle ceases to be "in all points" like our own; for each of us has to venture on life as onto an uncharted sea. Something inside Him carried Him forward—the something which has whispered to so many boys that there is a place for them in the world which lies beyond the hills. He went to John to be baptized and for a while John's influence molded Him. He, too, retired into the wilderness and there met the *first* crisis of His career. When He emerged, He had formed His own plan for His work; asceticism and denunciation, He knew, were not the role for Him.

His first success was swift beyond all expectations. Out of the Temple, shrieking and cursing, went the money-changers, while the crowd cheered His name until it echoed. That night the whole city was stirred. When He left, at the end of the feast, and went back into His own north country, He found that His fame had preceded Him. Crowds flocked to hear Him talk; news of His deeds of healing traveled ahead of Him everywhere. His vision of His work began to take definite shape. He would restore the self-respect of the people, abolishing the rule of formalism, and establishing a fresh, glorious conception of the Fatherhood of God and the brotherhood of man. It all seemed so natural, so easy, there in the warm sunshine of Galilee with the responsive faces of the multitude turned eagerly toward Him. The year or year and a half that followed were filled with the joy of increasing reputation and achievement. Apparently there was not a single cloud in the sky.

But there were people in Jerusalem with whose private affairs His ideas would seriously interfere. He was not left long in doubt as to their attitude. Incensed at His cleansing of the Temple, they sent their spies into the north country to report His movements, and they made every effort to turn the crowds away. Perhaps at first He had hope of winning even His enemies to His teaching—so altogether simple and satisfying His message seemed to Him. If so, the hope soon vanished. Opposition crystallized; it made itself felt in every audience He addressed, in every town He visited. Reluctantly He had to face the fact that the time was coming when He must compromise or fight. It was with this realization that He faced a second and a greater crisis.

He had crossed the lake one day in a little boat to get away from the crowds, but they were too quick for Him. They hurried around the end of the lake, gathering recruits as they went, and waited for Him at the landing place—more than five thousand strong. He was tired and wanted a chance to rest and think. But here were the people, pathetically eager, and He "had compassion on them." So He sat down among them and went on with His teaching until the day was almost over. Then, at last, the disciples came, hardly concealing their tired petulance, and demanded that He send them away.

"But they have made a long trip and have been with us all day without food," He replied. "We must feed them before they go."

The disciples regarded Him with blank amazement.

"Feed them—on what?" they demanded, "We have no money, and even if we had there are more than five thousand in the crowd!"

Jesus apparently did not hear them.

"Have them sit down," He commanded. "Gather up what-ever food you can find and bring it here to me."

Doubtingly, but too well-trained to argue, the disciples did as they were told. They arranged the crowd in companies of fifty and a hundred, collected the little supply of food which the more prudent members had brought, and laid the collection at His feet. He lifted His eyes to Heaven, blessed the food, ordered it redistributed and somehow the people ate and were satisfied.

Just what happened in the moment when the food was laid before Him is an impenetrable mystery, but there is no doubt at all as to what took place afterward. It was the event for which the people had waited, the unmistakable sign! Moses had fed their fathers on manna in the wilderness; here was one who likewise called on Heaven and supplied their wants. Surely He was the son of David, long foretold, who would overthrow the rule of their conquerors and restore the throne to Jerusalem!

Joyously they shouted the news back and forth. The day of deliverance had come; the tyranny of the Romans was about to end. Their enthusiasm carried them to their feet—fifty in this group, a hundred in that; almost as if by magic they found themselves organized. They were an army and had not realized it. Right there on the field they were enough to outnumber the garrison in Jerusalem; but they were only a nucleus of the host that would gather to their banners, once their southward march was formed. If they were five thousand now, they would be fifty thousand, perhaps a hundred thousand then. A wild enthusiasm seized them. Shouting His name at the top of their voices, they surged forward toward the little hill where He stood. . . .

And then——

He had foreseen their purpose, and even while they were perfecting their plan, doubt had raged through His spirit with the force of a tempest. Why not accept their nomination? Why not be their king? It would mean an alteration in His program, to be sure—a surrender of His vision of spiritual leadership. And yet it might not be such a surrender, after all. Solomon had been king, and a great spiritual leader; David had been king and had written the nation's highest ideals into his Psalms. He Himself was better balanced than David, wiser than Solomon—why not?

It was as splendid a picture as ever stirred the pulses of an ambitious man. For only an instant Jesus allowed His eyes to rest on it. Then He saw the other picture—the vast dumb multitudes of men, His brothers and sisters, the blind being led by the blind, their souls squeezed dry of vision and hope by the machinery of formalism. He saw generations born and die in spiritual servitude which nothing could end except the Truth that He had come to declare. To put Himself at the head of this army of fanatical patriots would be perhaps to risk His life and His message with it. But worse than the possibility of failure was the probability of success. To be king of the Jews would mean a lifetime spent in the defense of His throne and title, a lifetime of bloodshed and intrigue, while His message remained unspoken. Living, He would give His people only a semblance of national life; eventually He would die and leave them to be re-enslaved by the Roman power. And the Truth which He had come to declare, which was capable of continuing its work of emancipation throughout the world as long as time should last, would be traded for a glittering crown and an empty name. In a flash He saw it all and made His decision. Even as the multitude surged forward, He gave a few crisp orders to His disciples and disappeared.

The Gospel story puts the dramatic climax into a single sentence:

When Jesus therefore perceived that they would come and take him by force, to make him a king, he departed again into a mountain himself alone. (John 6:15)

In that hour of crisis He proved His title to be the companion, guide and master of every man and woman in every time. His understanding was universal. There is no worthy work of mind or muscle that cannot lead to Him, that does not inherit from Him its most valid charter and most useful policy.

There is no mere theorizing in His words; He speaks out of what He Himself has proved. If He says that a man's work is more eternally important than any title, He has a right to speak. He Himself refused the highest title. If He says that there are things more vital than merely making money, let no one question His authority. He was handed the wealth of a nation and handed it back again. Idealist He is, but there is nothing in the whole hard world so practical as His ideals. "There is a success which is greater than wealth or titles," He says. "It comes through making your work an instrument of greater service and larger living to your fellow men and women. This is my Father's business and He needs your help."

He told one story which should be published every year in all business magazines, all trade papers, all house organs. It concerned a certain rich man whose enterprises prospered beyond all his expectations. His land "brought forth plentifully," so much so that he said to himself: "What shall I do, because I have no room where to bestow my fruits?"

And he said, This will I do: I will pull down my barns and build greater; and there will I bestow all my fruits and my goods.

And I will say to my soul, Soul, thou hast much goods

laid up for many years; take thine ease, eat, drink, and be merry.

But God said unto him, Thou fool, this night thy soul shall be required of thee . . . (Luke 12:18-20)

The poor fool had regarded his business as nothing but a means of escape from business. He had hoarded his wealth, denying every generous impulse; spent his health, forfeiting every chance for wholesome enjoyment; sacrificed the joy of living for a selfish satisfaction that he hoped was coming when he had made his pile. And fate laughed in his face. He thought he had provided for every contingency, but the one great event which is always unexpected came like a thief and found him unprepared. . . .

With that anecdote should be published another, which is also a tragedy. It concerns the little hotel in Bethlehem, "the inn."

The mother of Jesus of Nazareth knocked at its doors and could not come in. It might have sheltered the greatest event in human history, and it lost its chance.

Why? Why was Jesus born in a stable? Because the people in the inn were vicious or hostile? Not in the least. The inn was full, that was all; every room was taken by folk who had affairs to attend to and money to spend. It was busy.

There was no "room in the inn."

Men's lives are sometimes like that inn.

You know a man whose heart is broken because his son is a fool. Yet deep within himself he knows that the fault is his own. All through the formative years of the boy's development, he never gave him any time. Not that he didn't love the boy, but he was busy. There was no room for family life, and his son is a fool.

You know men whose health is gone; men whose taste for reading and music and art is gone. Men who have literally no interests in life beyond the office which has become a mere treadmill on which their days are ground away.

In the process of being successful they have sacrificed success. Never once forgetting themselves, they have forgotten everything else. This is not Jesus' idea of what a life should be. He, who refused to turn aside from His business to become a king, was never too busy to turn aside for a sick man, a friend, a little child. He never forgot that one night His mother had stood on a threshold where there was no welcome.

The threshold of the little inn in Bethlehem. It was so busy that the greatest event in history knocked at its doors
—and could not come in.

chapter 7

The Master

So WE come to the end. To the final tests of a man's living . . .

How does he bear disappointment?

How does he die?

For two years it seemed almost certain that Jesus would prevail. We have marked the dramatic success with which His work began. We have watched the crowds flock about Him in the market place; we have heard the cheers that greeted His victories over shrewd antagonists and the murmured awe when a sick man rose and walked. Reports of His triumphs preceded Him everywhere so that men competed for the honor of being His host, there was friendliness in His audiences that made almost anything seem possible. And why not? If, by accepting His message, men could be lifted up, transformed into sons of God, heirs of eternity, why should any be so stubborn or so foolish as to oppose? Surely such truth must conquer.

If you read the story carefully, you can see how His tone and manner grew in confidence. In hours of exalted communion He stood face to face with God, felt Himself God's son, knew that He could lift the hearts of men as no other had ever lifted them. The knowledge thrilled Him beyond ecstasy. "I am the Way," He cried, and He called on His friends to free themselves, to cast their burdens upon the Lord, to believe more, rejoice more, *expect* more of God.

Those who listened in those days were profoundly impressed. Even the most callous yielded grudging admiration. "Never man so spake," said they. As for the multitude, its enthusiasm would brook no halfway measures. They would take Him by force and make Him king.

Then came the change.

His home town was first to turn against Him. Picture, if you will, the enthusiasm with which He planned His visit to it. Nazareth was little and despised, a jest among the wits of the day. It had produced no great men, been the scene of no historic achievement. Jesus knew all this. Those familiar streets and faces must often have been in His memory. When He healed a sick man in Capernaum, it could well have pleased Him to think that the report would be carried back to Nazareth. When He drove the plunderers from the Temple, He might have realized that, in the fame which had come to Him, His home town would have a share. "Jesus of Nazareth," His world called Him, linking its name with His. He had lifted the little village out of obscurity. And now, in the height of His glory, He was going back.

Did He arrive in the dusk and slip almost unnoticed through the streets to His mother's house? Perhaps she was in the kitchen; on hearing that footstep which she could never mistake, she ran and threw her arms around His neck.

"Jesus," she cried, patting His cheek and looking up at Him with glistening eyes. "Jesus, my boy, my boy!"

Hearing the name His brothers and sisters came hurrying from other parts of the house. All sorts of reports had drifted back—almost unbelievable reports. Every day the gossips of the village had stopped them to ask whether a letter or a message had come.

"Seems to be doing great things," said the gossips with ill-concealed envy. "Hope He doesn't try to go too far," they said in tones which revealed all too clearly their real hope that He *would* go too far and come to grief.

Against cynicism and innuendo, we can believe His brothers had stood their ground proudly. He *was* doing great things. The reports were not a bit exaggerated. Someday He would come back and show them all; the townspeople would wish then that they had believed. . . . And now He was back. He looked healthy and confident, but not otherwise different. Nazareth was a bit disappointed and He felt it. People, we reason, hardly knew what it was. Perhaps they had expected that He would be somehow bigger or better dressed or tagged with some outward sign of authority. . . . With forced enthusiasm they bustled about, asking Him questions, praising His appearance, but through it all ran a note of restraint.

"Come now, you must get to bed early," His mother may have said. "They will all be wanting to see you at the synagogue tomorrow."

So He went up to the room, His old room, alone. The homecoming was not quite what He had dreamed. They loved Him; they were proud of Him, but they doubted—that was clear enough. And they dreaded the test that must come next day.

He awoke refreshed and heartened. Some neighbors dropped in after breakfast, for the report of His arrival had spread quickly through the little town. When He and His mother reached the door of the synagogue, a crowd was waiting outside. They returned His greeting with a mixture of regard and curiosity and pushed promptly through the door behind Him, filling the little room. There was much whispering and craning of necks. He made His way to the front of the room, picked up the roll of the prophet Isaiah, turned around toward them and smiled.

Instantly all His illusions vanished. Instead of sympathetic understanding there was only cynicism on those faces. The old woman, His neighbor, whom He had planned to heal, was sitting prominently in front. She was willing to take a chance on anything, for she had been a long time sick, but her look was less a hope than a challenge. The substantial men of the town settled solidly in their appointed seats, and dared Him with their hard eyes to try His tricks on *them!* "You may have caused a stir in Capernaum," they seemed to say, "but Nazareth isn't so slow. We know you. You're no prophet; you're just the son of Joseph the carpenter, and you can't fool us!"

Slowly He opened the roll, and in tones that stirred them in spite of themselves He began to read:

> The Spirit of the Lord is upon me, because he hath anointed me to preach the gospel to the poor; he hath sent me to heal the brokenhearted, to preach deliverance to the captives, and recovering of sight to the blind, to set at liberty them that are bruised,
> To preach the acceptable year of the Lord. (Luke 4:18-19)

He closed the book and handed it back to the attendant. "This day is this Scripture fulfilled in your ears," He said simply. There was an ominous silence in the synagogue. "And the eyes of all . . . were fastened on him." He knew what they were thinking; they wanted Him to do some such mighty work as He had done in Capernaum. But He knew, He must have known, also the uselessness of trying. Scorn and ignorant self-sufficiency were miracle-proof. They would never receive Him, never be proud of Him. They merely wanted Him to exhibit Himself and they hoped that He would fail. "No prophet is accepted in his own country," He said to them sadly. Elisha before Him had said, "Neither is this the city." With a look of soul weariness He turned to leave.

Then the storm broke. All the pent-up envy of the little town for one who has dared to outgrow it burst out. The townsmen roared and surged forward, hurrying Him through the main street to the edge of a precipice where they would have thrown Him over. But the wrath which had been sufficient to conceive His destruction grew suddenly impotent when He turned and faced them. They shrank back, and before they could re-form their purpose, He had passed "through the midst of them" and was on His way. In His ears sounded the buzz of malicious comment, but He was too heart-sick to look back. From henceforth Capernaum became "his own city." Nazareth, the home of His youth, the dwelling place of His boyhood friends and neighbors, had given its verdict.

He had come unto His own, and His own received Him not.

His brothers deserted Him. We ought not to blame them too much perhaps. No man is a hero to his valet. The close relatives of any great man, who have lived with him through the familiar experiences of everyday life, must be always a little mystified by the world's worship. The brothers of Jesus had been witnesses of His defeat, and were left behind by Him to bear the ignominy of it. How the sardonic laughter must have rung in their ears! How endlessly the wits must have cracked their jokes about that morning in the synagogue. . . . These home-town sneers were bad enough, but the reports that came back from other towns threw the simple unimaginative family into a panic. It was said that He made seditious speeches; that He claimed to have a special relationship to God; that He utterly disregarded the Code of the Pharisees and denounced them openly before the crowds. Such conduct could mean only one thing. He would get Himself into jail, and His relatives with Him. Hence, the members of His family, who should have been His best helpers, spent their energy in the effort to get Him to go further away from home. Once when the Feast of Tabernacles was being celebrated in Jerusalem, they urged Him to "depart hence" and taunted Him, saying that if He could really do all that He claimed, the place for Him to make His reputation was at the capital. Anything to get Him out of Galilee. They were all unsafe while He stayed near them—so they thought.

"For neither did his brethren believe in him." (John 7:5)

He was teaching one day in Capernaum, to a crowd that hung spellbound on his words, when suddenly an interruption occurred. A messenger pushed through the audience to tell Him that His mother and brothers were outside and insisted on speaking to Him right away. A quick look of pain shot across His face. He knew why they had come; they had been sending Him hints of their coming for weeks. They had made up their minds that He was just a little bit out of His head, and they were determined His extravagances should not ruin them all. He drew Himself up to His full height and pointing to His disciples turned to the messenger:

"My mother and brethren?" He repeated. "Behold those who believe on me, *they* are my mother and my brethren."

They *were* indeed His real kindred, and many times they proved themselves worthy of the name; but even their devotion could not entirely remove the hurt. When later He had His brief hour of triumph, when the crowds flung their garments into the streets before Him and shouted their "Hosannas," even then His heart must have been sore at the thought that in all that multitude there was not one of the brothers for whom He had sacrificed so much of His youth. A warm hand clasp from one of them would have meant more than all the high homage of the multitude. But they were far away, still ashamed of the relationship, still regarding Him as well meaning but not quite sane.

His best friend died doubting Him. To that friend, John the Baptist, He owed His initial success. John had introduced Him to the people; His first disciples had come because John pointed Him out as a greater prophet than he himself. The two men were entirely unlike in character and method. John was austere, harsh, denunciatory—a lonely spirit, dwelling apart. Jesus was cheerful, friendly, never happier than when in a crowd. John laid down for his disciples a rigid program of ceremonies and fasts; Jesus disregarded forms and encouraged His disciples to disregard them. He recognized that He and John must do their work in different ways, but it had not occurred to Him that their differences would ever loosen the bond of friendship. He was cut to the quick, therefore, when two messengers came from John with a wistful, doubting question:

"Are you *really* a prophet, as I told people that you are?" John asked. "Instead of fasting, you banquet. Instead of calling on men to abjure pleasure, you share their pleasures. Are you the hope of the world, as I believed you to be, or must we look for another?"

Very tenderly, but sadly, Jesus sent back His reply. "Go tell John what you have seen and heard," He said, "how the blind see, lepers are cleansed and the poor have the good news preached to them."

It was a wonderful answer, but did it convince His friend? A few weeks later, in the dungeon of Herod's castle, John paid a last great penalty for his idealism and courage. Jesus, when He heard of it, "withdrew into a desert place alone." His closest friend and first adherent had gone out—a a sacrifice to the selfishness of a social order which He Himself was fighting. In that heartbreaking event He saw an omen for Himself. They who had been strong enough to murder John would one day destroy Him also. When He returned, there was a new seriousness in His face, a harder note in His teachings. He saw at the end of His path the shadow of the cross. And His heart was heavy because the friend who ought to have understood Him best had misunderstood Him and died in doubt.

The people deserted Him. When last we caught a glimpse of them, they were cheering His name beside the lake, seeking to force Him to be their king. He eluded them and retired into the mountain to think and pray. It must have been a dramatic moment when He reappeared. Only a single "Yes" was needed, and they would have lifted Him on their shoulders and born Him in triumph to the city gates. Hushed and expectant they waited for His answer—and what an answer! "I am not come to restore the kingdom to Jerusalem," He cried. "Mine is a spiritual mission: I am the bread of life. You have cheered me because I fed you in the wilderness, but I tell you now that what I have come to give you is myself, that by knowing me you may know your Father."

They could not have been more stunned if He had struck their leaders across the face. What did He mean by this senseless mysticism, this talk about "the bread of life"? Hadn't they seen Him heal the sick and conquer the Pharisees in debate— were not these signs that He was the leader, so long promised, who would rout the Romans and restore the throne of David? And now, when the hour was ripe, when they were ready to march, why this language which nobody could understand?

"The Jews therefore murmured concerning him, because he said 'I am the bread that came down from Heaven.'" It was sacrilege or nonsense, one or the other. In either event it proved Him an unsound leader. Gentiles might continue to follow Him if they chose, but His company was clearly no place for a self-respecting Jew.

Silently the cautious people slipped away, and afterward denied that they had ever had anything to do with Him. Those who were more daring or devoted continued with Him through the rest of the week, and on the Sabbath crowded into the synagogue where they knew that He would speak. The days had given Him time to reconsider and compose His thoughts; perhaps now He would make a reasonable reply to their hopes. But there was no compromise in His message that day. Again He repeated His seemingly senseless talk about the "bread of life." It destroyed the last hope of those who had looked to Him for the deliverance of Israel. "These are hard sayings," they protested, "who can understand them?"

And then the note of tragedy. *"Upon this many of his disciples went back and walked with him no more."* So Saint John notes in his Gospel the faithlessness of the crowds that had professed faith.

The tide had turned. He realized it clearly though the twelve could not. At every opportunity He sought to build up in them an increased sense of their responsibilities. He must "go into Jerusalem," He told them, "and suffer many things of the elders and chief priests and scribes, and be killed." They could not, would not believe it. Peter, hot-headed and enthusiastic, took Him aside and rebuked Him for what seemed a temporary loss of courage. "Be it far from thee, Lord," he exclaimed; "this shall never be unto thee." Generous loyal words, but they revealed an utter failure to appreciate the real situation. All hope of a revived and regenerated nation was gone; Jesus' one chance now for permanent influence was in welding His little group closer together and sealing their union with His blood.

For the first time in His public work He forsook Palestine and led His wondering but still dutiful followers into the foreign cities of Tyre and Sidon. The journey gave Him a chance to be alone with the twelve; and it was, in a small way, a repetition of His earlier triumphs. These foreign folk were friendly without ulterior motive. They cared nothing about the establishment of a throne in Jerusalem or the possibility of profit for themselves from His political triumph. They came to hear Him because His words thrilled them, because they felt their better selves touched and made vibrant by the wonder of His life.

He hated to leave these kindly strangers. Much more He dreaded the thought of another trip through Galilee. What a graveyard of high hopes it was! Every road, every street corner, almost every house and tree was alive with memories of His earlier triumphs. Now He must pass each one again, conscious that it might be the last time, His heart weighed down with the thought of high purposes that had brought no response and sacrifices seemingly in vain. Small wonder that He cried out against Chorazin and Bethsaida and even His own loved Capernaum, the cities for which He had done so much. "Woe unto you." He cried in His loneliness, "for if the mighty works which were done in you had been done in Tyre and Sidon they would have repented long ago, in sackcloth and ashes."

But neither Bethsaida nor Capernaum had ears for Him now. Some other novelty had taken hold of the public imagination. He had had His day; nothing more was to be expected from Him. So the spring and summer passed, and autumn came, bringing the Feast of Tabernacles, which He determined to celebrate in Jerusalem. It was a suicidal resolve. The report of His dwindling influence had been carried to the Temple clique, which was emboldened by the information. There were spies in every crowd that listened to Him; the echo of His smallest act was heard in the capital; He could not hope to arrive outside the city walls without imminent danger of arrest. All this He knew, but it did not weigh against His resolve. This might be His last feast. There would be visitors from all over the world, some of whom would surely take the seed of His message with them back to their homes. He must be true to His calling at whatever cost. So He went.

We catch one glimpse of Him on the Temple steps, surrounded by a partly curious, partly antagonistic crowd. It was His chance to recapture a little of the popular favor, to speak a placating word that might open the way to reconciliation; but no such thought entered His mind. The time for defiance had come. "I have offered you the truth," He cried, "the truth that would make you free." And when they shouted that they were sons of Abraham and hence already free, He replied that they were no children of Abraham, but "children of the devil."

They would have killed Him then and there, but their courage failed. After all He had still a considerable following, and it was better to wait. Give Him rope and He would tangle Himself inextricably. Every speech was alienating somebody. When the time was ripe, they would seize Him—perhaps at the next feast, if in the meantime He had not entirely discredited Himself and disappeared. So they argued among themselves, and He went back once more into His Galilee.

Just for a moment, in the next spring, there seemed to be a renewed popular interest. The crowds flocked around in the old familiar way; the disciples noted it joyously. "The multitudes come together to Him again," they exclaimed and at once their hopes were busy with new visions of His success. But dismay followed fast. Against their ardent protest He carried them off into close retirement. They were restless, lonely, distressed at the way in which He turned away supporters. Was it necessary to be so harsh with the Pharisees? After all there were many estimable men among them whose contributions would have been very helpful. Why should He have ridiculed them? Why tell people that their precious ritual was less acceptable to God than the cry for mercy of an untaught publican? Why slight their ready hospitality in favor of an outcast like Zacchaeus? His little group of friends were still groping for a clear vision of message and purposes when for the last time He led them down to Jerusalem and the final feast.

The one week of His life which everybody knows is the last week. Hence we pass over it in this book. It began with the triumphant shouts of "Hosanna"; it ended with the bloodthirsty cries of "Crucify." Between the first morning of triumph and the last hours of mortal agony it witnessed His finest verbal victories over His opponents. Never were His nerves more steady, His courage higher, His mind more keen. Deliberately He piled up the mountain of hatred, knowing that it would crush Him, but determined that there should be no doubt through the ages as to *what* He had stood for and *why* He had to die. Every man who loves courageous manhood ought to read these final chapters at least once a year. Any attempt to abridge or paraphrase them would result in failure or worse. We pass over them in reverent silence, stopping only for a glimpse of the three most wonderful scenes.

First, the final supper on that cool, quiet Thursday night. He knew that He would never meet with the disciples around the table again. All the memories of the three great years must have crowded into His mind as the meal progressed. How often they had sat together under a tree beside the lake, sharing the fish that their own nets had caught. How they had enjoyed that first meal at Cana when He turned the water into wine! What a glorious afternoon it was when He fed five thousand, and the shouts of gladness echoed back and forth among the hills! And this was the end. His relatives had turned their backs on Him; His home town had scorned His advances; His best friend had died doubting; the people had turned away, and His enemies were about to triumph—is there any other leader who would have stood forth unbroken by such blows? What was *His* attitude? One of complaint? Of faultfinding? Of weak railing at His own misfortunes or the willful wickedness of men? See, He rises in His place. He speaks, this proud young man who had refused to be a king and now is to die with common thieves. And *these* are His words:

Let not your heart be troubled . . . (John 14:1)
I have overcome the world. (John 16:33)

There is nothing in history so majestic! Already one of His disciples had slipped away to betray Him. That very night the soldiers would take Him, bind Him, throw Him into prison. The priests and Pharisees whom He had taunted would have their turn to taunt Him now. He would be harried through the streets like a hunted thing, the butt of every corner loafer's jest. All this He anticipated, and with the vision of it fresh before His mind, He lifted His head and looked beyond, into the far distant ages. "Be of good cheer," He said to them, in tones whose splendor thrills us even now. "I have overcome the world!"

They went out into the Garden where so many of their happy hours had been spent. The very air was fragrant with their most sacred confidences. Under this tree they had gathered for worship, while the setting sun gilded the towers of the city; in the waters of that brook they had found refreshment; to left and right of them the very stones cried out in heartrending reminder of the days that were gone. Even at that hour it was not too late for Him to save His life. Suppose He had said to Himself: "I have delivered my message faithfully, and it is no use. Judas has gone already to bring the soldiers; they will be here in half an hour. Why should I stay and die? It is only eighteen miles to Jericho, in bright moonlight and downhill all the way. Our friend Zacchaeus will be glad to see us. We can reach his house by daylight, rest tomorrow, cross the Jordan and do useful work the rest of our lives. The disciples can fish; I can open a carpenter shop, and teach in a quiet way. I have done everything that could be expected of me. Why not?"

It was all perfectly possible. The rulers in Jerusalem would have been glad to be rid of Him on such terms. He might so easily have continued on down the hill to peace and a comfortable old age—and oblivion. It was the last great temptation and decisively He dismissed it. He walked a little ahead in silence, followed by the eleven—for Judas was with them no longer. When they came to a quiet place, Jesus left them while He went away for His last hour of high communion with His Father, God.

A few minutes later He returned to find them sleeping. Even so short a vigil had proved too heavy for their feebleness. In the hour of His greatest need there was no help from them. Again He went away, His spirit torn with agony. He was young, thirty-three; He did not want to die. He cried out to God that the cup might pass from His lips; that He might have time to sweep away the charges of blasphemy and evil which His enemies had heaped on Him; time to build up the fragile stuff of His little band on whom the whole future of His message must depend; time to round out the full measure of His years and influence. So He prayed, and on coming back found them again asleep.

This time He did not disturb them. The high tide of His revolt had subsided; the courage which had never deserted Him throughout the three years cleared His soul, steadied His muscles.

"If it be not thy will that this cup pass from me," He prayed again, "then, Father, thy will be done."

It was victory after battle. With the calm peace of the conqueror without arms or armor, He could make ready for the end. He had not long to wait. The soldiers were already at the entrance of the garden. From His vantage point on the side of the hill He could mark the progress of their torches across the brook and up the path. The clang of their weapons rang through the trees; rough exclamations troubled the quiet evening air like profanity in a temple.

He waited until the armed men stumbled into His presence and then rose and stood before them.

"Whom seek ye?" He demanded.

Startled, awed, they could only mumble His name. "Jesus of Nazareth."

"I am He." The answer compounded of pride, humility, dedication.

They had expected angry denunciation, perhaps resistance—these they understood and could cope with. But such calm, such dignity went beyond the boundaries of their experience. Involuntarily they gave way and, rough veterans that they were, some of them "fell to the ground." It was a tribute, silent but magnificent.

"I told you," He repeated calmly, "that I am he." And then His thoughts turned at once to those who had shared His triumphs and His sacrifices through the years: "If therefore ye seek me let these others go their way." But He had no need to think of the disciples' safety. Already they had made their swift escape—the last of the deserters—

—first His home town
—then His best friend
—then His relatives
—then the crowd
—finally the eleven.

All who had stood at His side had gone and left Him to face His fate alone.

On a barren hill beyond the city walls they nailed His perfect body to the cross. Two robbers were crucified with Him. It was over. The rabble had sickened quickly of its revenge and scattered; His friends were hiding; the soldiers were busy casting lots for His garments. There was nothing left of the external influences which fire men's imaginations or grip their loyalty. Surely the victory of His enemies was complete; He could do no miracle there, hanging on a cross.

And yet——

"Jesus." It was the voice of one of the robbers. "Jesus," he says painfully, "remember me, *when thou comest into thy kingdom!*"

Read that, my friends, and bow your heads. You who have let yourself picture Him as weak, as a man of sorrows, uninspiring, glad to die. There have been many leaders who could call forth enthusiasm when their fortunes ran high. But He, when His enemies had done their worst, so bore Himself that a crucified felon looked into His dying eyes and saluted Him as king.

THE BOOK
NOBODY KNOWS

138

answer is that
bits of phi
bear

chapter 1

The History o

An INTELLIGENT and talkative la   herself
at dinner seated beside a bishop. Having a soci   , she knew
that most men are flattered to be met in conversation on their
own grounds, and so she started to talk about the Bible.

"I can't pretend that I read it as much as I should," she
confessed, "and really you know parts of it seem to me hopelessly out of date. Yet," she added broadmindedly, "I'll admit
that there are some very beautiful passages."

"Yes?" said the Bishop. "For instance?"

"Well, for example, that line about God tempering the
wind to the shorn lamb." (On the chance that there may be
one or possibly two readers whose knowledge is no more
exact than that of this fair lady, let us hasten to remark that
"God tempers the wind to the shorn lamb" is in Sterne's
Sentimental Journey, a book which resembles the Bible about
as much as *Robinson Crusoe* resembles the Encyclopedia
Britannica.)

"And now you must tell me your favorite verse," the lady
continued brightly.

"It would be hard for me to pick a single verse," the Bishop
answered. "But I can give you my favorite passage. It is the
one that tells about Eliza crossing the ice."

Not long ago I met a man who wanted to know which of
the Old Testament books contains the verse: "Thus saith
the Lord, Every tub shall stand upon its own bottom." The

both Jeremiah and Ezekiel give expression to
osophy that resemble this, but not in words that
ny resemblance to it whatever.

It would be easy to multiply such stories. They illustrate
a strange phenomenon.

The Bible is a book, or more properly a collection of books,
which is beyond comparison the world's best seller. New
novels grip the public fancy for a few weeks or months and
then disappear, but the Bible stands continuously at the
top of the list. Go "somewhere east of Suez," where there
"aren't no Ten Commandments," and what do you find? A
fine big bookstore in Rangoon—a city you have to visit "on
the road to Mandalay"—centrally located and up-to-date,
with a modern printing office in the rear. Modern presses are
turning out textbooks and literature of every sort. And Bibles,
rooms full of Bibles, literally rooms full of them. Go into the
finest hotel in any American city and on the stand at the
head of your bed—the last thing to meet your glance at night
and the first thing in the morning—is a copy of the Bible.
Nearly every home has at least one copy. Millions of copies
are given as birthday, graduation and Christmas gifts. It is a
book that everybody buys and concerning which almost
everybody is ready to engage in debate at the drop of a hat.
Yet how many read it? How many know what it really
contains?

It is *worth* knowing. Not all of it, of course. There are
long chapters of genealogy which are no more edifying than
pages of the telephone directory. There are First and Second
Chronicles, which recite the tedious mistakes and sins of kings
who were no better than the kings of England were and not
half so important in their influence on our lives. But when
you have passed over such passages and everything else that
for popular reading is tiresome or useless, what have you left?
These four great treasures:

1. A bird's-eye view of the development of civilization, a sort of review of the history of a people, a history that—in many of its aspects—is our great inheritance. The story begins with the origin of the earth. For the first eleven chapters the Bible deals with the human race as a unit. Coming down to the time when races were grouped and nations arose, it traces the development of the Hebrews—their beginnings as nomadic shepherds, their conquest and settlement of a home and their emergence into national life; their rise to splendor under kings David and Solomon; their overthrow and captivity, and the re-establishment of their national cult or worship, though with very limited authority in the matter of government, a century later. The recital brings us finally into definite touch with the civilizations of Greece and Rome. (Greece was the dominant power throughout the whole period of the New Testament.) Considered simply as a historic outline, this is a venture to command respect; certainly no one can claim to know history who has not read and understood the Biblical version.

2. Some of the greatest literature of all ages. Here, for instance, are some of the greatest of all poems, one of the greatest dramas, one of the finest love stories and a collection of proverbs which have entered into the common-sense philosophy of nearly every modern nation.

3. The best of all textbooks in human nature. A distinguished critic and educator, justly famous for his wise simplicity, said: "I thoroughly believe in a university education for both men and women; but I believe a knowledge of the Bible without a college course is more valuable than a college course without the Bible. For in the Bible we have profound thought beautifully expressed; we have the nature of boys and girls, of men and women, more accurately charted than in the work of any . . . novelist or playwright."

4. Finally, we have the story of Jesus, who lived the most

triumphant life ever lived on this planet, a life that changed the course of human thought and that still is able, after almost two thousand years, to transform individuals, communities and nations.

Surely it is worth while to see at least the soaring peaks of a book that contains all this. Let us start at the beginning with the title page of the most familiar version.

The first lines of the page read, "The Holy Bible." Since the word *biblia* in Latin is plural and means *library*, we know at once that we have here not a single book but a collection of very many different books.

The second element, "Containing the Old and New Testaments," means obviously that there are two main divisions and that the distinguishing feature is a difference in age, one group of books being more recent than the other.

The third part—in the King James Version—"Translated out of the original tongues," indicates that the Bible was not originally published in English but in more than one language foreign to us.

"And with the former translations diligently compared and revised," shows that the translation, which was made under the authority of King James I in 1611, is the successor to several earlier translations. Later notable translations of special interest to us include the American Standard Version, which was published in 1901 as an authorized revision of the King James Version, and the Revised Standard Version, a revision of the American Standard, of which the New Testament section was published in 1946 with the Old Testament following in 1952.

Turning over the pages we discover that the text is divided into numbered chapters and verses, which seems rather an unusual way to present a book until we learn that these divisions were not made by the original writers but were inserted in 1551 by Mr. Robert Stephens, a pious printer, who believed that more people would read the Bible if he made it easier to read. Several earlier attempts had been made to divide the books into chapters and verses, all of them unsatisfactory. The divisions imposed by Mr. Stephens are far from perfect and, indeed, the story goes that he made them while riding his horse between his home and the printing office, and that occasionally the horse stumbled and his pencil slipped. There are some glaring mistakes which would seem to lend color to this tale, but Mr. Stephens did remarkable work on the whole, and some such general scheme as his would appear to be helpful in any edition.

A single glance is enough to indicate that the Old Testament is much larger than the New—and here is an easy way to remember how many books are in each. The key number is three, which multiplied by itself gives nine. The Old Testament has thirty-nine books. Multiply three by nine and you have twenty-seven, the number of the books in the New Testament. Once you get that into your mind it is like "thirty days has September"; you can't forget it even if you try.

Cæsar, you remember, divided all Gaul into three parts. Similarly scholars have divided the Old Testament into three divisions—the historic books, beginning with Genesis and ending with Esther; the poetic books, beginning with Job and ending with the Song of Songs; and the remainder, which consists of sermons, or, as they are more commonly called, books of prophecy.

Of the historic books the first five have a certain unity which has long caused them to be regarded as one. They are called the Pentateuch, meaning the five-in-one book, and there is a tradition that Moses wrote them all. Whether he did or not we can leave to the scholars to dispute, but there is no doubt that he is the dominating figure in all five books. And what a figure! These are the five:

Genesis—the book of beginnings.

Exodus—the book of going out.

Leviticus—the book for the priests.

Numbers—a sort of amplified census report.

Deuteronomy—a Greek name meaning "second law," or review and digest of the laws.

There are some wonderful things in Leviticus for the student of history. For example, many of the laws of health and sanitation on which we moderns pride ourselves are also distinctly set forth here. We think of the disinfection of a house where there has been contagious disease as a comparatively recent development in medical science, but Moses prescribed that the blankets of the sick man should be burned and the house thoroughly purified. Numbers, also, has passages of great interest, but it may be said that these two books are less appealing to the general reader than the other three and may well be omitted if one wants to get the best in the most profitable way.

Start in then with the first chapter of Genesis, and you are gripped at once. Here is no preface, no argument, only a great declaration:

In the beginning God created the heaven and the earth. And the earth was without form, and void; and darkness was upon the face of the deep. And the Spirit of God moved upon the face of the waters. And God said, Let there be light: and there was light. (Gen. 1:1-3)

Viewed only as good writing that paragraph is unmatched in our language. What a way to begin a story! How dignified, how impressive! How swift and sure the movement! How nobly superior to the Greek mythologies, and free from their grossness and puerility!

If you argue that the astrophysicist tells the story in another way, your argument is only partly true. Some of the most "advanced" scientists believe that in the beginning there was nothing but incredibly rarefied nebulous matter; that it gathered itself first into larger bodies which eventually collected enough matter to become ancestors of the planets we know. Other scientific thinkers reason that our universe was originally a relatively small mass of inconceivably dense matter in which not even atoms had form. As the mass expanded, planets were born. All theories agree that these masses were heated and shaped by cosmic forces; they cooled, water appeared and land emerged; vegetation flourished on land and in water and the staggering fact of life was established as the basic—but always miraculous—first principle of our planet. Look back at Genesis, and you will discover a certain method of progress in its account which is not at all at variance with the best scientific knowledge. In fact, those swelling first lines of Genesis now seem to state, with incomparable majesty and economy, the prevailing view of science—a fact at which scientists as well as laymen marvel.

It, too, starts with matter fluid and formless, "without form, and void." But the matter is not wholly inert; the creative Spirit—call it energy if you like—is brooding over that vastness and forming something of purpose. The matter is in motion. It becomes masses. There is distinction between that which belongs to the earth and that which is of other bodies. Upon the earth the waters gather into oceans, and land is seen in continents.

Then we emerge into biology. Life appears first in low and simple forms. Life in the water and life in the air. Life that creeps and life that flies and life that walks. The higher animals appear, and last of all, man. His place at the top of the pyramid of creation is the same in both Genesis and geology, the difference being that Genesis expresses in a few hundred words what science states (in different form) in hundreds of volumes. And Genesis gives a reason for man's creation and a goal for his life, while science is more limited in its vision.

So we have man and woman entering into life on our planet. Science locates the beginnings of human life in the fertile and fragrant valley of the Euphrates. Genesis is more specific, naming the beautiful spot the "Garden of Eden," and identifying the first couple as Adam and Eve. Let us take a running look at these two interesting people and the more important of their descendants, for in the Old Testament, as in all other historical records, the history of peoples is principally the lives of a few outstanding individuals.

Adam, our first ancestor, does not make a very brave showing. He and Eve were given the run of the Garden, with permission to eat any fruit except that of one particular tree. They ate the forbidden fruit, and when God discovered them in their transgression Adam took refuge behind Eve. "The woman whom thou gavest to be with me," he complained, "she gave me of the tree, and I did eat." A cowardly excuse which profited him nothing. For their sin they were cast out, and the Garden was closed to them. No longer could they have food without effort.

> . . . cursed is the ground for thy sake; in sorrow shalt thou eat of it all the days of thy life;
> Thorns also and thistles shall it bring forth to thee . . .
> In the sweat of thy face shalt thou eat bread, till thou return unto the ground; for out of it wast thou taken: for dust thou art, and unto dust shalt thou return. (Gen. 3: 17-19)

Eve had two sons, Cain and Abel. As a shepherd Abel had nothing to do but sit on the side of a green hill and watch his flocks grow fat, making money for him the while. Cain was a farmer, and anyone who has ever worked on a farm understands why farmers in all ages have been discontented and will realize how Cain felt. In his jealousy over Abel's easy life and calm demeanor Cain slew him. "Am I my brother's keeper?" he demanded in surly tones when God made inquiry for Abel. The question has come down through the generations as a text for a million sermons.

Cain seems to have had good stuff in him, regardless of his envious nature and terrible temper; at least his descendants were capable men. One of them, Jubal, was the first musician; and another, Tubal-Cain, as the first blacksmith, founded the useful arts. We skip over a number of other interesting characters, noting only that "there were giants in those days," and that men lived to wondrous old age. Adam, in spite of the necessity for hard work, hung on for a matter of nine hundred and thirty years, but the prize for longevity goes to Methusaleh, who established the world's record of nine hundred and sixty-nine years. He passed away in the year of the flood; there is no telling how long he might have lived in a dry climate. Old as these patriarchs were, they did not all learn wisdom with their years. In fact their misdemeanors were so flagrant that

it repented the Lord that he had made man on the earth, and it grieved him at his heart. (Gen. 6:6)

There seemed to be no remedy but to wipe out the whole race and make a fresh start. One man and his family—Noah, his wife and his sons, Shem, Ham and Japheth—were selected for survival, and Noah was instructed to build an ark that would hold them, together with a male and female representative of each species of animal. He was allowed to warn his neighbors, but when in any age has the hopeful human race been willing to face bad news? They jeered at his stories of the coming storm; they stood around the dry dock where he was working on his ark and passed the same sort of crude jokes with which the folks of a later day greeted Fulton and his *Clermont*. Noah was angry, but he kept at work and had the last laugh. The rain began, and

> every living substance was destroyed which was upon the face of the ground, both man, and cattle, and the creeping things, and the fowl of the heaven; and they were destroyed from the earth: and Noah only remained alive, and they that were with him in the ark. (Gen. 7:23)

God has never again indulged in this wholesale effort at reformation, probably because He discovered that the first attempt did so little good. The descendants of Noah lived much shorter lives than the patriarchs, but they were up to pretty much all the bad tricks, as we shall see.

One thing which makes the Bible so interesting and so educational is the fact that it presents its great figures entire—with no cloaking of their mistakes, no effort to set them up on pedestals. We see ourselves in these pages, with all our passions and frailties, all our hopes and affections, our victories and defeats.

Years passed and grew to centuries, and the great figure of Abraham emerged, a wealthy shepherd having flocks that roamed over so wide an area that he was brought into conflict with rival ranchmen and had to fight for his rights. As a citizen Abraham was openhanded, hospitable and prosperous; and though his treatment of his wife left much to be desired, he had both vision and courage. When God commanded him to leave his country and go into another, he "departed as the Lord had spoken unto him" and was rewarded by becoming the father of a mighty people. A sense of humor was one of his assets, a quality not too common in the Bible. When it was promised to him that he and his wife Sarah should have a son,

Abraham fell upon his face, and laughed, and said in his heart, Shall a child be born unto him that is an hundred years old? and shall Sarah, that is ninety years old, bear? (Gen. 17:17)

But Sarah did bear, and they named the boy Isaac, which means laughter—a name which ought to have guaranteed him a merry life but did not.

Like many sons of great men Isaac lacked the qualities which make for greatness. He was a good man but something of a dreamer, who allowed his father to select a wife for him and promptly became subject to her will. The story of the wooing of Rebecca is the first romance in the Bible, and makes pretty reading. But Rebecca was a strong-minded woman who knew what she wanted, and her principal desire was to supplant her eldest son, Esau, and put her second son and favorite, Jacob, in line for Isaac's property.

Esau, a hard-working farmer and an outdoor man, was hairy; Jacob was smooth-handed, literally and figuratively. Isaac, the father, had grown old and blind. Rebecca made a pair of gloves of kidskin for Jacob and sent him to Isaac with food and a request for the inheritance.

And Isaac said unto Jacob, Come near, I pray thee, that I may feel thee, my son, whether thou be my very son Esau or not.

And Jacob went near unto Isaac his father; and he felt him [the hairy gloves], and said, The voice is Jacob's voice, but the hands are the hands of Esau. . . . so he blessed him. (Gen. 27:21-23)

Jacob, shrewd and unprincipled, met his match in Laban, who was to become his father-in-law. Laban had two daughters, a homely one named Leah and a beauty, Rachel. Jacob agreed to serve Laban seven years if he might have Rachel for his wife. At the end of the seven years Laban gave him

Leah instead and insisted that he serve a second seven-year period for Rachel. Jacob stuck to it. He and Rachel were finally married and proceeded to repay her loving parent in kind by taking all the best cattle and leaving him sickly ones. With this fine moral start they set up housekeeping, and Jacob lost no time in becoming the father of twelve sons, of whom the next to the youngest, Joseph, is the second important figure after the flood.

The oldest of the twelve brothers was Reuben, to whom Jacob on his deathbed said significantly, "unstable as water, thou shalt not excel." Reuben would have liked to protect Joseph from the envious hatred of the others, who saw all too clearly Jacob's favoritism, but Reuben was too weak to accomplish anything. The other brothers cast Joseph into a deep pit. It was their first intention to kill him, but at the suggestion of Judah, who wanted to save Joseph's life and could plan no other way, he was lifted out and sold to a passing caravan, which took him to Egypt.

A various parade now marches before us, actors playing fascinating roles in a great story—Potiphar, captain in the service of Pharaoh, who took a liking to Joseph and made him an overseer; Potiphar's wife, who fell in love with the bright youngster and, when out of his loyalty to her husband, Joseph refused her advances, caused him to be cast into prison; the royal butler, whose release Joseph secured by interpreting a dream, and who promised in turn to get Joseph out of jail:

> Yet did not the chief butler remember Joseph, but forgat him. (Gen. 40:23)

Success quickly banishes the memory of old-time friends.

Presently, however, Joseph secured his own release, having

been able to interpret a dream for Pharaoh himself. Pharaoh had seen in his dream seven fat cattle and seven lean cattle, and behold the seven lean cattle ate up the seven fat ones. What could it mean? "It means," said Joseph, "that we are going to have seven good years and then seven very bad ones; and we better get ready for the bad ones right away." Thus Joseph made the first cyclical economic chart showing that an area of financial inflation precedes one of depression and is of equal size and density. A popular economic analyst of our time publicly admitted that he got the idea from Joseph. It made him a fortune. For Joseph it brought promotion in public service until he was second only to the Pharaoh. Through Joseph's foresight and organizing ability, the Egyptians stored up food in the seven fat years and survived the lean years without complete disaster.

Joseph was big in nature as well as in ability. He sent for his father and brethren, forgave them, got them good jobs in the public service and settled them in luxury in his adopted country. Thus things went swimmingly for the children of Israel until Joseph died, after which calamity descended. The Pharaoh who had been so friendly also died, and "there arose a new king over Egypt, which knew not Joseph." Envy and jealousy of the Israelites was widespread; there was a universal demand that they should be evicted from the rich jobs and fat concessions. They not only were evicted but they were thrust down to the very bottom of the social ladder. Having been rulers, they were made slaves, and their bitter servitude prepared the way for the next great figure—one of the mighty men of all history—Moses, lawgiver, organizer, builder of a nation.

One of the wicked decrees of Pharaoh was that every son who was born to the Hebrews should be cast into the river. The mother of Moses managed to hide her baby for three

months, and then, unable to conceal him any longer, she made
a little cradle and set him afloat in the River Nile near the
spot where the daughter of Pharaoh and her maidens came
down to bathe. Pharaoh's daughter took compassion on the
pitiful little voyager, carried him with her to the palace and
reared him as her own. She gave him his name, Moses; "she
said, Because I drew him out of the water." The boy grew up
with all the educational advantages which the palace could
give, but his heart was true to his people. He developed
physical strength which was needed when he ran afoul of an
Egyptian taskmaster who was abusing a poor Hebrew work-
man. Moses slew the man and hid his body, and formed then
and there the determination to set the Hebrews free.

With his brother Aaron, who was a good talker, as Moses
was not, he carried on extended negotiations with Pharaoh,
enforcing his arguments by a divinely induced series of ten
plagues that descended on the Egyptians. In the end he was
allowed to lead the Hebrews forth into the wilderness, but
Pharaoh changed his mind at the last moment and gave pur-
suit. It was a fatal decision. The Red Sea, which had separated
to let the Hebrews pass through, closed up on Pharaoh and his
army and drowned them every one. So Moses was launched
on his career as leader of a grumbling, shortsighted and discontented lot of former slaves, who continually annoyed him
with their complaint that they would rather be back in their
slavery than wandering free in the wilderness.

Moses was not only a leader but an organizer as well,
thanks partly to his father-in-law, Jethro. That wise old
gentleman, visiting him in the wilderness on a day when he
was holding court, saw the tremendous pressure which was
on him in his combined capacity of ruler and judge, and
protested:

Thou wilt surely wear away, both thou, and this people that is with thee: for this thing is too heavy for thee; thou art not able to perform it thyself alone. (Exod. 18:18)

Acting on the old man's sound advice, Moses associated certain other upright men with him as judges, and thus it came about that the people were provided not only with a law— through the Ten Commandments and the comprehensive Mosaic Code—but with a judiciary as well.

The Ten Commandments are, of course, the outstanding monument to Moses' wisdom and influence. Read them over. How direct; how simple; how free from superfluous or trivial injunctions! They drive straight to the heart of human and divine relationships, and are the cornerstone on which nations have erected their legal and ethical codes. But they are not the only survival of Moses' leadership. The long, carefully molded Mosaic Law is hardly less remarkable. It embraces both a civil and a criminal code and foreshadowed by centuries not only our modern jurisprudence but much of our modern health regulation and medical practice.

On the civil side there is protection of property and reputation. There are exemption laws providing that the outer garment of a poor man, given by him in pawn, shall be returned to him at night; laws providing that the land that has been mortgaged and forfeited shall be restored to the family at the end of a period of years; laws punishing libel and protecting the good name of man and woman. There are laws providing that a poor man's wages are not to be retained to his injury. On the other hand, judges are warned not to favor a poor man but to render equal justice. Taxes were light and levied in proportion to a man's property, but there was one tax concerning which it was provided that the rich should not be permitted to pay more nor the poor allowed to pay less. It was a small tax, but it represented manhood and self-respect and equality before the law.

Some of the regulations went far beyond ordinary legal limits and prescribed the conduct of a gentleman:

> Thou shalt not curse the deaf, nor put a stumbling block before the blind, but shalt fear thy God: I am the Lord. (Lev. 19:14)
> Thou shalt not go up and down as a talebearer. . . . (Lev. 19:16)
> Thou shalt not hate thy brother in thine heart. . . . (Lev. 19:17)
> Thou shalt rise up before the hoary head, and honour the face of the old man, and fear thy God: I am the Lord.
> And if a stranger sojourn with thee in your land, ye shall not vex him.
> But the stranger that dwelleth with you shall be unto you as one born among you, and thou shalt love him as thyself. . . . (Lev. 19:32-34)

The criminal code was severe and swift, but inflexibly just. Life was protected and murder punished with death. Even accidental homicide did not go without penalty to him by whose carelessness it occurred, but he was not condemned to death. "An eye for an eye and a tooth for a tooth" sounds severe in these days when the definitions of crime and punishment grow ever more complex, but it made for a law-abiding people, careful of one another's rights.

The sanitary code was extended, minute and enforced with strict penalties. Can you imagine the feat of bringing a horde of escaped slaves across a wilderness without losing them by dysentery, typhoid fever or hookworm? It was made possible by a simple but powerfully effective system of sewage disposal. That priests and rabbis should have personal supervision of slaughterhouses may seem at first sight like a strange mingling of the spiritual functions with the material; but it preserved the nation from scrofula and other disorders, as the isolation of communicable diseases and the strict disinfection under priestly supervision prevented the spread of plagues. Most important of all, the laws of Moses were of such a nature as to minimize venereal disease. The healthy sex life of the Jews of ancient times is one of the chief reasons for their amazing racial continuity.

The distance from Egypt to the Promised Land is no longer than the trip from New York to Buffalo. Moses might easily have led his people over the route in a few weeks, instead of which the wanderings occupied forty years. Guided by divine wisdom, he saw the necessity for a long period of isolated discipline. They were slaves when he started with them; they were an organized self-governing nation when, at length, he climbed to the pinnacle of Mount Pisgah and looked across into the Promised Land, which he was permitted to see but not to enter.

> So Moses the servant of the Lord died there in the land of Moab, according to the word of the Lord.
> And he [the Lord] buried him in a valley in the land of Moab, over against Bethpeor: but no man knoweth of his sepulchre unto this day. (Deut. 34:5-6)

How well he had done his work was immediately apparent. Joshua, whom he had chosen to succeed him, took hold without a hitch and completed the journey into Canaan. He, too, was a man of vision. As a young man, he had been sent by Moses with eleven others to spy out the Promised Land. Ten of the twelve came back with a fainthearted report. They said it was a land

> that eateth up the inhabitants thereof; and all the people that we saw in it are men of a great stature.
> And there we saw the giants, the sons of Anak, which come of the giants: and we were in our own sight as grasshoppers, and so we were in their sight. (Num. 13:32-33)

Thus you can always get a majority vote to do nothing, to take no chances. But there was a minority report. Joshua and Caleb, without minimizing the difficulties, protested stoutly that the land was fertile and worth fighting for. They brought back samples of fruit to prove their contention, but it was a long time before the people had the courage to move on.

Joshua was a soldier and was much needed for the work which Moses had left to be done. He led his people across the Jordan, engineered the successful attack upon Jericho, the walled city of the unfortunate people who happened to be in possession of the Promised Land, and conducted a triumphal campaign which was about as savage as any war could be. Finally, his work completed, he called his people together for a farewell address of great dignity and power. "Behold, this day I am going the way of all the earth," he told them; and with that he laid aside his arms and died.

There comes a little later a picturesque succession of leaders, presented in a book called Judges, with whom we can tarry only a moment in this rapid survey. There was a woman, Deborah, among them, whose stirring battle hymn is one of the first recorded poems. There was a keen fighter named Gideon, a shrewd strategist, who equipped his slender force of three hundred men with chariot lights and trumpets and attacked at night. The enemy, roused from complacent slumber, hearing the din of trumpets and seeing the lights charging down upon them from every hillside, imagined that a host of chariots was attacking, and took to flight. So Gideon won a bloodless victory.

Some of the judges made their way up from the lower ranks, for national necessity knows no respect for pedigree. Of these, Abimelech was the son of a housemaid, and Jephthah the son of a harlot. There was Samson, the strong man, who had been promised that his strength should remain with him as long as he did not cut his hair. A good-natured, easy-going fellow he was, fond of athletic sports and overfond of women. Delilah wormed his secret from him, cut off his hair while he slept and delivered him to the Philistines, who put out his eyes and amused themselves with his labors as a slave.

In their triumph they did not notice that his hair was growing every day, and when at a great feast they sent for him to make sport, he bribed his guide to let him stand between the pillars of the temple. With one mighty heave he thrust them apart, burying himself and his enemies in a common grave.

> So the dead which he slew at his death were more than they which he slew in his life. (Judg. 16:30)

Finally there was Samuel, stern, uncompromising, incorruptible. He was not a particularly lovable character, and his powerful one-man rule does not seem to have left a place for any associates. At least the people saw no one capable of carrying on in his place, and reminded him brutally that his own sons were failures.

> Behold, thou art old, and thy sons walk not in thy ways: now make us a king to judge us like all the nations. (1 Sa. 8:5)

Angrily Samuel agreed but not without a warning. Their king would be tyrannical, he told them; they would repent their demand. Nevertheless, he acceded to it, and searching through the tribes he found a clean-cut young man named Saul, who stood head and shoulders above all the rest. Him he selected and anointed as Israel's first king.

"God save the king," shouted the people happily—the first time in history that the cry had been raised—and indeed it looked as though their happiness were justified. They had a brave and handsome monarch whose modesty was as striking as his courage. What now could stop them from complete success? But Saul's career is one of the great tragedies. He might have been to his people what George Washington was to us, but he could not stand prosperity, and so little permanent imprint did he leave that the writer of Hebrews, in enumerating the great characters of the nation, does not even mention his name. He was modest and likable, but he was a prey to sullen moods and a slave of jealousy. He was jealous of Jonathan, his son, and would have slain him but for the determined protest of the people. He was most jealous of David, who, when the armies of Israel were standing in helpless terror before the giant leader of the Philistines, Goliath, took his shepherd's sling, picked up a smooth stone from the brook and planted it squarely in the giant's forehead. For this victory, and the acclaim that followed it, Saul never forgave him.

Saul was not without military genius. He led his people more than once to victory. Throughout his career fighting was constant, with the Amalekites, the Philistines and other hostile tribes, and sometimes one side won and sometimes the other. But much of the energy and time that ought to have gone into the nation's battles was spent in the vain effort to destroy David; and the net result of Saul's reign was little. "Tomorrow," said the ghost of Samuel, appearing grimly before him, "tomorrow shalt thou and thy sons be with me." Saul marched into battle on the morrow knowing that his fate was sealed; and when the final moment of defeat arrived he called on his swordbearer to run him through, preferring to die like a man rather than be the captive of his enemies.

And David reigned in his stead.

If you find it strange that Napoleon, the penniless young lieutenant, could leap to the throne of an empire; if your imagination is warmed by the rise of the gaunt, homely, country boy Lincoln to the White House, then there is a real treat for you in David's career as it is related in First Samuel. What a romantic story! The simple shepherd lad, tending his sheep and playing his lute, receives a sudden summons home. Saul, the king, who is passionately fond of music, has sent out a call for a musician. The boy goes to court and by his modesty and quick intelligence becomes a favorite. The blustering Goliath affords his courage a golden opportunity; in a single hour he wins the gratitude of the nation and with it incurs the jealous hatred of the king. Jonathan, the handsome crown prince, loves him, and between the two boys there springs up one of the sublime friendships of history. Compelled to flee the court, a rebel not by his own wish but because of the insane envy of Saul, David lives for years by his wits, surrounded by the ragtag and bobtail of insurgency.

> And every one that was in distress, and every one that was in debt, and every one that was discontented, gathered themselves unto him; and he became a captain over them: and there were with him about four hundred men. (1 Sa. 22:2)

At length Saul dies and David ascends the throne. With firm hand and statesmanlike vision he enforces order within the kingdom and respect without. So successful are his campaigns that he is able to establish a garrison in far-off Damascus and levy tribute on the Syrians, while Hyram, the powerful king of Tyre, is glad to claim him as an ally and a friend. He is one of the most real characters in all literature. You can see his sturdy body and strong but kindly face; you hear his tones and feel his presence, for there is no attempt to make him anything more than human. In fact, his sin—the great blot on his kingly career—is set forth in complete detail. It has been the theme of countless poems and plays.

Walking one afternoon upon the roof of his palace, David

saw a beautiful woman in her bath. It was love at first sight. He sent immediately to inquire her name, and though he learned that she was the wife of Uriah the Hittite, he took her into his harem. The act was made more heinous by the fact that Uriah was away, fighting his king's battles at the front. After a period the girl, Bathsheba, brought David the news that she was with child. Then came the act of complete villainy. David conferred with Joab, his general, and arranged that Uriah should be sent into the front rank at the next battle. Loyally the brave soldier fulfilled his orders and, as had been expected and hoped by the king, he was reported among the casualties. Bathsheba became the favorite of the palace and bore a famous son, Solomon, for whom she secured the succession through her influence over David.

It is not a pretty story, and the prophet Nathan, a rugged old preacher who feared nothing, did not allow the king to forget his sin. Until his dying day David was conscience-stricken. We are quite sure that many of the Psalms which are attributed to him must have been written by others, but we know that he did write this one, a bitter cry of repentence:

> Have mercy upon me, O God, according to thy loving-kindness: according unto the multitude of thy tender mercies blot out my transgressions. (Psa. 51:1)
> For thou desirest not sacrifice; else would I give it: thou delightest not in burnt offering.
> The sacrifices of God are a broken spirit: a broken and a contrite heart, O God, thou wilt not despise. (Psa. 51:16-17)

We know also that the great shepherd Psalm was David's, composed probably during the brief insurrection of his son Absalom, when the king was forced to abandon the capital city and flee like a hunted thing in the wilderness:

The Lord is my shepherd; I shall not want.

He maketh me to lie down in green pastures: he leadeth me beside the still waters.

He restoreth my soul: he leadeth me in the paths of righteousness for his name's sake.

Yea, though I walk through the valley of the shadow of death, I will fear no evil: for thou art with me; thy rod and thy staff they comfort me.

Thou preparest a table before me in the presence of mine enemies: thou anointest my head with oil; my cup runneth over.

Surely goodness and mercy shall follow me all the days of my life: and I will dwell in the house of the Lord for ever. (Psa. 23)

If David had done nothing more than compose these two poems he would have established his right to immortality. But he was one of the great statesmen-kings, lifting his people up to their high point of national independence and self-respect. His reign is the climax in this history of a people. Through his leadership and that of his great predecessors, the children of Abraham, who started as wandering shepherds and passed through the purifying fire of Egyptian slavery and the harsh schooling of the wilderness, achieved at last a sense of solidarity which has persisted through the ages.

chapter 2

Proverbs, Poems
and Prophets

TEN FAIRLY representative people were asked,
"What do you know about Solomon?" Four of the ten
answered, "Nothing." Other answers were: He had two
thousand wives; he was the husband of the Queen of Sheba;
he built Solomon's Temple; he was the wisest man who ever
lived.

The statistics regarding Solomon's marriages as given in
the Book of Kings are "seven hundred wives, princesses, and
three hundred concubines." The Queen of Sheba was not
officially among this company. A monarch in her own right,
she was so impressed by the stories of Solomon's splendor and
wisdom that she made a long journey to visit him and after
a series of receptions and banquets returned to her home. The
present kings of Ethiopia claim their descent from Solomon
through a son, Menelek, born to this queen. It may have been
true, as she said of Solomon, that "the half has not been told."
All that we know certainly is that she never appears in the
Bible again. Other histories, however, record social and economic links between the Hebrews and Ethiopians.

Solomon did build the Temple, and it remained the pride
and glory of Jerusalem until the destruction of the city by the
Babylonians in 586 B.C. But the most enduring monuments

left by this great ruler were not in stone or bronze but in words—the Proverbs, a rich mine of wisdom in which every nugget is solid gold. One can only marvel after reading them how a man so wise in other ways could have been so unwise about women.

He made a fine start as king. The Lord appeared one night in a dream, asking him to name his heart's desire, and Solomon answered:

> . . . thou hast made thy servant king instead of David my father: and I am but a little child: I know not how to go out or come in.
>
> Give therefore thy servant an understanding heart to judge thy people, that I may discern between good and bad: for who is able to judge this thy so great a people? (1 Ki. 3:7, 9)

To which the Lord replied:

> Because thou hast asked this thing, and hast not asked for thyself long life; neither hast asked riches for thyself, nor hast asked the life of thine enemies; but hast asked for thyself understanding to discern judgment;
>
> Behold, I have done according to thy words: lo, I have given thee a wise and an understanding heart . . .
>
> And I have also given thee that which thou hast not asked, both riches, and honour: so that there shall not be any among the kings like unto thee all thy days. (1 Ki. 3:11-13)

Without this wise choice on the part of Solomon we probably never should have had the Proverbs; but something more than inspired knowledge went into them. They bear evidence of comprehensive experience with every phase of human nature and conduct. Some of them, as might be imagined from Solomon's own record, contain warnings against the unrighteous woman.

For she sitteth at the door of her house, on a seat in the high places of the city,

To call passengers who go right on their ways:

Whoso is simple, let him turn in hither: and as for him that wanteth understanding, she saith to him,

Stolen waters are sweet, and bread eaten in secret is pleasant.

But he knoweth not that the dead are there; and that her guests are in the depths of hell. (Prov. 9:14-18)

Most of the Proverbs could hardly be called religious. They are the shrewd guideposts to worldly wisdom, by which a man may make his way through life with most profit to himself and least discomfort to other people:

The fear of the Lord is the beginning of knowledge: but fools despise wisdom and instruction. (Prov. 1:7)

Reprove not a scorner, lest he hate thee: rebuke a wise man, and he will love thee. (Prov. 9:8)

As vinegar to the teeth, and as smoke to the eyes, so is the sluggard to them that send him. (Prov. 10:26)

A false balance is abomination to the Lord: but a just weight is his delight. (Prov. 11:1)

He that is surety for a stranger shall smart for it: and he that hateth suretiship is sure. (Prov. 11:15)

As a jewel of gold in a swine's snout, so is a fair woman which is without discretion. (Prov. 11:22)

He that keepeth his mouth keepeth his life: but he that openeth wide his lips shall have destruction. (Prov. 13:3)

The simple believeth every word: but the prudent man looketh well to his going. (Prov. 14:15)

In all labour there is profit: but the talk of the lips tendeth only to penury. (Prov. 14:23)

The eyes of the Lord are in every place, beholding the evil and the good. (Prov. 15:3)

Better is a dinner of herbs where love is, than a stalled ox and hatred therewith. (Prov. 15:17)

He that is greedy of gain troubleth his own house . . . (Prov. 15:27)

He that is slow to anger is better than the mighty; and
he that ruleth his spirit than he that taketh a city.
(Prov. 16:32)

Many of the phrases and sentences have entered into our
common talk. Everybody knows them, but not everybody
knows where they originated.

> Go to the ant, thou sluggard; consider her ways, and
> be wise: (Prov. 6:6)
> Hope deferred maketh the heart sick ... (Prov. 13:12)
> A soft answer turneth away wrath: but grievous words
> stir up anger. (Prov. 15:1)
> It is naught, it is naught, saith the buyer: but when he
> is gone his way, then he boasteth. (Prov. 20:14)
> Where there is no vision, the people perish ... (Prov.
> 29:18)
> He that spareth his rod hateth his son ... (Prov. 13:24)
> A man that hath friends must shew himself friendly ...
> (Prov. 18:24)
> Wine is a mocker, strong drink is raging: and whoso-
> ever is deceived thereby is not wise. (Prov. 20:1)
> A good name is rather to be chosen than great riches
> ... (Prov. 22:1)

Some of the wisest and most memorable observations are
set forth in poetic guise, which adds to their impressiveness:

> There be three things which are too wonderful for me,
> yea, four which I know not:
> The way of an eagle in the air; the way of a serpent
> upon a rock; the way of a ship in the midst of the sea;
> and the way of a man with a maid. (Prov. 30:18-19)

> For three things the earth is disquieted, and for four
> which it cannot bear:
> For a servant when he reigneth; and a fool when he is
> filled with meat;

For an odious woman when she is married; and an handmaid that is heir to her mistress.

There be four things which are little upon the earth, but they are exceeding wise:

The ants are a people not strong, yet they prepare their meat in the summer;

The conies are but a feeble folk, yet make they their houses in the rocks;

The locusts have no king, yet go they forth all of them by bands;

The spider taketh hold with her hands, and is in kings' palaces. (Prov. 30:21-28)

These latter selections are not Solomon's, but come from a man named Agur, the son of Jakeh, about whom we know nothing. Another group of sayings is given under the heading, "These also are the sayings of the wise"; and the last chapter of Proverbs is the work of an anonymous writer, presumably a woman, and possibly Bathsheba, whose story has just been told.

There are two other Old Testament books which come to mind in connection with Solomon. The first is introduced as "The song of songs, which is Solomon's," but whether this means it is by Solomon or concerns Solomon is a question. It is a poem about a young girl who lived in the northern hills. Though they are now regarded as unhistorical, many interpretations have viewed it as a description of the rivalry between Solomon and a shepherd for the love of a shepherdess. Solomon is supposed to have seen her on his travels and have wanted her for his harem, but her heart was true to her shepherd lover. When the ladies of the court praised Solomon to her and demanded, "What is thy lover more than any other?" she answered stoutly, "My beloved is mine, and I am his."

She was carried off to Jerusalem, but she slept fitfully. "I slept but my soul was awake," she said. In her dreams she found herself wandering all about the streets of a strange city, looking for her lover. Finally her loyalty was rewarded. Solomon would not hold her against the hunger of her heart and returned her to her Galilean swain.

This is the story, somewhat involved in the telling but clear enough to anyone who will take time to puzzle it out. When you read the italic type included in most editions at the head of each chapter, however, what do you discover? That this old-fashioned love song is *"an allegory of Christ and the church"!* Nothing could be more absurd. The "Song" is not a religious book in any sense; the name of God does not once occur in it. Its theme is the triumph of virtuous love over all the riches that a king can offer. Simply that and nothing more. When you see how diligently certain anno-tators have worked to squeeze all the life and humanity out of the Bible, you wonder how the Book has lasted so long. Its vitality, in spite of the bad offices of its friends, is the most powerful argument for its inspiration.

Ecclesiastes is the other book commonly attributed to Solomon because the first verse reads:

The words of the Preacher, the son of David, king in Jerusalem. (Eccl. 1:1)

Modern scholars seem to think that some obscure writer of a much later date wrote the book and that the resplendent Solomon gets the credit—a quite plausible conjecture. It is too bad we cannot be sure about the authorship, for the writer, whoever he was, left us one of the great masterpieces. Fred-erick the Great called it the "book for kings," and insisted that every monarch ought to read it regularly. Whenever someone recommends that you buy a current novel which claims to be ultramodern in its cynical appraisal of life, save

your three dollars and fifty cents and take down your Bible
and read Ecclesiastes again. You will find in it everything
that our self-styled "advanced" writers have ever said, and
it's much better said than they ever thought of saying it.

It is the book of an old man who had sought pleasure in
every conceivable form but had nowhere found satisfaction.

> Vanity of vanities . . . all is vanity.
> What profit hath a man of all his labour which he
> taketh under the sun?
> One generation passeth away, and another generation
> cometh: but the earth abideth for ever.
> The sun also ariseth, and the sun goeth down, and
> hasteth to his place where he arose. . . .
> All the rivers run into the sea; yet the sea is not full;
> unto the place from whence the rivers come, thither they
> return again.
> All things are full of labour; man cannot utter it: the
> eye is not satisfied with seeing, nor the ear filled with
> hearing.
> The thing that hath been, it is that which shall be; and
> that which is done is that which shall be done: and there
> is no new thing under the sun. (Eccl. 1:2-9)

Being in a position of power, and with educational opportunities beyond those of other men, the writer set forth to
make himself the wisest of all. But

> I perceived that this also is vexation of spirit.
> For in much wisdom is much grief: and he that in-
> creaseth knowledge increaseth sorrow. (Eccl. 1:17-18)

He tried to find satisfaction in mirth and wine, and again
in achievement—the building of palaces and gardens, the
accumulation of property, gold and silver, servants.

> Then I looked on all the works that my hands had

wrought, and on the labour that I had laboured to do: and, behold, all was vanity and vexation of spirit, and there was no profit under the sun. (Eccl. 2:11)

So, disillusioned and old, he continues for eleven gloomy chapters, and then suddenly there comes a change in the tempo. He has found the answer, the one thing that gives satisfaction, the one safeguard against a lifetime of fruitless searching and reiterated disappointments.

Remember now thy Creator in the days of thy youth, while the evil days come not, nor the years draw nigh, when thou shalt say, I have no pleasure in them; (Eccl. 12:1)

There are scholars who say that this majestic twelfth chapter of Ecclesiastes does not jibe with the other eleven and must have been added by a later hand. True, perhaps, but improbable. It makes a grand conclusion to a very wonderful book, and it belongs just where it is.

From the deep shadows of Ecclesiastes you turn with a sense of relief to the Psalms, filled with the grandeur of the mountains, the fragrance of spring air, the vast stretches of the firmament and the joy of the Lord. To be sure, there are other notes, for the Psalms are a complete emotional record of human life. In them are love, hope, despair, the bitterest of sorrow, the most exultant delight, sweet affection and deep hatred, confession of sin and joy in forgiveness. But the dominant note is optimistic and believing.

There is good reason to believe David wrote many of the earlier Psalms, and there are some that grew out of his personal experience; but no one man makes a hymnbook. Some Psalms were written hundreds of years after David's death. The man who wrote—

By the rivers of Babylon, there we sat down, yea, we wept, when we remembered Zion.

We hanged our harps upon the willows in the midst thereof. (Psa. 137:1-2)

that man gave a page of vivid autobiography that dates itself five hundred years after David. When another singer wrote:

O God, the heathen are come into thine inheritance; thy holy temple have they defiled; they have laid Jerusalem on heaps.

The dead bodies of thy servants have they given to be meat unto the fowls of the heaven. . . (Psa. 79:1-2)

thus telling of a time when Jerusalem was captured in a bloody battle by a massacre, and the Temple was defiled but not destroyed, we know that the Psalm was written in the times of the Maccabees. It may be that a thousand years separates the oldest of these songs from the latest.

Of the whole, a hundred and fifty songs, which are best worth knowing? First of all, the Twenty-third, of course. Nearly every child learns it; every child should. If, in addition to this, you would like to pick three others as a part of your children's education, you will be pretty safe if you follow the number nine—the Nineteenth, the Ninetieth and the Ninety-first.

Moses has been credited with the Ninetieth—the noble chant of an old man, who, seeing his own generation disappear and a new generation rise up to take its place, nevertheless faces the future with serene trust.

Lord, thou hast been our dwelling place in all generations.

Before the mountains were brought forth, or ever thou hadst formed the earth and the world, even from everlasting to everlasting, thou art God. (Psa. 90:1-2)

For a thousand years in thy sight are but as yesterday when it is past, and as a watch in the night. (Psa. 90:4)

So teach us to number our days, that we may apply our hearts unto wisdom. (Psa. 90:12)

The Nineteenth acclaims the firmament and the moral law:

The heavens declare the glory of God; and the firmament sheweth his handywork.

Day unto day uttereth speech, and night unto night sheweth knowledge. (Psa. 19:1-2)

The Ninety-first is a majestic confession of faith.

He that dwelleth in the secret place of the most High shall abide under the shadow of the Almighty.

I will say of the Lord, He is my refuge and my fortress: my God; in him will I trust.

Surely he shall deliver thee from the snare of the fowler, and from the noisome pestilence. (Psa. 91:1-3)

There is another Psalm, a very short one, which in my boyhood was always read aloud at the beginning or completion of a journey. It is a grand hymn of trust for going away and praise for returning safely home, and since it is so short we can quote it in full:

I will lift up mine eyes unto the hills, from whence cometh my help.

My help cometh from the Lord, which made heaven and earth.

He will not suffer thy foot to be moved: he that keepeth thee will not slumber.

Behold, he that keepeth Israel will neither slumber nor sleep.

The Lord is thy keeper: the Lord is thy shade upon thy right hand.

The sun shall not smite thee by day, nor the moon by night.

The Lord shall preserve thee from all evil: he shall preserve thy soul.

The Lord shall preserve thy going out and thy coming in from this time forth, and even for evermore. (Psa. 121)

If the human race lasts for a million years and produces ten million poets, there will not be a grander hymn of faith than those eight verses of the Hundred and Twenty-first Psalm.

"Why do you call the Psalms poetry?" somebody asks. "They don't rhyme." Hebrew poetry does not consist of rhyme or meter, but in balance of thought, a parallelism. One line says a thing and the next repeats it with slight and skillful variation.

In the way of righteousness is life; and in the pathway thereof there is no death. (Prov. 12:28)

Or the second line is an adversative clause:

Wealth gotten by vanity shall be diminished: but he that gathereth by labour shall increase. (Prov. 13:11)

Thus the balance and rhythm are not in the words but in the thought. Having in mind this distinctive characteristic, it is easier to understand why the Book of Job is called sometimes "the greatest poem" and sometimes "the greatest of all dramas."

Everybody knows Job, "the most patient man who ever lived"—a bit of knowledge based on the remark in the New Testament: "Ye have heard of the patience of Job." As a matter of fact, Job was about as impatient as a man could possibly be, and properly so perhaps, for he was the victim of trials quite undeserved. The word "patience" as the New

Testament writer uses it does not denote the moral quality of submission with cheerfulness to a hard experience, but mere endurance. "You have heard how much Job endured, and know that in the end he had better fortune"—that seems to be about what the writer means.

In the story Job is a rich farmer, cattle owner and public-spirited citizen, who heads all subscription lists and has the satisfaction of seeing his enterprises succeed and his children grow up with good promise. Suddenly calamity descends on him. He does not know it, but Satan has made a bargain with God to try his soul. The outcome of the trial is to determine whether Job, or any other man, is righteous merely for the love of righteousness or whether he must be bribed to righteousness by prosperity and the promise of heaven.

Job's crops are destroyed, his barns burned, his children taken sick, and he himself breaks out all over with horrible boils. In this condition he is visited by a group of three friends—professional moralists and Pollyannas—and between them and him the dramatic debate ensues. They tell him just where he has been wrong and urge him to confess his sins to God and beg forgiveness. He responds sarcastically,

> No doubt but ye are the people, and wisdom shall die with you. (Job 12:2)

He denies that he has sinned and refuses to tell God that he has because it would be a lie; and he won't lie even to be relieved from all his misfortunes.

His conversation is far from meek, but you can't fail to admire his indomitable courage. In the end it triumphs. God says to him in effect:

"Job, you have talked a good deal of nonsense, and you have been very impatient, but you have helped me to win out in my contest with Satan. He said that nobody on earth loves goodness for its own sake, and I told him that you do. He said I was wrong, but you have proved me right. I am proud of you, and I was never so proud as when you protested that you would not lie even to please me."

It is a grand book. It does not furnish any answer to the perplexing problem of suffering. It does not explain why a good man, Job or any other, should have sorrow visited on him in a world which is supposed to be under the control of a loving God. What it does proclaim is that God has staked His reputation on His ability to produce human beings who can stand anything that fate or fortune may bring—men who will be good without a bribe. It insists that in this trial of creative strength and moral goodness God is winning out.

"Every man has his price," says the cynic, but Job did not have his price. He was stripped of his possessions, he lost his health, he had a fool for a wife, and his friends were no comfort to him. But he remained constant. "Even if God does not reward me, and treats me like a wicked man; even if He has made a mistake about me, nevertheless I stand on my record. I am glad I fed the hungry and helped people when I could. I have nothing to repent, and I refuse to lie and say that I have. The words of Job are ended." It is a brave speech of a brave man, and small wonder that God responded to it, restored him his property, blessed his sons and daughters, and allowed him to live in prosperity for a hundred and forty years.

So Job died, being old and full of days. (Job 42:17)

So much for the poetry of the Old Testament, and the drama.

To pick up our historical outline where we left it, we must go back to King Solomon, who has built his Temple and palaces, written his Proverbs and grown old, his heart being "turned away" by his harem. With a thousand mothers to look after them the children of a king ought to be properly brought up, but the net results in Solomon's household were not so good. His heir, Rehoboam, was a typical rich man's son—soft, conceited, sure of his own opinion and contemptuous of advice. As soon as it was known that "Solomon slept with his fathers," a rough and ready soldier named Jeroboam organized an insurrection, demanding that King Rehoboam lower the taxes and conduct himself in a less arbitrary fashion than had his father.

The old men who had been Solomon's counselors urged Rehoboam to compromise, but the hothead young courtiers were all for the Big Stick, and Rehoboam sided with them.

> And the king answered the people roughly, and forsook the old men's counsel that they gave him;
> And spake to them after the counsel of the young men, saying, My father made your yoke heavy, and I will add to your yoke: my father also chastised you with whips, but I will chastise you with scorpions. (1 Ki. 12:13-14)

This made it all very easy for Jeroboam, who promptly persuaded the ten northern tribes to separate and elect him their king. Rehoboam kept only Judah and the little tribe of Benjamin.

> And there was war between Rehoboam and Jeroboam all the days of his life. (1 Ki. 15:6)

The beginning of the end of the Jewish nation—until the establishment of modern Israel only a few years ago.

All of this took place around 1000 B.C., which is a useful date to remember in connection with David and Solomon. From the death of Solomon until 586 B.C. when Jerusalem was destroyed by the Babylonians, the history of the two little kingdoms is a sad tale of intrigue, sinfulness, bad management and steady decline. Sometimes the kingdoms fought and sometimes they were allies. In periods of peace the crown prince of one kingdom was usually named after the reigning monarch of the other, so that the record in the Book of Kings is confusing enough to the average reader. You get the gist of it in verses like these:

> In the thirty and first year of Asa king of Judah [the smaller kingdom] began Omri to reign over Israel [the larger] . . . (1 Ki. 16:23)
> But Omri wrought evil in the eyes of the Lord, and did worse than all that were before him. (1 Ki. 16:25)
> So Omri slept with his fathers, and was buried in Samaria: and Ahab his son reigned in his stead. (1 Ki. 16:28)
> And Ahab the son of Omri did evil in the sight of the Lord above all that were before him. (1 Ki. 16:30)

Each king, you see, excelled his predecessor in wickedness and incompetence. We have no time for them in this rapid survey except for a single glance at two of the most dramatic figures—Jezebel, the strong-minded old queen, and Jehu, who slew her. Jezebel was a princess of the proud kingdom Tyre, and when Ahab, king of Israel, married her, he thought he had achieved a great diplomatic victory. As Queen Mother, Jezebel's powerful influence lasted after the death of her husband and throughout the reign of her son Joram, king of Israel, and Azariah, her son-in-law, who was king in Jerusalem. Attaliah was another Jezebel and dominated Jerusalem as the mother did Samaria. Jehu was a kind of Cromwell, stern, bloody, unmerciful. He killed kings Joram and Azariah both, and raced back to the capital to make away with Jezebel and all the members of the royal family. When Jehu started for a place, he arrived in a hurry—

the driving is like the driving of Jehu the son of Nimshi; for he driveth furiously. (2 Ki. 9:20)

Jezebel could have fled, but her queenly pride scorned such cowardice. Instead, she

painted her face, and tired her head, and looked out at a window. (2 Ki. 9:30)

When Jehu drove through the streets, she taunted him as a dog who had slain his master. And Jehu

lifted up his face to the window, and said, Who is on my side? who? And there looked out to him two or three eunuchs.

And he said, Throw her down. So they threw her down: and some of her blood was sprinkled on the wall, and on the horses: and he trode her under foot. (2 Ki. 9:32-33)

With such unedifying spectacles the record is thickly dotted. The Hebrew writers were nothing if not honest; they give us the story in all its ignominy and shame. The kings of Jerusalem make a little better showing than the kings of Israel, but we have to remember that the record is written from the Jerusalem point of view. Neither set deserves a place in our memories. Their doings are significant only as a dark background for the shining words and works of the prophets, one of the most remarkable succession of men in human history. It was a case of

Truth forever on the scaffold, Wrong forever on the throne,—
Yet that scaffold sways the future, and behind the dim unknown,
Standeth God within the shadow, keeping watch above his own.

In every wicked reign there was a righteous man of God who could be neither bribed nor intimidated. He stood forth crying, "Thus saith the Lord," and though the king writhed and fumed and sought to destroy, the prophet was the victor.

The first of this exalted company was Nathan, who was court preacher in the reign of David. When that mighty monarch had stolen the wife of the brave soldier Uriah and compounded the crime by sending Uriah into the front line of the battle, Nathan appeared at the court and announced that he had come to tell the king a story. There were two men in a certain city, he said, the one rich, having many flocks and herds, and the other so poor that he possessed only one little ewe lamb. And the rich man, desiring a banquet, had spared all of his own big flocks and appropriated the poor man's one lamb.

> And David's anger was greatly kindled against the man; and he said to Nathan, As the Lord liveth, the man that hath done this thing shall surely die:
> And Nathan said to David, *Thou art the man.* (2 Sa. 12:5, 7)

Picture to yourself the spectacle. The king surrounded by rich possessions, supported by his lords and soldiers; the penniless preacher, clothed in rough skins, with no power but truth, no protection but the flaming sword of moral courage. "*Thou art the man.*" The effect was immediate.

> And David said unto Nathan, I have sinned against the Lord. (2 Sa. 12:13)
> ... and David fasted, and went in, and lay all night upon the earth. (2 Sa. 12:16)

After Nathan came Elijah the Tishbite, a hairy man, living alone in the woods, drinking the water of mountain streams and fed by ravens. He it was who stood out against the four hundred prophets of the religion of Baal which the wicked Queen Jezebel had imported, and challenged them to a life and death contest. They were to build their altar and lay their sacrifice thereon; he would lay a similar sacrifice on the altar of the Lord. Whichever god sent down fire from Heaven was the one who deserved to be worshiped. From morning until noon the false prophets leaped upon their altar, calling out to Baal, while Elijah taunted them.

> And it came to pass at noon, that Elijah mocked them, and said, Cry aloud: for he is a god; either he is talking, or he is pursuing, or he is in a journey, or peradventure he sleepeth, and must be awaked. (1 Ki. 18:27)

At evening when the four hundred had failed to prove their god's power, Elijah laid up his own altar, placed the sacrifice on it, stacked up the wood and poured water over it to make the test harder. Then he prayed.

> Then the fire of the Lord fell, and consumed the burnt sacrifice, and the wood, and the stones, and the dust, and licked up the water that was in the trench.
> And when all the people saw it, they fell on their faces: and they said, The Lord, he is the God; the Lord, he is the God.
> And Elijah said unto them, Take the prophets of Baal; let not one of them escape. And they took them: and Elijah brought them down to the brook Kishon, and slew them there. (1 Ki. 18:38-40)

He knew well that the same fate would have befallen him had he lost, and indeed it threatened him anyway. Queen Jezebel was nothing if not courageous, as we have already seen. When she heard what he had done to her prophets, she sent a messenger unto Elijah, saying, So let the gods do to me, and more also, if I make not thy life as the life of one of them by to morrow about this time. (1 Ki. 19:2)

Elijah was forced to flee, and suffered a breakdown from which he never fully recovered. But he had strength enough left to plant himself squarely across the path of King Ahab. That royal gentleman desired to extend his estate and tried to buy the vineyard of a self-respecting citizen named Naboth, who refused to sell. Ahab caused Naboth to be accused of treason, and he was put to death, and his estate, according to the law, was confiscated. King Ahab hurried over to look at his new acreage, and there was Elijah waiting for him.

And Ahab said to Elijah, Hast thou found me, O mine enemy? And he answered, I have found thee: because thou hast sold thyself to work evil in the sight of the Lord.

Behold, I will bring evil upon thee, and will take away thy posterity . . . (1 Ki. 21:20-21)

And it came to pass, when Ahab heard those words, that he rent his clothes, and put sackcloth upon his flesh, and fasted, and lay in sackcloth, and went softly. (1 Ki. 21:27)

All the starch went out of the kings when the prophets spoke up. Elijah was one of the most heroic of them all, and Mount Carmel, where he faced the idol worshipers, is a monument on the path of human progress. It marks the spot where one man stood against tremendous odds and by his own singlehanded courage turned back a nation to spiritual worship. Of him we might say what Whittier wrote of another champion of righteousness:

The world redeemed from superstition's sway
Is breathing freer for thy sake to-day.

We are told that Elijah never died but was snatched up to Heaven in a chariot of fire. Elisha, who had been his assistant, put on his mantle and continued his work, a power in the land for many years. So great was his vitality that even death could not destroy it.

> And it came to pass, as they were burying a man, that, behold, they spied a band of men; and they cast the man into the sepulchre of Elisha: and when the man was let down, and touched the bones of Elisha, he revived, and stood up on his feet. (2 Ki. 13:21)

The earlier prophets did not write down their sermons, but about 800 B.C. some of them began doing so. The first of these was Amos. He was not trained in the theological school and did not belong to the priestly party or wear the union label, so that when he began to preach an officious priest tried to stop him. Amos would not be stopped; he had plenty of courage. A little later we shall refer to him again, and to Hosea, who belongs to the same period. The prophets seem to have come in pairs—

Amos and Hosea,
Isaiah and Micah,
Ezekiel and Jeremiah.

Micah was a down-state man who had the same prejudice against Jerusalem that many people now feel toward New York. It was hopelessly wicked, he said, and merited destruction for its sins:

> Zion shall be plowed like a field, and Jerusalem shall become heaps, and the mountain of the house as the high places of a forest. (Jer. 26:18)

Isaiah, on the contrary, was a city man, loving town life, at home in the bustle of the market place and the activities of the court. Jerusalem was a grand town to live in, he said, in spite of its sins, and God would take care of it.

> Therefore thus saith the Lord ...
> For I will defend this city to save it for mine own sake, and for my servant David's sake. (Isa. 37:33, 35)

These two quotations encourage us with the knowledge— much needed in these controversial days—that two men can be equally good and acceptable to God and yet hold absolutely contradictory views. Micah and Isaiah agreed in their stern insistence on righteousness as the only path to salvation, but they disagreed violently in respect to Jerusalem. Both were right and both wrong. God did defend the city for a long time after the northern kingdom surrendered to its enemies in 722 B.C. But ultimately, in 586 B.C., the destruction which Micah had prophesied came true. The beautiful Temple of Solomon was laid in ruins, and the proudest families of Jerusalem were carried away captive to Babylon.

In speaking of Micah and Isaiah as a pair, we mean that they lived at the same time, not that they were on the same level, intellectually or in the importance of their message. Isaiah was one of the outstanding religious leaders of all history. He was of high birth, and may even have been related to the royal family, for he had free access to the palace, and he appears to have been a preceptor for one king, Hezekiah. His ministry began in "the year that King Uzziah dies," the king who had been his hero and whose reign, brilliantly begun, ended lamentably.

Isaiah had to rebuke sin in high places, to offend princes and priests and politicians, for he belonged to the stormy period when the Assyrians were invading adjacent realms, and his own little kingdom was trying vainly to make its future secure by an alliance with Egypt. This he denounced and thereby

gained the ill will of many powerful interests. But when
Jerusalem needed Egypt's help, Egypt had her own hands
more than full. On a desperately tragic day the Assyrian
army camped before Jerusalem, and the king and his counselors were in terror. The king covered himself with sackcloth
and sent for Isaiah, the one unterrified man in town.

Isaiah's day had come. He wasted no time rubbing in his
reproaches, but spoke with a voice which put new courage
into the king and all his forces.

> Therefore thus saith the Lord concerning the king of
> Assyria, He shall not come into this city, nor shoot an
> arrow there, nor come before it with shields, nor cast a
> bank against it.
> By the way that he came, by the same shall he return,
> and shall not come into this city, saith the Lord. . . .
> Then the angel of the Lord went forth, and smote in
> the camp of the Assyrians a hundred and fourscore and
> five thousand: and when they arose early in the morning,
> behold, they were all dead corpses. (Isa. 37:33-36)

We are not dependent on the Bible alone for the story of
this invasion. Scholars in their probings into ancient records
have found the account written by Sennacherib, the Assyrian
king himself, and his own confession that the expedition failed
to capture Jerusalem.

While Isaiah denounced both Assyria and Egypt, and urged
Jerusalem to avoid entangling alliances with either of them,
he had a conception of international relations which is amazingly modern in the best sense of the word.

> In that day shall there be a highway out of Egypt to
> Assyria, and the Assyrian shall come into Egypt, and the
> Egyptian into Assyria, and the Egyptians shall serve with
> the Assyrians.
> In that day shall Israel be the third with Egypt and
> with Assyria, even a blessing in the midst of the land:

Whom the Lord of hosts shall bless, saying, Blessed be
Egypt my people, and Assyria the work of my hands,
and Israel mine inheritance. (Isa. 19:23-25)

This is precisely as if, while we were still at war with
Germany, having Great Britain as our nearest ally, we had
said: "Someday the war will be over and the Divine plan will
include and need us all. The United States is to be one of
three powers in the future glory of the world, and the other
two are to be Great Britain and Germany, for the Lord has
blessed them all, saying, 'Blessed be England my people, and
Germany the work of my hands, and America mine inheritance.' "

Isaiah had to be a pessimist as to the immediate future, but
his superb optimism is shown all through his work, and comes
to its worthiest expression in the poem with which his own
book of sermons ends:

> Strengthen ye the weak hands, and confirm the feeble
> knees.
> Say to them that are of a fearful heart, Be strong, fear
> not: behold, your God will come . . .
> Then the eyes of the blind shall be opened, and the ears
> of the deaf shall be unstopped.
> Then shall the lame man leap as an hart, and the tongue
> of the dumb sing: for in the wilderness shall waters break
> out, and streams in the desert.
> And the parched ground shall become a pool, and the
> thirsty land springs of water . . . (Isa. 35:3-7)

When we say that Isaiah's own book ends with this magnificent poem, somebody may raise an objection. "The book
of Isaiah has sixty-six chapters," he may say, "and how can it
end with Chapter 35?" The answer is that beginning with
Chapter 40, this book has another author. We do not know
his name, nor why he took such great pains to conceal it.

Following the exile one hundred years or more after the work and writing of Isaiah himself, there were some useful but rather commonplace prophets, Haggai and Zechariah, whose messages helped with the work of rebuilding the Temple but who cannot be called great men. Yet one truly great voice did speak out, the voice of this splendid unknown prophet, the author of the last chapters of the book which is all labeled with Isaiah's name. It was he who proclaimed that the time had come to build a road back to Jerusalem and to restore the devastated city.

He described himself as "the voice of a herald," crying, "Make straight in the desert a highway for our God." He called men to grade the roads, cutting down the hills and filling the valleys and preparing to go back to Zion. He does not name Isaiah or refer to any king or event contemporary with him. On the contrary, these chapters were clearly written a hundred and fifty years later, in the time of Cyrus, the new king of Persia, and the unknown one sees in his rise to power a divinely given opportunity.

> Thus saith the Lord to his anointed, to Cyrus, whose right hand I have holden, to subdue nations before him. . . .
> I will go before thee, and make the crooked places straight: I will break in pieces the gates of brass, and cut in sunder the bars of iron:
> And I will give thee the treasures of darkness, and hidden riches of secret places, that thou mayest know that I, the Lord, which call thee by thy name, am the God of Israel.
> For Jacob my servant's sake, and Israel mine elect, I have even called thee by thy name: I have surnamed thee, though thou hast not known me. (Isa. 45:1-4)

Even though Cyrus was a heathen, he was God's Messiah for that event. Talk if you like about being broadminded!

Then think of the prejudices that prophet had to overcome to make such a declaration. And think what came of it: a new nation, a new and purer worship, a new epoch in the spiritual history of mankind.

Here is his vision for the rebuilding of Jerusalem:

Arise, shine; for thy light is come, and the glory of the Lord is risen upon thee.

For, behold, the darkness shall cover the earth, and gross darkness the people: but the Lord shall arise upon thee, and his glory shall be seen upon thee.

And the Gentiles shall come to thy light, and kings to the brightness of thy rising. (Isa. 60: 1-3)

And this is his dream of a regenerate society and a peaceful world; a new heaven and earth, that is, a new theology and a new political economy:

For, behold, I create new heavens and a new earth: and the former shall not be remembered, nor come into mind.

But be ye glad and rejoice for ever in that which I create: for, behold, I create Jerusalem a rejoicing, and her people a joy.

And I will rejoice in Jerusalem, and joy in my people: and the voice of weeping shall be no more heard in her, nor the voice of crying.

There shall be no more thence an infant of days, nor an old man that hath not filled his days: for the child shall die an hundred years old; but the sinner being an hundred years old shall be accursed.

And they shall build houses, and inhabit them; and they shall plant vineyards, and eat the fruit of them.

They shall not build, and another inhabit; they shall not plant, and another eat: for as the days of a tree are the days of my people, and mine elect shall long enjoy the work of their hands.

They shall not labour in vain, nor bring forth for trouble; for they are the seed of the blessed of the Lord, and their offspring with them.

And it shall come to pass, that before they call, I will answer; and while they are yet speaking, I will hear.

The wolf and the lamb shall feed together, and the lion shall eat straw like the bullock: and dust shall be the serpent's meat. They shall not hurt nor destroy in all my holy mountain, saith the Lord. (Isa. 65: 17-25)

These are words of splendor, and it is a pity that the author of them should have been so determined to conceal his identity and so successful in doing it.

Between the days of Isaiah himself and the times of the unknown prophet whose chapters conclude the book came the dark period of the exile, when Jerusalem was destroyed and its best families were carried away captive to Babylon. To this dark period Ezekiel and Jeremiah belong. Ezekiel, living in Babylon, sought by his exhortations to keep up the spirit of his fellow countrymen and fix their hopes on a restoration of the Holy City and the re-establishment of their national life. Jeremiah, in Jerusalem, held high the ideal of personal and civic righteousness and spoke plain truths to the vassal king, who was allowed by the conquerors to maintain a pitiful remnant of authority and kingly show.

Jeremiah is one of the noblest characters of history and perhaps the bravest figure in the whole Old Testament. It is too bad that his book is so badly mixed up that the unguided reader can hardly follow it. He preached in the Temple, in the palace and on the street corners and even on the city dump; and neither promises nor threats could swerve him. Jehoiakim, the weak and futile king, let the Temple go to ruin but fixed up his own palace with a rich lining of cedar and invited Jeremiah to inspect it.

"Very nice indeed," sneered Jeremiah. "As a king you're a

fine judge of cedar. Your father did justice to the poor and needy, and it was well with him."

> But thine eyes and thine heart are not but for thy covetousness, and for to shed innocent blood, and for oppression, and for violence, to do it.
> Therefore thus saith the Lord concerning Jehoiakim . . .
> He shall be buried with the burial of an ass, drawn and cast forth beyond the gates of Jerusalem. (Jer. 22:17-19)

For such plain speaking and for his warnings that the Assyrians were sure to visit punishment upon the city, Jeremiah was cast into prison. Then occurred one of the most interesting business transactions of the Old Testament. The Assyrians, as Jeremiah had prophesied, *did* come, and they made their camp in Anathoth, where he had his own little farm. Jeremiah had long wanted to buy an adjoining piece of land owned by a relative, Hanameel. That wily old man, seeing an army of Assyrians camped on the land, said to himself: "Jeremiah is down there in prison and probably hasn't heard that the Assyrians have arrived. This is a good time for me to unload on him." So he hurried to the prison and offered the land, and Jeremiah bought it. But Jeremiah was not fooled. He knew he was buying ten thousand Assyrians, and he took care to have the purchase properly recorded in the presence of witnesses and the documents safely put away.

> Thus saith the Lord of hosts [he exclaimed], the God of Israel; Take these evidences, this evidence of the purchase, both which is sealed, and this evidence which is open; and put them in an earthen vessel, that they may continue many days.
> For thus saith the Lord of hosts, the God of Israel; *Houses and fields and vineyards shall be possessed again in this land.* (Jer. 32:14-15)

The punishment which he had foretold as a result of national sin had come, but he knew that a period of national calamity brings repentance followed by better days, and that the time to trust in the Lord and buy good real estate is when everybody else has lost faith and is eager to sell. We shall refer again to Jeremiah when we come to discuss the Bible's ten greatest men.

Everyone who has read the Old Testament at all knows about Daniel, who spent a night with the lions rather than give up his religion; and about Shadrach, Meshach and Abednego, his three sturdy associates. They were cast into a fiery furnace but walked comfortably on the hot coals and came forth without even smelling of smoke. Similarly, we are well acquainted with Esther, the beautiful Jewess, who became queen and had the satisfaction of seeing Haman, the wicked prime minister, hung upon the high gallows which he had built for Mordecai the Jew. These are two heroic figures, Daniel and Esther, and it is sad indeed to be told that the scientists, in digging around among the ruins of those faraway times, have been unable to find any trace of a prime minister named Daniel or a queen called Esther. We are forced reluctantly to conclude that the two books bearing these honored names are splendid pieces of nationalistic propaganda, written by patriotic gentlemen who sought to uphold the spirits of their fellow exiles and, in the case of Daniel, nerve them for one of the most heroic struggles in history—one that in spite of overwhelming odds succeeded.

As with Daniel, so with Esther. The author of the book that bears her name made her victory complete, as we shall have occasion to note more fully when we come back to her again. You will remember that her uncle Mordecai, a Jew, was a prime minister.

And Mordecai went out from the presence of the king

in royal apparel ·of blue and white, and with a great
crown of gold, and with a garment of fine linen and pur-
ple: and . . .
    The Jews had light, and gladness, and joy, and
honour.
And many of the people of the land became Jews; for
the fear of the Jews fell upon them. (Esth. 8:15-17)

But these verses, which make so brave a showing for the
Jews, are not a historic document but only a pious hope.
The Jews, in reading them, buckled their belts a little tighter
and took courage. We can read the Book of Esther and the
Book of Daniel with pleasure and appreciation, not as history
but just as we read other dramas which deserve the high
name of literature.

In taking leave of the Old Testament we must stop to pay
reverent tribute to two great truths which give eternal significance to these ancient books.

1. We have in the record of the division and downfall of
the Jewish nation the first instance in human history where
the god did not go with the land. In earlier days each tribe
and nation had its own particular deity or set of deities, and
when a man transferred from one country to another he, of
course, changed gods. Naomi, urging her two beautiful
daughters-in-law to go back to their own country after their
husbands had died of starvation, said to Ruth:

Behold, thy sister in law is gone back unto her people,
and unto her gods: return thou after thy sister in law.
(Ruth 1:15)

It was the custom that when a woman married she took the
gods of her husband; if he died and she must go back to her
own people, she abandoned her husband's gods and took theirs
again. But when the ten tribes of Israel split away from the
tribes of Judah and Benjamin, Jehovah did not go to either

one or the other, *but remained with both*. His worship was often neglected, but in their hearts the people knew that He was still their God, and always at the time of tribulation they threw down their idols and returned to Him.

The idea of One God—unseen and not to be worshiped in visible form—had been born in the world, and had taken firm hold on human minds. This is the outstanding achievement of the Hebrews, the thing which gives the Old Testament eternal truth and inspiration.

2. In its total effect the Old Testament is a record of God's progressive revelation of Himself to men. This is the second element in its greatness. Steadily—from Genesis to Micah—the conception of His nature and quality grows clearer, bigger, finer.

A God who had to be persuaded by argument and sacrifices, who drove hard bargains with any who sought to disobey or cheat Him—this was the God of Abraham, of Isaac and of Jacob. But gradually other thinking began to stir in the minds of men, and to find expression in the courageous utterances of the prophets. We have referred already to Amos, who was not a priest and had nothing but scorn for the formulas and ritual of the established religion. He saw the Temple courtyards red with blood and men seeking through sacrifices to buy the right to be iniquitous, and he cried out: "God cares nothing for sacrifices; He is a God of Justice."

> I hate, I despise your feast days, and I will not smell in your solemn assemblies.
> Though ye offer me burnt offerings and your meat offerings, I will not accept them: neither will I regard the peace offerings of your fat beasts.
> Take thou away from me the noise of thy songs; for I will not hear the melody of thy viols.
> But let judgment run down as waters, and righteousness as a mighty stream. (Amos 5:21-24)

As a conception of the Almighty this represented a great step upward. In those same days another preacher, Hosea, was adding another item to the expanding fund of truth. Hosea was a married man, and his wife was a flirt. The town was full of gossip about her, so much so that Hosea was compelled finally to put her away. His friends said "good riddance," and even the most critical agreed that he had been amply justified in his action. But Hosea, buttressed about by public opinion, was nonetheless torn by lonesomeness, sorrow and regret. This woman who had wronged him—he still loved her, wanted her, could not live without her. Pocketing his pride, he went to her with forgiveness and took her back to his home.

And out of that domestic tragedy there came to Hosea a great new truth. "If I, being only a man, can love so much and forgive so much, surely God must be capable of even more," he said. Amos had told the world that God is *just*. Hosea added, "And *kind*."

In Isaiah and Jeremiah we find the new thought of God's kindness gaining added force, but the book bearing the name of Jonah gives the most interesting and probably the least appreciated glimpse of the development of the idea. Because of Jonah's mishap, which resulted in a three days' sojourn in the belly of a big fish, that book of four little chapters has been too often passed over lightly or treated with contempt. It deserves recognition and reverence, for it contains the most compassionate note in the Old Testament.

Jonah was a preacher, you remember, and was ordered by God to go to Nineveh and denounce the city for its sins. Instead of carrying out his orders Jonah ran away, was caught in a storm at sea, thrown overboard by the panic-stricken sailors and held in the belly of a great fish until he was thoroughly repentant and ready to obey. After this severe lesson he went to Nineveh and announced to all and sundry that the city would be destroyed for its sins within forty days. So convincing were his words and manner that the rulers of the city ordered a general period of fasting and repentance.

> Who can tell [they cried] if God will turn and repent, and turn away from his fierce anger, that we perish not?
> And God saw their works, that they turned from their evil way; and God repented of the evil, that he had said he would do unto them; and he did it not. (Jon. 3:9-10)

This was good luck for the people of Nineveh but it was hard on Jonah and "he was very angry." He reproached God, saying, "I knew you wouldn't go through with your threat and that's why I tried to run away from this assignment"

> for I knew that thou art a gracious God, and merciful, slow to anger, and of great kindness, and repentest thee of the evil. (Jon. 4:2)

He went outside the city and sat down in a chair to watch and sulk and to see what would happen. The sun was hot, and God caused a great gourd to grow up over Jonah and shelter him. But the next morning when Jonah thought he should be sitting pretty, God sent a worm to cut the stem of the gourd and it withered away. Then come the final three verses which picture Jehovah with a nobler, more compassionate quality than any that the Old Testament writers had ever ascribed to Him before:

> And God said to Jonah, Doest thou well to be angry for the gourd? And he said, I do well to be angry, even unto death.
> Then said the Lord, Thou hast had pity on the gourd, for which thou hast not laboured, neither madest it grow; which came up in a night, and perished in a night:
> And should not I spare Nineveh, that great city,

wherein are more than sixscore thousand persons that cannot discern between their right hand and their left hand; and also much cattle? (Jon. 4:9-11)

What a noble utterance! What a long upward climb has been made since the days when the Israelites plundered cities and wiped out men, women and children under the conviction that they were working the will of God! The Old Testament contains the record of this upward progress. It begins with savage people, merciless prophets and a terrible God.

> Thus saith the Lord of hosts, I remember that which Amalek did to Israel, how he laid wait for him in the way, when he came up from Egypt.
> Now go and smite Amalek, and utterly destroy all that they have, and spare them not; but slay both man and woman, infant and suckling, ox and sheep, camel and ass. (1 Sa. 15:2-3)

And it ends with a people who have learned humility through suffering and righteousness through adversity, and with prophets who utter the will of God in more and more exalted language, ending with Micah, who reached the grandest elevation of all.

> *He hath shewed thee, O man, what is good; and what doth the Lord require of thee, but to do justly, and to love mercy, and to walk humbly with thy God?* (Mic. 6:8)

chapter 3

The Great Life

In the first section of this book the author wanted to see Jesus as if he were discovering a new figure in history. He hoped to strip away all that for him had robbed Him of realness and vitality.

Here the task is different. The focus is broader and the view less intimate. We see Jesus and the events that revealed Him in terms of a magnificent history and literature. We see Matthew, Mark, Luke and John record the great life and part of the great book. It would be impossible to avoid some repetition. It would also deprive the reader unjustly. This story may always begin again at its ending. After two thousand years it still has something new to say to us in each retelling. Matthew, Mark, Luke and John knew that.

On a spring evening (before this story had been told the first time) a band of hard-faced men stole out of Jerusalem, crossed a little valley and made their way into the Garden of Gethsemane. Armed with clubs and spears, they carried torches which cast weird shadows through the trees, and, though they doubtless tried to move quietly, the noise of their progress must have jangled cruelly in the peace of that lovely night. At the gate that opened into a garden on the slope of the hill stood Jesus of Nazareth, awaiting them. A pathetic little company of disciples trembled about Him, but as the heavy steps drew closer and the spear points gleamed in the flickering light, the disciples melted away until He was left alone.

Not quite alone.

> And there followed him a certain young man, having a linen cloth cast about his naked body; and the young men [soldiers or members of the mob] laid hold on him:
> And he left the linen cloth, and fled from them naked. (Mark 14:51-52)

These words are our introduction to an important historical character. There is evidence that the young man who left his linen cloth and fled naked was Mark, author of the so-called "second Gospel," which, in point of composition, is actually the first. Before any other mind had thought of it, he conceived the grand idea of making a written record of the works and words of Jesus. Subsequent New Testament writers were debtors to young Mark, and so are we all.

He was not one of the original twelve disciples; indeed, he may never have seen Jesus except on that fateful night. His mother was a believer, and the Last Supper was held at her house. You can picture the active-minded boy, lying curious in his bed in the family room downstairs, overhearing the wonderful farewell words of Jesus, the final hymn and the rustle of preparation for departure. On the impulse of the moment he jumped out of bed and followed to the Garden. Whether or not he was a witness to any of the events of the next few days we have no means of knowing. We do know, however, that he was associated for a time with Paul and later with Peter. Hearing them talk about Jesus, gathering an incident here and a saying there, he began gradually to compose his book. It is a brief straightforward story, with brisk action and very little discourse, just those high spots of activity and achievement that would appeal most naturally to a young man.

For a time his book was the only life of Jesus. Then a man named Matthew, apparently the same one who had been a tax collector and was called to discipleship, must have looked it over and said to himself: "This book would be much more useful if it had a lot of Old Testament references. And besides, it ought to have more of what Jesus said." So he made these additions, sprinkling his narrative with the phrase, "that it might be fulfilled as was written by the prophets." His book contains the word "fulfilled" more times than any of the others; it is obvious that he was bent on giving the life of Jesus all the Old Testament authority possible and that his object was to write what might be termed "The Gospel (or Good News) as Adapted to Hebrew Readers."

Paul, the most adventurous of the early Christian missionaries, was often sick, and had as a physician a Greek gentleman named Luke. Luke had a friend named Theophilus who, as he thought, would be interested in the story of Jesus, but not in the form set forth by Mark or Matthew. Accordingly, Luke wrote:

> Forasmuch as many have taken in hand to set forth in order a declaration of those things which are most surely believed among us,
> Even as they delivered them unto us, which from the beginning were eyewitnesses, and ministers of the word;
> It seemed good to me also, having had perfect understanding of all things from the very first, to write unto thee in order, most excellent Theophilus, (Luke 1:1-3)

You will note that he does not criticize the accounts already written but observes merely that he does not find them adapted to Theophilus. He did not claim to have been, and in fact was not, an original disciple, but he said that he had enjoyed exceptional opportunities for hearing the story from reliable men who had firsthand knowledge. These are perfectly straightforward reasons for writing a book, and they furnish a pleasing introduction both to the Good News as Luke wrote it and to that later book, partly compiled from his own experiences as a companion of Paul, the Acts of the Apostles.

Luke did not care a fig about quotations from the Old Testament which might be very convincing to Jesus' own people. Theophilus, like Luke, was a stranger to Hebrew tradition. But Luke did tell of the Good Samaritan, and of the Prodigal Son, and some other exalted stories of the appreciation of Jesus for people outside His own nation. Matthew never could have written this book any more than Luke could have written Matthew's.

One other fact is significant about the third Gospel. In some way the writer got hold of a fresh source of information about the women of that early Jerusalem community. Who told him and what was told we can only guess, but the fact is clear that Luke knew more and tells more about the women who were friends of Jesus than any of the other writers. That element gives an added quality of fineness to his book, which is probably the most beautiful book in the world.

Years later in Ephesus, where Greek philosophy had tinged the thought and vocabulary of all educated people, a man named John wrote another story of Jesus. It is hardly the life story: rather it is an interpretation, and a very fine one. We should have lost some of the most beautiful sayings of Jesus if it were not for this fourth Gospel, and one has only to read it through to understand why in every age it has been so greatly loved.

These four books have much duplication, which was an inconvenience when copying had to be done by hand, so that very early in the history of the church there began to be made compilations like Tatian's *Diatessaron*, which attempted to cut up the four books and knit them together into a connected story. We may be glad that none of these attempts proved successful and that, with all their duplication and occasional contradictions, we have these four different records, with the earmarks of their separate authorship perfectly clear. The four are a hundred times more convincing than one account could possibly be, and the very fact that they do not always agree is the best possible proof that they tell a real and not a manufactured story.

But the four stories have not eliminated dispute. How many cruel debates have arisen over the question of His miracles. Yet nothing is clearer than that He did not attach the same importance to these mighty works that His followers did. He was often reluctant to perform them, and was so fearful that He might be advertised abroad as a wonder-worker and thus have the real significance of His teaching blurred that He frequently urged those whom He had healed to "go and tell no man."

The question of baptism has split Christian communions. Jesus, when His success began to bring great crowds to Him so that His disciples were baptizing more than John the Baptist, ceased Himself to baptize anybody.

> When therefore the Lord knew how the Pharisees had heard that Jesus made and baptized more disciples than John,
> (Though Jesus himself baptized not, but his disciples,)
> He left Judæa, and departed again into Galilee. (John 4:1-3)

The question of forms and ceremonies and revisions of prayerbooks occupies the time and discussion of many church assemblies. But there is no record that Jesus ever prayed in public. The one prayer which He gave to His disciples is the simplest imaginable and consists of sixty-six words. As for the place and manner and form of worship, He dismissed the

whole subject with one great and unforgettable sentence. It
was a part of one of the most remarkable discourses of His
ministry, delivered to an audience of one, the woman of
Samaria. Said she:

> Our fathers worshipped in this mountain; and ye [be-
> ing a Jew] say, that in Jerusalem is the place where men
> ought to worship.
> Jesus saith unto her, Woman, believe me, the hour
> cometh, when ye shall neither in this mountain, nor yet
> at Jerusalem, worship the Father. (John 4:20-21)
> God is a Spirit: and they that worship him must wor-
> ship him in spirit and in truth. (John 4:24)

He was much more tolerant toward heretical opinions than
were any of His followers, either those of His immediate
circle or those who have taken His name in later days. His
attitude was set forth clearly on the day when one of His
disciples came boasting that he had found a man doing good
in His name and, since this man was an outsider and not of
their own number, the disciple had forbidden him. He doubtless expected praise, but he met a rebuke.

> And Jesus said . . . Forbid him not: for he that is not
> against us is for us. (Luke 9:50)

His was the broadest sort of invitation to fellowship, having
no petty barriers of creed or formulas or ceremony. "He went
about doing good." "Never man so spake." These—His good
works and His good words—are the things for which He
wished to be remembered; they constitute the story of His
life.

He was born in troubled times. In previous chapters we
have traced the rise of the Jews from their beginning as
nomadic shepherds to their glory as a nation under David and

Solomon (about 1000 B.C.). We have seen the kingdom split into two parts, and the long sad years of bickerings, intrigues, foreign entanglements and decline, eventuating in the capture of Jerusalem and the exile of its leading families into Babylon. In this running survey we have no time to trace the various re-establishments of the sacred city—though this means the elimination of some fine figures, such as Nehemiah—nor its various phases of destruction. The successive conquests of the ancient world reached their climax in Alexander, who overran more territory than any other conqueror and, weeping because there were no more worlds to conquer, died, probably of dissipation, in his early thirties in 323 B.C.

Immediately his vast kingdom was broken up. That part of it which included Palestine came under the control first of Egypt in the days of the Ptolemies, who built the great library at Alexandria, translated the Old Testament into Greek in the version known as the Septuagint (work of seventy scholars), and opened a home in Egypt for many thousands of Jews. Egyptian domination gave place to that of the sporadic Grecianized Syrian kingdom, in which King Antiochus is the most interesting figure to us, since his tyranny inspired the revolt of the Maccabees.

The Maccabæan family, a heroic Jewish priest and his seven brave sons, began a war with no higher hope than that of dying for the faith, and they achieved the impossible result of winning the freedom of their country. Again a race of Jewish kings ruled in Jerusalem, this in the middle of the second century before Christ (about 150 B.C., as a rough easy date). A sturdy little kingdom it was but unable to stand very long against invaders from without and political and religious decay within. Inevitably it came under the conquering power of Rome, but the vigor of the Maccabees promised to perpetuate itself in a new line of kings. Herod, a military leader from across Jordan, allied himself with Rome and was made a kind of feudal king. He married a Maccabæan princess, Mariamne, whose beauty and tragic fate gripped the imaginations of the people and made the name Mary so common in New Testament times and later. Herod murdered her, and she was only one among his many victims.

Rome passed from a nominal republic into an empire. Cæsar Augustus was emperor and Herod (beneficiary of the brave Maccabees) reigned in Palestine when Jesus was born.

The policy of Rome was tolerant; local customs and even local prejudices were not greatly interfered with, and the Jews were permitted to carry on their worship and, to a large extent, the internal affairs of their government as they chose under their own rulers. But Rome was the real power, and naturally the Jews were not happy. They had become a nation whose ideals were bound up in a book. If they no longer had their independence, they still did have the Law, the Prophets and the Writings. They studied these and thought they found promises that Jerusalem was again to have political power. They looked back to the days of David and Solomon, idealizing the reigns of these great kings. They were sure that someday another king of David's lineage would sit on the throne in their sacred city, and they even found in Micah a verse which some imagined to mean that their king would be born in Bethlehem:

> But thou, Bethlehem Ephratah, though thou be little among the thousands of Judah, yet out of thee shall he come forth unto me that is to be ruler in Israel; whose goings forth have been from of old, from everlasting. (Mic. 5:2)

It is necessary to have this little historic background in order to understand why there were two rulers simultaneously in the days of Jesus: Herod the King, whom Jesus characterized as "that fox," and Pilate, the Roman governor; and why the Jewish crowds, fired by patriotic enthusiasm, sought to take Jesus, "Son of David," by force and make Him their king; and why, when He refused, they melted away from Him and allowed the shouts of "Hosanna" of Palm Sunday to be drowned out on Friday by the shout of "Crucify."

As nearly as scholars can figure it out, Jesus was born about 4 B.C. The Christian chronology was not fixed until the sixth century, and our subsequent study of the Roman records which mention the great taxation in the reign of Cæsar Augustus indicates that a mistake of about four years was made.

His life preceding His thirtieth birthday is cloaked in mystery. We catch one glimpse of Him going up to the Temple with His parents, where He was lost from them for a day and subsequently discovered in the midst of a group of wise old men, asking questions and amazing them by the keen penetration of His comment. Except for this single episode the Gospels throw little light on His boyhood. We know the names of His brothers, James and Judas and Joses and Simon, and there were at least two sisters. For some years He apparently was the man of the house, and His earnings in the carpenter shop were the main support of the family. Perhaps this was a disappointment to Him, for He must have been a studious boy who would have preferred to read and study. But He was strong and vigorous, and the family needed His help and His younger brothers His protection. At thirty, however, He had discharged His obligations; He was free legally and morally to find His own occupation and to do as He liked.

But what should He do? He had no professional education. He had attended the village school in the synagogue, as every Jewish boy of His time was supposed to do, and He could read, as we know, for He did read later in public. His conversation and discourses showed a considerable degree of famil-

iarity with the literature of His people, the Law and the Prophets and the Psalms. It requires no great imagination to sense
the brooding that must have gone on within Him as He lifted
up His eyes from the bench to see a caravan passing through
the valley below on its way to the greater world, or as He sat
at night under the stars wondering at the eternal mysteries behind them.

One day in the slack season, about the first of the year as
we count it, He took a vacation, turned the shop over to His
brothers and went away to attend a kind of camp meeting
conducted by His brilliant, fiery young cousin, John. The two
cousins had known each other more or less, for John's father
was a priest, and there is little doubt that as Jesus went up to
Jerusalem for the annual feasts He met John there. John had
turned his back on the priesthood to become an independent
preacher. It is rather a solemn thought that at nearly every important period of Jewish history the established church failed
to meet the requirements of the situation. Neither the prophets nor the Psalm writers were official priests, but unsalaried
and unofficial. John the Baptist refused the priesthood; Jesus
was a layman. The facts need not be read as a criticism of organized religion, but they suggest strongly the need for tolerance in the church and for the spirit of humanity toward new
truth, whether from inside or outside the ranks.

John drew great crowds. He must have been a powerfully
dramatic figure, his leathern girdle about his loins, eating his
locusts and wild honey, and denouncing the eminent Pharisees
and Sadducees as a "generation of vipers."

> ... who hath warned you to flee from the wrath to come?
> Bring forth therefore fruits meet for repentance:
> And think not to say within yourselves, We have Abra-
> ham to our father: for I say unto you, that God is able of
> these stones to raise up children unto Abraham. (Matt.
> 3:7-9)

Jesus felt the contagion of the movement. He also went to John and asked to be baptized, and John, looking up and seeing Him on the bank, uttered a noble testimony to the sort of boy and young man that Jesus must have been:

I have need to be baptized of thee, and comest thou to me? (Matt. 3:14)

It is noteworthy that no sense of guilt or shame appears to have had a part in His religious experience at this point. He did not argue with John about their relative fitness to baptize each other. He felt that the spirit of devotion which was in Him demanded some outward expression; John's way through baptism was the way that presented itself, and He took advantage of it.

It was a wonderful day for Him. He had made His decision; He had put the old life behind Him. John, His popular and powerful cousin, had recognized His inherent power. From thenceforth He would be a carpenter no longer but a preacher like John, rebuking men for their sins, calling them to repentance. The day ended and night fell, and with it came the reaction. He went away into the wilderness and remained for more than a month in solitude, tortured by questionings and doubts. He felt power stirring within Him. How should He use it, and for what? The Gospel narrative dramatizes that period of self-searching by the appearance of Satan in person, with a threefold temptation.

And when the tempter came to him, he said, If thou be the Son of God, command that these stones be made bread. (Matt. 4:3)

The temptation to use His power for the material success—money, comfort, ease.

Then the devil taketh him up into the holy city, and
setteth him on a pinnacle of the temple,
And saith unto him, If thou be the Son of God, cast
thyself down ... (Matt. 4:5-6)

The temptation to achieve cheap fame by performing wonders for the admiration of the crowd.

Again, the devil taketh him up into an exceeding high
mountain, and sheweth him all the kingdoms of the
world, and the glory of them;
And saith unto him, All these things will I give thee, if
thou wilt fall down and worship me. (Matt. 4:8-9)

The temptation to become a political leader, to use the popular discontent and His strategic position as a workingman's
leader as a tool for His own advancement.

To all this He answered, "Get thee behind me, Satan," and
He emerged from the wilderness with a clear-cut picture of
His mission and His program. He saw very quickly that He
could not adopt John's methods. John was an ascetic, a re-
former, a denouncer. Jesus was fond of people, loved social
life and liked to be in a crowd. John said, "Flee from the
wrath to come." Jesus said, "God is your Father, and has
made the world as a happy place for His children." The two
messages were complementary, but, while the friendship of
the cousins was firm and their respect for each other deep and
true, they were utterly unlike in personality. Each must speak
the truth as he saw it and in his own chosen way.

It was an age when philosophers in cities like Athens and
religious teachers in Palestine went from place to place and
gathered together the men who were attracted by their character of learning and wished to become their pupils. It is
interesting to remember that the name by which Jesus most
liked to be called was "Master," not a master of servants but

a master of pupils, a schoolmaster. And the name He gave to His associates, "disciples," means simply "pupils." The story of the way in which He gathered these men is full of interest. He seemed to have no studied method. As we noted earlier, He called one and another as He passed by, saying, "Follow me," and the man who was called left his fishing, or whatever his work might be, and followed instantly.

The significant thing to remember is His amazing faith in plain ordinary folk. He did not look over the Blue Book or the Directory of Directories, saying to Himself, "This is the most important mission that anyone ever undertook; I must have the very best and ablest assistants." On the contrary, it was almost as though He said, "For my purpose I need men who are strong enough in body to stand hardships, strong enough in faith to overcome doubt. I can trust this message of mine to their keeping and feel sure that it will never die out." That supreme confidence in common humanity sets Him apart from most other leaders who have attempted large things, and the magnificent way in which His faith was justified is one of the finest proofs of His divinity.

Though they have appeared before in these pages it might be worth while to look again at these pupils of His. How many of us know much about them, or could even write a list of their names? The first two of the permanent disciples were John, the son of Zebedee (with whom was afterward associated his brother, James), and Andrew. Andrew was apparently the sort of man who likes to discover good things and then tell them to a brother or to someone else with more initiative. That is the fate of many of the world's most useful people. He had been with Jesus only about an hour when he slipped away and brought his brother Simon. Almost at once Simon began to achieve a degree of prominence which Andrew could never have attained. Andrew accepted the situation loyally and so far as we know was never jealous of his more emphatic and outspoken brother, though he might have thought he had good reason for being. The next day Jesus found another Galilean named Philip, who also had a friend, Nathanael. These are the first six—

John and James.

Andrew and Simon.

Philip and Nathanael.

All play important parts.

Then came two others who never were prominent; James, the son of Alphaeus, and Thaddaeus, whose other name was Lebbaeus. Finally, there were four more, each of whom was important and is known by name to all of us. Levi, or Matthew, was a taxgatherer whom Jesus called "as he passed by." Whether Matthew went through any ceremony of repentance and baptism is not recorded, but you will recall that he made a great feast to which pretty much the whole town was invited. It was because of His attendance at such feasts, with their indiscriminate guest lists, that Jesus was criticized as a "wine bibber" and a "gluttonous man." To such criticism He responded with some of the noblest of His parables, the Lost Sheep, the Lost Coin and, best of all, the Prodigal Son.

The tenth in our list is Thomas, a moody fellow who insisted on thinking things out for himself. "Doubting Thomas" he has been called because after the resurrection, when some of the disciples claimed to have seen Jesus, Thomas answered stoutly:

Except I shall see in his hands the print of the nails, and put my finger into the print of the nails, and thrust my hand into his side, I will not believe. (John 20:25)

It is unfair to Thomas to remember only his doubt and to forget that when the disciples were trying to dissuade Jesus from His last dangerous journey to Jerusalem it was this same Thomas who exclaimed, "Let us also go, that we may die with him."

There was as number eleven another Simon, whose surname, "the zealot," does not mean that he personally was of an over-zealous disposition but that he had been a participant in one of the sporadic revolutions against Roman authority. You might term him a socialist if you wanted a not very exact but sufficiently convenient description. And finally there was Judas, the only one of the twelve who was not a Galilean but who, as a member of the royal tribe of Judah, felt himself superior to the crowd of fishermen, publicans and common folk. Better educated than the rest, a man of business ability, he was treasurer and "carried the bag." When Jesus said, "Take no thought for the morrow, saying, what shall we eat or what shall we drink," it may have sounded all right to the other eleven, but you can imagine the look of mingled cynicism and worry on the face of Judas, who had to pay the bills. Equipped by talent and training to be of larger service than any of the others, he was the only traitor.

These, then, were the twelve who were destined to change human history.

The public life of Jesus appears to have covered just three years: a year of organization and small beginnings; a year of dramatic deeds and great successes; a year of diminishing popularity and disappointments. He started quietly in the little towns near His home, talking to whoever would listen and taking advantage of any occasion that brought people together. There was a marriage in the neighboring village of Cana, to which He was invited with His mother. The meaning of what happened there will reward another quick review of the details. At a critical moment in the celebration Mary caught a look of distress in the eyes of the hostess and with quick feminine instinct divined the situation. The wine had given out. There occurred then the first miracle of Jesus, the transforming of water into wine. Very few sermons are preached about this miracle, and it is usually glossed over as being not quite in keeping with the character of His life and work. But to those of us who picture Him as the Great Companion, sociable, loving crowds, followed everywhere by bands of laughing children, this beginning of His public activity seems splendidly significant. He had refused to employ His miraculous power to turn stones into bread to satisfy His own hunger; He had not yet employed it to heal the sick or convey a moral lesson. But He did not think it beneath the dignity of His mission to perform a miracle in order that the happiness of a company of friendly folk might be continued and a hostess preserved from embarassment.

And, if you will, think again for a moment of the other miracles.

In Capernaum, another near-by place, He healed sick people and attracted crowds by His preaching so that His reputation spread and there were rumors about Him even in Jerusalem, the capital. His entrance into that city was dramatic; it lifted Him instantly out of the class of ordinary country philosophers and made Him a national figure. It was in the outer court of the Temple, the center of the religious life of the nation, a spot that ought to have been more holy than any other, but which had been degraded by greed into a noisome market place. He

found in the temple those that sold oxen and sheep and doves, and the changers of money sitting:

And when he had made a scourge of small cords, he drove them all out of the temple, and the sheep, and the oxen; and poured out the changers' money, and overthrew the tables;

And said unto them that sold doves, Take these things hence; make not my Father's house an house of merchandise. (John 2:14-16)

That night His name was on every tongue; His great success had begun.

Immense crowds flocked about Him. Once He had to push out into the lake in a little boat, using it as a pulpit. Again He sat down with them on the green slopes of a mountain and there delivered the one long discourse of His ministry, a talk which contains many of the most sublime thoughts ever put into human language.

Blessed are the poor in spirit: for theirs is the kingdom of heaven. (Matt. 5:3)

Blessed are the merciful: for they shall obtain mercy.

Blessed are the pure in heart: for they shall see God. (Matt. 5:7-8)

Ye have heard that it hath been said, Thou shalt love thy neighbour, and hate thine enemy.

But I say unto you, Love your enemies, bless them that curse you, do good to them that hate you, and pray for them which despitefully use you, and persecute you;

That ye may be the children of your Father which is in heaven: for he maketh his sun to rise on the evil and on the good, and sendeth rain on the just and on the unjust. (Matt. 5:43-45)

Lay not up for yourselves treasures upon earth, where moth and rust doth corrupt, and where thieves break through and steal:

But lay up for yourselves treasures in heaven . . .

For where your treasure is, there will your heart be also. (Matt. 6:19-21)

Behold the fowls of the air: for they sow not, neither do they reap, nor gather into barns; yet your heavenly Father feedeth them. Are ye not much better than they?

Which of you by taking thought can add one cubit unto his stature?

And why take ye thought for raiment? Consider the lilies of the field, how they grow; they toil not, neither do they spin:

And yet I say unto you, That even Solomon in all his glory was not arrayed like one of these.

Wherefore, if God so clothe the grass of the field, which to day is, and to morrow is cast into the oven, shall he not much more clothe you, O ye of little faith? (Matt. 6:26-30)

His miracles caused His reputation to spread before Him, and the most dramatic of them, the feeding of a host of people, was followed by one great moment of triumph, which, however, marked the beginning of the end.

We have seen the miracle as Jesus might have regarded it. Let's look now at the crowd. That multitude of people whom He had seated in groups of fifty and a hundred rose to their feet after their miraculous meal and discovered that they were an army. They looked up with new eyes at the strong young man who had fed them as Moses had fed their ancestors in the wilderness. They remembered the words of the prophets. Here indeed was a son of David; here was the promised leader who should free his people, drive the Romans before him and sit again upon the throne in Jerusalem. With a great shout they surged forward.

Did He hesitate for a moment? Was there an instant in which the temptation to seize this proffered leadership battled with His real ideals? We know only the final decision, which was quickly made:

When Jesus therefore perceived that they would come and take him by force, to make him a king, he departed again into a mountain himself alone. (John 6:15)

From that hour His popularity waned. Most of those who had followed Him in the hope of reward through a successful revolution began to drop away.

From that time many of his disciples went back, and walked no more with him. (John 6:66)

Even the twelve were disappointed and disheartened. Why was it necessary for Him to be so inflexible? Why must He always abuse the Pharisees and other influential people? Why turn away so abruptly from those who could be of so much help? Jesus alone saw clearly. He led them away from Galilee into the foreign shores of Tyre and Sidon. He wanted to be alone with them, to try to make them understand why He must refuse temporal power; why, indeed, it would be necessary for Him to ensure the permanency of His message by sealing it with His blood. He must "go into Jerusalem," He told them, "and suffer many things of the elders and chief priests and scribes, and be killed." Indignantly they sought to dissuade Him. "Be it far from thee, Lord," the hotheaded Peter exclaimed; "this shall never be unto thee." Their remonstrances were in vain. Quietly, courageously, He turned about and prepared for the journey to Jerusalem which would be the end.

We are again impressed by the fact that the whole last year of His ministry has a different tone. He is far more emphatic, far more audacious. Knowing that compromise is useless, He lashes out against the smug complacency of the Pharisees, who render lip service to Jehovah but are rotten at the core with selfishness and greed. He knew what fate held in store for Him; the warnings had been coming in quick succession for more than a year. The death of John the Baptist was the first one. Cast into prison for denouncing the licentious marriage of Herod, John was sacrificed to the wicked request of the wife, Herodias, and her abandoned daughter, Salome.

And when the daughter of the said Herodias came in, and danced, and pleased Herod and them that sat with him, the king said unto the damsel, Ask of me whatsoever thou wilt, and I will give it thee.

And she went forth, and said unto her mother, What shall I ask? And she said, The head of John the Baptist.

And immediately the king sent an executioner . . . and
he went . . .
And brought his head in a charger, and gave it to the
damsel: and the damsel gave it to her mother. (Mark
6:22, 24, 27-28)

As we have seen from another vantage point, all events now
had a tragic emphasis. The death of John cast a permanent
shadow over the heart of Jesus and added greatly to the force
and bitterness of His denunciations. His rejection by His
home town, Nazareth, was another blow. It is easy to imagine
the high hopes with which He had turned His steps toward
it. He had already succeeded in Capernaum and near-by cities;
He had made a great stir in the capital. For the first time in
history the name of Nazareth was linked with the name of a
national figure. He would go back to His old friends and
neighbors, give them the glad tidings, heal their sick and
share with them the joys of success. But the town received
Him scornfully. "You may have fooled them in Capernaum,"
the cynical faces said, "but little old Nazareth isn't so slow.
You're no prophet; we know you. You're just the boy who
used to work in the carpenter shop."

And he did not many mighty works there because of
their unbelief. (Matt. 13:58)

His mother and brothers wavered, feeling it unsafe to be
closely connected with one who was stirring up so much opposition. They urged Him to go up to Jerusalem.

For neither did his brethren believe in him. (John 7:5)

So, deserted by those who ought to have stood by Him most
stanchly, abandoned by this popular following, supported
only by His original little group of disciples, and they waver-

ing and in doubt, He made His way back to Jerusalem to face the events of that last week which the Gospels give us in such full detail. In the final hour of tragedy even His disciples were missing. Only a few stricken women huddled at the foot of the Cross, and the last word of faith was not spoken by a friend but fell from the lips of a crucified thief:

Lord, remember me when thou comest into thy kingdom. (Luke 23:42)

So He died, and those who had demanded His blood regarded their triumph as complete. Surely a little group of unlettered peasants could do nothing without leadership. Jerusalem and the Roman power would now be safe from the menace of one who gave common people the foolish idea that they were sons of God and, hence, the equals of the king. What actually happened is set forth with force and conviction in each of the four Gospels separately. His disciples declared that He still lived. On their report the tomb was examined and found empty. In the city where He had been put to death disciples set to work with results so immediate and astonishing that even the Roman authorities were shortly compelled to take notice. They began to produce a literature, and with this we shall deal in the next chapter.

The pious men who broke the Bible up into chapters and numbered verses contributed something to our convenience, but they destroyed the swing and charm of the unbroken narrative. The Scriptures are fed to us in Sunday school in measured doses of about eight verses a week; we read the Bible, when we read it at all, one or two chapters a day. This is not our habit with other thrilling literature; we give a good story a real chance by reading it straight through in a single interested sitting. Try this plan someday with the book of

Luke and follow it with Acts. Forget that you have ever seen the Bible before; read the whole account of the great beginnings as you would read any other finely told chapter of history. See if it is not indeed an invigorating experience.

It is the story that changed the whole world. In saying that we are not unmindful of the limitations of the work of Jesus. He did not overthrow the oppressive government of Rome. He did not lower the tax rate. He did not improve sanitary conditions in Jerusalem, nor did He erect a public library at Nazareth. He did not increase the wages of Christians over those of infidels. He taught no sure cure for disease. The economic status of His followers was exactly as it had been: He found them fishermen, He left them fishermen. He did nothing to justify those who talk as though the "economic interpretation of history" were the last word in wisdom.

But His fishermen were different men, transformed, endowed with power, capable of great faith and magnificent achievement. Through them and their successors He started more philanthropies than all others who have ever lived. Hospitals and clinics, charities and libraries, schools and colleges have multiplied where He has inspired the souls of men. His religion is the best asset of civilization. That part of the world outside of which very few of us would willingly spend our days is named for Him, Christendom.

chapter 4

The Acts and the Epistles

THE PERIL of building around a single person is that when he dies or withdraws organization falls to pieces. "An institution is the lengthened shadow of a man," but there have been many men eminent in their day who cast no such shadow. The good they did is indeed "oft interred with their bones." Surely this process of disintegration, natural enough following the death of any leader, would be inevitable when the Leader had died a felon's death and the followers were unlettered peasants. The authorities at Jerusalem took this complacent point of view and rested easy.

They received a rude shock within a very few days. Peter and John, in preaching on the streets of the city and performing deeds of healing, gathered crowds that interfered with traffic and caused them to be arrested. Thinking to overawe these simple fellows, the High Priest Annas and his colleagues presided personally at the trial. Picture their amazement when Peter broke into vigorous denunciation of them as the murderers of the Lord in whose name only could salvation be found.

> Now when they saw the *boldness* of Peter and John . . . they marvelled; and they took knowledge of them, that they had been with Jesus. (Acts 4:13)

Those words deserve notice for the light they throw on the figure and manner of the real Jesus as contrasted with the unsatisfying portraits of Him that have come down to us through the ages. Painters have painted Him and writers have written about Him as a "man of sorrows," a physical weakling, a "lamb," an unhappy man who was disappointed and thus glad to die. The conquering attitude of the disciples does not tally with such descriptions. The Bible does not say of them, "seeing the lamb-like character of Peter and John" or "seeing that Peter and John were men of sorrow and acquainted with grief," but "seeing the *boldness* of Peter and John" the authorities knew that such men must have been the friends and companions of Jesus.

So characteristic was this boldness, so vigorous were the disciples in the propagation of the faith, that within less than twenty years the rulers of the far-removed city of Thessalonica were troubled by the report that

> These that have turned the world upside down are come hither also;
> . . . and these all do contrary to the decrees of Cæsar, saying that there is another king, one Jesus. (Acts 17:6-7)

Only a little later, not more than forty years after the death of Saint Paul, Pliny the Roman governor of Bithynia is compelled to write to the Emperor Trajan for instructions as to how he may check the growth of this extraordinary new sect. Since his letter and Trajan's reply are the only genuinely ancient records outside the Bible itself which bear directly on early apostolic activities, they are worth quoting at some length:

> *To the Emperor Trajan:* It is my invariable rule, Sir, to refer to you in all matters where I feel doubtful; for

who is more capable of removing my scruples, or inform-
ing my ignorance? Having never been present at any
trials concerning those who profess Christianity, I am
unacquainted not only with the nature of their crimes, or
the measure of their punishment, but how far it is proper
to enter into an examination concerning them. Whether,
therefore, any difference is usually made with respect to
ages, or no distinction is to be observed between the
young and the adult; whether repentance entitles them
to a pardon; or if a man has been once a Christian, it
avails nothing to desist from his error; whether the very
profession of Christianity, unattended with any criminal
act, or only the crimes themselves inherent in the profession are punishable; on all these points I am in great
doubt. In the meanwhile, the method I have observed
towards those who have been brought before me as
Christians is this: I asked them whether they were Christians; if they admitted it, I repeated the question twice,
and threatened them with punishment; if they persisted,
I ordered them to be at once punished: for I was persuaded, whatever the nature of their opinions might be,
a contumacious and inflexible obstinacy certainly deserved correction. . . .

This contagious superstition is not confined to the
cities only, but has spread its infection among the neigh-
bouring villages and country. Nevertheless, it still seems
possible to restrain its progress. The temples, at least,
which were once almost deserted, begin now to be fre-
quented; and the sacred rites, after a long intermission,
are again revived; while there is a general demand for the
victims, which till lately found very few purchasers.
From all this it is easy to conjecture what numbers might
be reclaimed if a general pardon were granted to those
who shall repent of their error.

Trajan to Pliny: You have adopted the right course,
my dearest Secundus, in investigating the charges against
the Christians who were brought before you. It is not
possible to lay down any general rule for all such cases.
Do not go out of your way to look for them. If indeed

they should be brought before you, and the crime is proved, they must be punished; with the restriction, however, that where the party denies he is a Christian and shall make it evident that he is not, by invoking our gods, let him (notwithstanding any former suspicion) be pardoned upon his repentance. Anonymous informations ought not to be received in any sort of prosecution. It is introducing a very dangerous precedent, and is quite foreign to the spirit of our age.

So rapidly has the shadow of the Cross extended that in less than a single century it falls across the emperor's throne. Let us turn back to the Bible record and trace the dramatic steps by which this incredible success was won.

The book of the Acts of the Apostles opens significantly:

The former treatise have I made, O Theophilus, of all that Jesus *began* both to do and teach, (Acts 1:1)

That sentence tells us first that the book was written by the same man who wrote the book of Luke and to the same man, Theophilus; and, second, that the writer, in common with the other disciples, regarded the three brief years of Jesus' public work as merely the beginning of His larger life and influence. So the events proved.

Jerusalem of those days was a populous and crowded city, and the disciples were countrymen from an outlying province. Yet, after a brief period of bewilderment, they organized themselves and became immediately a center of power. Thousands of men, some of them prominent in the city's life, came out to their meetings, confessed to the crime that had been done in the murder of Jesus, and became His truest followers.

Jesus and the original twelve had pooled their revenues in the "bag" which Judas carried, and he had paid all the expenses. For a time the Jerusalem community attempted to operate on this basis and, while there was no hard and fast rule, the sentiment was in favor of a common purse, and most of the group acceded to it. This led to the first tragedy.

A man named Ananias and his wife Sapphira wanted credit for having given their all, but they kept back half of the price of the land they had sold. Peter called Ananias to account, and he brazenly repeated his lie. Peter looked hard at him and said:

> Ananias, why hath Satan filled thine heart to lie to the Holy Ghost, and to keep back part of the price of the land?
>
> Whiles it remained, was it not thine own? and after it was sold, was it not in thine own power? why hast thou conceived this thing in thine heart? thou hast not lied unto men, but unto God.
>
> And Ananias hearing these words fell down, and gave up the ghost: and great fear came on all them that heard these things.
>
> And the young men arose, wound him up, and carried him out, and buried him. (Acts 5:3-6)

Three hours later Sapphira repeated the lie and met a similar fate. The incident profoundly impressed the young community. It appears from the narrative that the disciples were not required to give up their property and that some of them did not do so and suffered no reproach. But the sham of pretending to do so met with tragic rebuke. Communism failed even under the most sacredly favorable circumstances and probably always will fail, short of the millennium. The fact that it was attempted at all, however, indicates the earnest idealism of that early group and helps to explain the spirit which carried their faith to the ends of the world and laid the strong foundations of the church.

The Jews of that period were widely scattered. Their families were large and their country was small. There were colonies in almost every important city in the Mediterranean section, but they had times of home-coming at the several annual feasts in Jerusalem. The disciples took advantage of these occasions to preach to crowds that came from widely scattered places, and so quite early there began to be followers of Jesus, not only throughout Palestine but in Egypt and as far north as Antioch. It was in Antioch that need was first discovered for a name that should distinguish between Jews who did not accept Jesus and those who recognized His leadership. And "the disciples were called Christians first in Antioch." Up to that time the followers of Jesus had simply spoken of themselves as of "the Way." The first name of Christianity was "the Road."

In all these early movements Peter was the foremost figure. He developed a gift of speech that surprised his friends, and he never lacked courage. But presently there came on the stage a new figure of vast influence. One of the early preachers, Stephen, had given special attention to those Christians in Jerusalem who had not been born Jews but had come in as proselytes. He was arrested and condemned to death, and was executed by stoning. Doubtless the people who did the actual throwing of the stones were for the most part of the rabble, but "a young man named Saul," a zealous Pharisee, looked on with approval at a sentence which he as a member of the Sanhedrin, or high court, had helped to pass. Those who threw the stones

> laid down their clothes at a young man's feet, whose name was Saul. (Acts 7:58)

This young man named Saul was an ardent persecutor. He heard that the Christian faith was spreading as far as Damascus, and he obtained letters to the Jewish authorities there for the arrest of any who were of "the Way." He left Jerusalem very eager to carry out his errand, but with a growing inward uneasiness. He was mentally "kicking against the pricks" or goads of his own conscience. He remembered Stephen, whose face during his trial and execution had been "like the face of an angel." Riding along the road toward Damascus at midday, which is not a good time for a man to be riding there, he was stricken down by what may have been sunstroke; but with it came, as he believed, a voice, saying, "Saul, Saul, why persecutest thou me?" Saul's companions saw the blinding light but did not hear the voice. Saul asked, "Who art thou, Lord?" And again the voice came, "I am Jesus whom thou persecutest."

Saul's conversion was instantaneous, yet its development was most interesting. Instead of arresting anyone in Damascus, he at once announced his change of convictions, and had to escape from the city by means of a basket let down from the wall. Then he retired to Arabia for three years. When he emerged he had a definite plan. He would go back to Jerusalem to be welcomed by the disciples, who (Saul might well have thought this) would naturally choose him as their leader. It was a grand plan, but it met with bitter disappointment. When he arrived in Jerusalem, the disciples were afraid of him and, even after he had been vouched for by Barnabas, gave him a very grudging welcome.

Rebuffed but still ardent, he went to his old home in Tarsus, the Greek city where he had been born, a Jew but with full right of Roman citizenship, a fact of which he was immensely proud and of which he took full advantage. For a while he had little to do. Then Barnabas, a discoverer of men greater than himself, one of whom was Mark, went to Tarsus and invited Saul to come to Antioch where the work was making great progress. Saul went, and a new chapter in the ethical and spiritual history of the world began.

After a very successful work in Antioch, Barnabas and

Saul proposed to visit the old home of Barnabas in the island of Cyprus, and to preach as they went. This they did, and took with them Mark, who was a nephew of Barnabas. In Cyprus they had great success and established a friendship with the Roman governor, Sergius Paulus. Saul, named for the Old Testament king, now changed his name to Paulus, probably after this governor. From Cyprus they went into the nearer regions of Asia Minor.

And now an occasion of irritation arose. Barnabas was the leader of this journey, but Paul everywhere became the more prominent figure. Barnabas was evidently a tall impressive man; Paul was much smaller, more active and nervous. In one place on the mainland they were received with such honor that there was a proposal to deify them:

> And they called Barnabas, Jupiter; and Paul, Mercurius, because he was the chief speaker. (Acts 14:12)

Mark did not like the way things were going. His uncle Barnabas was the really great man, but Paul was taking the lion's share of the honors. Mark and Paul finally disagreed so completely that Mark left the two older men and went back to Jerusalem. In due time Paul and Barnabas followed, and both at Antioch and later at Jerusalem gave a vivid account of a most successful tour.

Thus far there had been no serious quarrel in the church, but the calm was about to be broken. Barnabas and Paul had found that many Gentiles were eager to know about Jesus, and the question now arose whether these people in becoming converts must become Jewish proselytes. Barnabas saw no reason why Christianity should be a mere sect of Judaism, and Paul agreed heartily. But the older disciples, all Jews, could not see how a man could be a Christian and not keep the whole Old Testament law.

A strange thing had happened at Jerusalem. The brothers of Jesus had not believed in Him during His ministry, and at one time even thought Him insane, but after His death they became loyal converts. Two of them, Jude and James, wrote short books, which are in the New Testament, and James went to Jerusalem and became very active in the church there. He was a "just man," a phrase that had been used of his father, Joseph, and was a very devout student of the Old Testament law. It is said that during his long periods of prayer his knees became callused like those of a camel. James was the head of the conservative faction, and Peter was at first of the same persuasion. James, by reason of his relationship to Jesus, had risen above Peter in Jerusalem, and he it was who presided over the first heresy trial in church history—the trial of Paul and Barnabas for baptizing Gentiles without insisting that they conform to the whole Jewish ritual.

It was a decidedly surprising experience for Paul. He had sat in Jerusalem as one of the seventy-one members of the Sanhedrin, the supreme court of the nation. Now he found himself back in the same city before Peter and James and John in positions not unlike that which he had occupied. He saw "those that were reputed to be somebody," as he rather loftily described them, and said, "whatsoever they were it maketh no matter to me"; he declared that they got more from him than he had ever got from them, that he neither went out under their authority nor recognized their right to tell him what he should preach. All the same, he cared greatly for their good will and the effect of their endorsement.

The story is told in the fifteenth chapter of Acts, one of the great documents in the history of the liberation of the human spirit. Paul's accusers presented their case, and Paul and Barnabas replied, and after a long debate a compromise was arrived at. The church in Jerusalem, consisting entirely of Jews, would stand firm for the old fundamentals, but the churches abroad, being Gentile, might follow a more liberal faith. At the suggestion of James a letter was sent from Jerusalem to the Gentile brethren in the churches which Paul had organized:

> Forasmuch as we have heard, that certain which went out from us have troubled you with words, subverting your souls, saying, Ye must be circumcised, and keep the law: to whom we gave no such commandment: (Acts 15:24)
> For it seemed good to the Holy Ghost, and to us, to lay upon you no greater burden than these necessary things;
> That ye abstain from meats offered to idols, and from blood, and from things strangled, and from fornication: from which if ye keep yourselves, ye shall do well. Fare ye well. (Acts 15:28-29)

Here was the first issue that divided Christians into two kinds, the fundamentalist and the liberal, and they were not to quarrel. Christians who had been reared as Jews were to be required to keep the whole Mosaic law, and those who were not so reared were to be accepted on their love of Jesus and a very simple code of morality. Paul left Jerusalem jubilant. He had won out. Telling later about "those who would have taken away our liberties," he says,

> To whom we gave place by subjection, no, not for an hour; that the truth of the gospel might continue with you. (Gal. 2:5)

He and Barnabas were now ready to start on another missionary journey and a longer one. But they had a quarrel. Paul, who did not like Mark, would not go if Mark went along, and Barnabas would not leave Mark behind.

And the contention was so sharp between them, that they departed asunder one from the other: and so Barnabas took Mark, and sailed unto Cyprus;

And Paul chose Silas, and departed, being recommended by the brethren unto the grace of God. (Acts 15:39-40)

Paul did not get on very well. He met a series of hindrances and changed his route several times. At length he came to Troas, the site of ancient Troy, where he fell ill and saw in a vision a man of Macedonia, saying, "Come over into Macedonia, and help us." Read carefully the next sentence; it is notable for its pronouns:

And after *he* had seen the vision, immediately *we* endeavoured to go into Macedonia . . . (Acts 16:10)

Where do we get this *we*? Who were the *we*?

Paul was one of them, but he is not the writer. Silas and Timothy were two others, but they are not the writers.

Who is it that comes into the narrative just at this point, under the shelter of this little word "we"? It is the author of beautiful books, the bearer of good news, Luke the Physician.

From here on the book of Acts is made up of two kinds of material, that which says "we" and that which says "he" or "they." The "we" sections show the times when Luke was present; the rest of the story he got from others. You will find it interesting to read the book of Acts from Chapter 16 to the end and discover just how much Luke actually saw and how much he heard from witnesses.

And now the good news took on a new character. Paul had crossed into Europe and found a fresh field. He preached in Philippi, in Thessalonica, which is modern Salonica, in Berea and even in proud Athens. That sophisticated city was the capital of the smart world.

> For all the Athenians and strangers which were there
> spent their time in nothing else, but either to tell, or to
> hear some new thing. (Acts 17:21)

Partly out of curiosity, partly from genuine intellectual
interest, the Athenians allowed Paul to make his way up to
Mars Hill and there set forth this new religion of which he
was the representative. Earlier in this book we've considered
how nobly he met a keen test of his mental agility. You will
recall how Paul faced the hostile, cynical crowd and spoke
only the truth, but with such diplomatic skill that the sophisticated and doubting were interested. He behaved bravely, to
be sure. But he avoided anger and challenge and accomplished
his purpose because he was a magnificent diplomat, because he
knew how to appeal to men's hearts *and* their minds.

From Athens Paul went to Corinth, then the Panama of
the ancient world, where a boom was in progress waiting a
government appropriation for the digging of the canal, which
had still to wait seventeen hundred years. Bachelor though
he was, Paul utilized more than any of the other apostles the
abilities of women. In Corinth he was fortunate in finding a
woman of talent, Priscilla, who with her husband, Aquila,
took him in. Like Paul they were tentmakers, and for a time
he worked with them. Paul soon began to gather converts.
The orthodox ruler of the synagogue, Sosthenes, did not like
the way things were going and stirred up a crowd which
hurried Paul before the Roman deputy, with the character-
istically intolerant charge:

> This fellow persuadeth men to worship God contrary to
> the law. (Acts 18:13)

The deputy, Gallio, was brother to the philosopher Seneca
and a man of solid common sense.

And when Paul was now about to open his mouth, Gallio said unto the Jews, If it were a matter of wrong or wicked lewdness, O ye Jews, reason would that I should bear with you:

But if it be a question of words and names, and of your law, look ye to it; for I will be no judge of such matters.

And he drave them from the judgment seat. (Acts 18:14-16)

With characteristic fickleness the crowd now turned on Sosthenes and administered a sound beating, which was in process when Gallio stepped out of the courtroom:

And Gallio cared for none of those things. (Acts 18:17)

Paul, who had been beaten repeatedly and once stoned and left for dead, rather enjoyed the spectacle, and the thrashing did Sosthenes good, for he subsequently became a convert. Indeed, when Paul was at Ephesus a few years later Sosthenes was with him and appears in the enviable position of joint author of the letter to the home folk, the Corinthians:

Paul, called to be an apostle of Jesus Christ through the will of God, and Sosthenes our brother,

Unto the church of God which is at Corinth . . . (1 Cor. 1:1-2)

Sometimes it takes a sound beating to open a hard-shelled mind to new truth, and the subsequent results may be of great benefit.

It was in Corinth that Paul developed what came to be his method: simply to move along the Roman roads from city to city, selecting important and favorable centers and "digging in" for a stay of considerable length; establishing a work that would radiate in different directions through the agency of his own helpers and such visitors as came to see him and took away with them the essentials of his message.

But another thing happened in Corinth in that autumn, a momentous thing. There the writing of the New Testament began.

We have already considered the writing of the four Gospels. The date of the first of them, Mark, is about 61; Paul reached Corinth ten years earlier, in 51. Up to that time the story of the life of Jesus had been told orally. No one felt the need of a written biography; no one felt qualified to write it. So it was not with the Gospels that the actual writing of the New Testament began, but with the letter which Paul in Corinth wrote to his old church in Thessalonica, the Epistle to the Thessalonians. You will be interested in the story.

Go back to the period before Paul's arrival in Corinth, to his crossing from Troas to Europe. He had seen a vision of a man of Macedonia inviting him into Europe, and he went. The little boat that carried him and his three companions, Timothy, Silas and Luke, bore the most precious freight that ever landed on the western shore of the Mediterranean. But Paul did not meet the man of Macedonia. For a good while he had a hard time. As we have already noted, he was beaten and imprisoned in Philippi, mobbed in Thessalonica, driven out of Berea and flouted in Athens. "Our flesh had no rest," he wrote about those days. "Without were fightings and within were fears." When he arrived in Corinth, he was alone, having left Silas at Berea and Timothy at Thessalonica.

The weeks while he waited for them to come to him were a period in which Paul was very near to nervous prostration. If it had not been for Priscilla's good cooking and the companionship which he found with her and her husband, he might have broken down entirely. His whole work since coming to Europe seemed a total failure; it had brought only hardship and humiliation.

He was afraid Timothy and Silas would never come. He was afraid they would be mobbed to death. And if they came he feared they would say: "It's no use. These people just will not hear the good news. In Philippi they say that if they had us back in jail we would never get out. In Berea they are ready to quote the Jewish law against us and say that Jesus did not measure up to the prophecies. In Thessalonica we dared not go on the streets in daylight. In Athens your sermon is a joke."

So in his lonesomeness he conjectured and was tortured by his imagination. But one day two dusty travelers arrived in Corinth and there inquired if a certain man was boarding somewhere in town, a small, wiry, nervous man of defective sight, a man named Paul. To their joy they learned that he was staying with Aquila and Priscilla; they hunted him up, and there was a glad reunion. Paul could hardly restrain himself.

"How is the work going?" we can imagine him asking.

"Fine," cried Timothy and Silas.

"You mean in Philippi?"

"Yes, there and everywhere else."

"In Berea?"

"Yes, the church is growing every day."

"But surely not in Thessalonica?"

"Yes, in Thessalonica, too. And they remember you with gratitude and want you to come back."

Paul was almost intoxicated with joy. The heartbreaking anxiety found relief in an ecstasy of satisfaction. The work was going well everywhere, even in Thessalonica! Eagerly he called for parchment and, with Timothy as a volunteer stenographer, he dictated a letter to send back to Thessalonica.

He told them how he had left with his two companions, but on reaching Athens had changed his mind and sent Silas and Timothy back:

Wherefore when we could no longer forbear, we thought it good to be left at Athens alone;

And sent Timotheus, our brother, and minister of God, and our fellowlabourer in the gospel of Christ, to establish you ... (1 Th. 3:1-2)

It almost killed him to think that they might have forsaken their faith. But they had not; they were standing fast.

But now when Timotheus came from you unto us, and brought us good tidings of your faith and charity, and that ye have good remembrance of us always, desiring greatly to see us, as we also to see you:

Therefore, brethren, we are comforted over you in all our affliction and distress by your faith:

For now we live, if ye stand fast in the Lord. (1 Th. 3:6-8)

So he dictated, as fast as Timothy could write, and sent the letter by a messenger going north from Corinth. He put in sundry exhortations and a little doctrinal teaching, and started the message forth on its eventful journey. He did not know, of course, that he had begun a great book. He never suspected that this impetuously composed first letter to the Thessalonians was to be the first volume in a new sacred library. But it was; and that is the way the New Testament began.

He had to write a second letter to the Thessalonians to answer some questions growing out of the first one. These letters were lent to near-by churches and copied and read to the congregations. Paul heard how widely they were used and so he wrote more and more. He had learned to supplement the living voice with the written page. If he were at work today he would not only preach; he would be a regular contributor to the press. He would love the smell of printer's ink.

After eighteen months in Corinth he went back to Jerusalem and gave account of his second missionary journey. He had a string of new churches through Asia Minor, Macedonia and Greece. He had developed his method, and he was happy in the knowledge of a great success. He remained in Palestine only a few months; it had grown too small for him. But while he was there he wrote one letter that must have attention. He learned that in Galatia, in Asia Minor, where he had established churches, he had been followed by fundamentalists who were telling the people that Paul was not really an apostle; that he possessed no real authority; that the good news as he had taught it was defective because he did not teach the Mosaic law.

Now Paul had great respect for the Mosaic law, and he did not object to the fundamentalists, provided they kept on their own side. But to have them invading a field which he had developed and to start a divisive doctrine there, looking, according to his view, not forward but backward, was too much for his hot temper and strong conviction. At once he called for his trusty pen, and after the formal greeting he plunged straight into his message:

I marvel that ye are so soon removed from him that called you into the grace of Christ unto another gospel:

Which is not another; but there be some that trouble you, and would pervert the gospel of Christ.

But though we, or an angel from heaven, preach any other gospel unto you than that which we have preached unto you, let him be accursed. (Gal. 1:6-8)

For do I now persuade men, or God? or do I seek to please men? for if I yet pleased men, I should not be the servant of Christ.

But I certify you, brethren, that the gospel which was preached of me is not after man. (Gal. 1:10-11)

He goes on to remind them of his history—how he was

the chief persecutor of the church, but was converted; how he received his message not from the group in Jerusalem but directly from God in his hours of quiet retreat in Arabia. He went to Jerusalem, he says, and met with James, "the Lord's brother"; he and Peter agreed concerning the right of Gentiles to be received into communion without being compelled to comply with the Mosaic law, and he won his fight. When later, at Antioch, Peter backslid into the old hard-shell theology, Paul had refuted him openly.

> But when Peter was come to Antioch, I withstood him to the face, because he was to be blamed. (Gal. 2:11)

By subsequent battles and by many persecutions, of which he bore the scars, he had won the right of his churches to freedom. Were they now proposing to abandon this great freedom because some strict constructionists from Judea had come among them, stirring up trouble?

> Stand fast therefore in the liberty wherewith Christ hath made us free, and be not entangled again with the yoke of bondage. (Gal. 5:1)
> For all the law is fulfilled in one word, even in this; Thou shalt love thy neighbour as thyself. (Gal. 5:14)
> If we live in the Spirit, let us also walk in the Spirit.
> Let us not be desirous of vain glory, provoking one another, envying one another. (Gal. 5:25-26)
> Be not deceived; God is not mocked: for whatsoever a man soweth, that shall he also reap.
> For he that soweth to his flesh shall of the flesh reap corruption; but he that soweth to the Spirit shall of the Spirit reap life everlasting.
> And let us not be weary in well doing: for in due season we shall reap, if we faint not. (Gal. 6:7-9)

That white-hot letter to the Galatians, product of intense

moral indignation, whose curses remain untranslated because
the translators have feared to put them into plain English, is
the Magna Charta of Christian liberty. It is the rebuke of
bigotry and the battle cry of freedom.

Paul soon set forth on his third and last missionary journey.
He started northward as he had done before, passing from
Antioch by land around the end of the Mediterranean,
preaching as he went, till he came to Ephesus. There he found
an opening in the Jewish synagogue; but after three months
a sharp clash arose, and he rented a schoolroom from a
philosopher named Tyrannus, the philosopher using it half
the day and Paul the other half. He took a two years' lease
of this place and developed his extension service so fully

> that all they which dwelt in Asia [the province, not the
> continent] heard the word of the Lord Jesus, both Jews
> and Greeks. (Acts 19:10)

The growth of his body of adherents was so remarkable
that in this city, where the beautiful temple of Diana stood,
and her shrine was sacred, the idol makers were almost out of
work. A large mass meeting of the silversmiths and allied trades
convened in the theater. There was a great shout for two
hours, "Great is Diana of the Ephesians," But then, as often,

> the more part knew not wherefore they were come
> together. (Acts 19:32)

So the crowd shouted itself tired without violence, and the
town clerk said a tactful word that dismissed the assembly.

In Ephesus, before this riot made his withdrawal wise, Paul
heard occasionally from his churches in Macedonia and
Achaia, and he kept in touch with them by means of his
letters, which were increasingly comprehensive. From here he
wrote his two letters to the Corinthians. If you will read them,

you will see that he canvassed pretty nearly every subject of church organization and of practical sociology: Ought the church to retain in its membership a fornicator? Ought Christians to observe the festivals of the moon? What about eating meats that had been offered to idols? Ought Christians to marry? Ought women to have part in public worship? Ought Christians to be involved in lawsuits? Prompted in part by questions submitted to him, his letters grew to include more and more of doctrinal instruction and of practical application of truth to life. Read these letters and see how there come into them such sublime passages as the chapter on charity:

> Though I speak with the tongues of men and of angels, and have not charity, I am become as sounding brass, or a tinkling cymbal.
>
> And though I have the gift of prophecy, and understand all mysteries, and all knowledge; and though I have all faith, so that I could remove mountains, and have not charity, I am nothing. (1 Cor. 13:1-2)
>
> Charity suffereth long, and is kind; charity envieth not; charity vaunteth not itself, is not puffed up,
>
> Doth not behave itself unseemly, seeketh not her own, is not easily provoked, thinketh no evil;
>
> Rejoiceth not in iniquity, but rejoiceth in the truth;
>
> Beareth all things, believeth all things, hopeth all things, endureth all things. (1 Cor. 13:4-7)
>
> And now abideth faith, hope, charity, these three; but the greatest of these is charity. (1 Cor. 13:13)

And his great chapter on life after death:

> For this corruptible must put on incorruption, and this mortal must put on immortality.
>
> So when this corruptible shall have put on incorruption, and this mortal shall have put on immortality, then shall be brought to pass the saying that is written, Death is swallowed up in victory.

O death, where is thy sting? O grave, where is thy victory? (1 Cor. 15:53-55)

Therefore, my beloved brethren, be ye stedfast, unmoveable, always abounding in the work of the Lord, forasmuch as ye know that your labour is not in vain in the Lord. (1 Cor. 15:58)

The Epistle to the Hebrews, which in our Bible is attributed to Paul, was almost certainly not written by him. The style is very different from his, and it does not seem likely, since all his letters were to congregations, that he would have addressed a letter to a whole people. The best Greek composition in the New Testament is in this letter, and so delicate and persuasive is it that there are those who think they detect a woman's hand. Some have conjectured that Priscilla might have been the writer. Paul had lived in her home, and she and Aquila, her husband, had been among his very best friends.

The letter is general, but its definite purpose is to convince thoughtful Jews that they will lose nothing by embracing the new faith but, on the contrary, will gain. It says: "You can have all that you cherish most and even more in the Christian faith. Do you love your Law? Well you may, but here is the same law written more beautifully. Do you love your Temple, your priesthood, your traditions? Everything you have cared for is here, and all the better."

It is noble in its conception of the basic principle of all heroism—faith. It calls the long roll of the faithful in all the ages and says that widely as they differed in many things they were all animated by one common inspiration. Read this grand roll call in Chapter 11:

They were stoned, they were sawn asunder, were tempted, were slain with the sword: they wandered about in sheepskins and goatskins; being destitute, afflicted, tormented;

. . . they wandered in deserts, and in mountains, and in dens and caves of the earth. (Heb. 11:37-38)

Wherefore seeing we also are compassed about with so great a cloud of witnesses, let us lay aside every weight, and the sin which doth so easily beset us, and let us run with patience the race that is set before us. (Heb. 12:1)

Others of the apostles now began to write. James, the brother of Jesus, had never felt wholly satisfied with Paul's doctrine of faith; he wrote a letter, a strange one for a man of such devotion to the law, of which one might almost say that it was not religious at all, so little did it regard form or ceremony. It was a very practical little homily on the importance of good works:

Pure religion and undefiled before God and the Father is this, To visit the fatherless and widows in their affliction, and to keep himself unspotted from the world. (Jam. 1:27)

A younger brother of Jesus, named Jude, also wrote a short letter. It was rather an apology for not writing a longer one which he had in mind to write on "our common Christianity." It grew out of a special occasion, which it may be presumed to have met well.

John, the son of Zebedee, also wrote, though later, three letters, one a remarkably sweet and beautiful letter addressed to no one in particular, and two short ones. Of these two, one was to a Christian lady whose name we do not know and the other to a friend, Gaius. Peter, also, wrote two letters and rather fine ones, as might have been expected of this blunt courageous man. But no one employed the letter-writing method to the extent that Paul did. His letters were copied and lent and read and became a kind of unofficial manual for the administration of the churches.

Paul left Ephesus after the riot, but not to return to Jerusalem; he was going across into Europe again. We may imagine the conversation that took place, for we get a wonderful glimpse into his mind in the letters to the Corinthians.

"You are going over the same ground again, Paul?"

"Yes, but every time widening the circle. This is my third time out. Each time I make a little larger swing and see the work growing."

"When do you get back to Jerusalem?"

"Next spring at Easter. I am going to take back the biggest collection that the Jerusalem church ever received."

"Are you going to stay there?"

"Stay there? Do you think I could ever be content to settle down and stay in Jerusalem?"

"But you are getting to be an old man, and travel is hard on you and dangerous."

"Yes, I have been in dangers of many kinds. It has been my privilege to travel farther than any of the other apostles,"

in labours more abundant, in stripes above measure, in prisons more frequent, in deaths oft.

Of the Jews five times received I forty stripes save one.

Thrice was I beaten with rods, once was I stoned, thrice I suffered shipwreck, a night and a day I have been in the deep;

In journeyings often, in perils of waters, in perils of robbers, in perils by mine own countrymen, in perils by the heathen, in perils in the city, in perils in the wilderness, in perils in the sea, in perils among false brethren;

In weariness and painfulness, in watchings often, in hunger and thirst, in fastings often, in cold and nakedness. (2 Cor. 11:23-27)

"That is a long list of perils, Paul. It must nearly have broken you down."

"I have a still heavier burden—my anxiety for all the churches I have established."

"Do you carry them on your mind and feel responsible for them?"

Who is weak and I am not weak? who is offended, and I burn not? (2 Cor. 11:29)

"You have done a great work and have much to be proud of."

"I am proud of it, and have been criticized as being vain about it. I have sometimes been ashamed of myself for letting people know my pride and joy in all this. Yet, while I have sometimes made myself a fool by seeming to boast, I really am not boastful. God forbid that I should glory, save in the cross of Christ and in the joy of service."

"When you go out again where shall you go?"

"Back again over the same ground, but more widely, to all the Roman capitals in Asia Minor and Greece, and then to Rome."

"Rome? And what then?"

"Oh, then I rather think I shall go to Spain."

Spain was a long way off and was bounded by the Pillars of Hercules, which we now call the Straits of Gibraltar. They were supposed to bear a banner in the sky above them, saying, *Ne plus ultra*—nothing more beyond. Paul was going the limit.

He set forth on his journey, and it was while he was on the road, at Cenchrea, that an incident happened which gave us the greatest of all his epistles. A woman named Phebe, "who had been a succourer of many, and of myself [Paul] also," was going to Rome; she asked Paul for a letter of introduction, which he, never having been to Rome, agreed to write. Phebe suggested that it would be well for Paul to tell the Roman Christians some of his teachings, as she was afraid she

might not be able to answer their questions. He agreed to
do it if she could find him a stenographer, and Phebe produced a young man named Tertius. He proved a good helper,
and so Paul expanded his teachings into a more fully developed system than anywhere else in his writings. He was not
sidetracked by questions concerning local matters, and he
swung out free into his orbit. Phebe took the letter with her
and delivered it safely to the Romans. It is a great achievement
and was written just before Paul, with his committee of
provincial Christians and his goodly collection for the mother
church, went up to Jerusalem for what proved to be his last
visit.

He had been warned. A certain prophet, Agabus, who had
come down from Judea, met him at Cæsarea, took Paul's
girdle and bound his hands and feet, saying:

> Thus saith the Holy Ghost, So shall the Jews at Jerusalem
> bind the man that owneth this girdle, and shall deliver
> him into the hands of the Gentiles.
> And when we heard these things [says Doctor Luke],
> both we, and they of that place, besought him not to go
> up to Jerusalem.
> Then Paul answered, What mean ye to weep and to
> break mine heart? for I am ready not to be bound only,
> but also to die at Jerusalem for the name of the Lord
> Jesus. (Acts 21:11-13)

So, seeing that they could not dissuade him, they went with
him. He took the large collection, as he had expected, and
was well received by the apostles, though still looked at a
little askance because of his free doctrines. Only a few days
had passed, however, when he was seized by the local authorities as "the man, that teacheth all men every where against
the people, and the law," and was thrown into jail. There,
weary of delays in the local courts, he finally exercised his

right as a Roman citizen and appealed to Cæsar, who at that time was Nero. Thus it was that Paul came to Rome.

Luke stayed with him through the two years of imprisonment which preceded his appeal, journeyed with him in a winter voyage and shipwreck and a sojourn of three months in Malta, all of which he describes vividly in Acts. They reached Rome together, and there the book of Acts ends abruptly:

> And Paul dwelt two whole years in his own hired house, and received all that came in unto him,
> Preaching the kingdom of God, and teaching those things which concern the Lord Jesus Christ, with all confidence, no man forbidding him. (Acts 28:30-31)

Probably no one came up from Jerusalem to Rome to appear against him, for five years had elapsed since his arrest, and so he was acquitted at his first trial and allowed to live under surveillance but in comfort. During those years he wrote more letters, including some of the finest, like Ephesians and Colossians, and especially Philippians. He had a special love for the places where he was whipped and imprisoned and where he compelled the magistrates to come down to the jail and invite him to walk out. It was in this period, also, that he wrote the charming little letter to Philemon.

It happened in this way. Philemon was a Christian man of wealth who lived in Asia Minor. He had a slave named Onesimus, a wild and disobedient lad who ran away and got to Rome, where he led a gay life. But he knew Paul, who had been at his master's house, and he went to hear him preach. Homesick and conscience-smitten, he asked what he ought to do. Paul kept him awhile to test him and then suggested that he go back to his master, not under bonds but of his own free will. Paul wrote a letter requesting his old friend to take this lad back on a new basis, "as a brother in the Lord." Paul was in a good and almost merry mood when he wrote this letter: "I will get around in your neighborhood after a while. Have a room ready for me."

It was not at all a depressed and broken-down apostle who was writing, you see. In some ways he was having a very good time. He was not in prison but was living under guard in "his own hired house," a splendid host, entertaining pilgrims from far and near. Where did he get the money? We can only guess. In some way apparently he had come into funds. Perhaps his father had died and left him an inheritance. Perhaps his well-to-do friends kept his purse filled. It must have cost him $30,000, as an eminent scholar once computed, for those five years, $6,000 a year for rent in Rome, where rents were high and the housing problem was acute, and for food for his rather large household, and for his expense of transportation for himself and his companions. Thirty thousand dollars for a man who had boasted that he was poor yet made many rich, and that his own hands had supported him much of the time while preaching!

Wherever the money came from, it is a fine thing for us all that during those five years Paul had it. Never, probably, has the world better spent $30,000. He had a guard whom, of course, he had to feed and fee, and this guard had to listen to Paul, who was always talking to visitors and telling about Jesus. The soldier who guarded him today might be on guard at the palace the next day, or at least might sleep that night with palace guards. It was not long till Paul could write:

> But I would ye should understand, brethren, that the things which happened unto me have fallen out rather unto the furtherance of the gospel;
> So that my bonds in Christ are manifest in all the palace, and in all other places;
> And many of the brethren in the Lord, waxing confi-

dent by my bonds, are much more bold to speak the word without fear. (Phil. 1:12-14)

Before many months there were disciples under the very roof of Nero, and Paul could add:

> All the saints salute you, chiefly they that are of Cæsar's household. (Phil. 4:22)

After about two years, as we suppose, the case against him was dismissed for lack of prosecution, and he made another journey, of which we get scattered glimpses in his two epistles to Timothy and the one to Titus. He had been in Crete and other islands and again at Troas. There is a verse which seems inconsequential, but it is luminous; it comes in the sad but triumphant ending of his last letter to Timothy, pleading with him to come to Rome and help care for him, and to bring Mark. Paul had learned that Mark was a better man than he had thought.

> Only Luke is with me. Take Mark, and bring him with thee: for he is profitable to me for the ministry. (2 Tim. 4:11)
> The cloke that I left at Troas with Carpus, when thou comest, bring with thee, and the books, but especially the parchments. (2 Tim. 4:13)

When had Paul been at Troas? The only occasion on which we saw him there was in 51, and this was 58! Was he asking for a cloak that he had left seven years before? No, he must have been out of prison and making another great swing around his circle when he was arrested a second time.

His second imprisonment was very different. No longer was he in his own house but, if we may trust tradition, was in the Mamertine prison, of which Hawthorne wrote, "Methinks there cannot be on earth another so evil a den, so full of haunting memories and vague surmises." The difference was that the first offense was only against the Jews, while now Christianity had grown so fast that the Roman Government had begun to fear. How long his second imprisonment lasted we do not know, but there came the dark day when they led him out and killed him. Peter, if we are to believe tradition, had also come to Rome. When sentenced to die, he asked to be crucified head downward, deeming himself unworthy to be killed in the same manner as his Lord—a magnificent touch of sentiment in a rough old saint.

It is almost certain that Nero blotted out both these great lives. We have an epistle of Peter's written from "Babylon," by which we suppose he meant Rome, and at the time of writing it he seems not to have been in any immediate danger. But the test came, and he met it gloriously. As for Paul, he died triumphant.

> For I am now ready to be offered, and the time of my departure is at hand.
> I have fought a good fight, I have finished my course, I have kept the faith:
> Henceforth there is laid up for me a crown of righteousness ... (2 Tim. 4:6-8)

And nobly had he won it. But to the end he wanted books and white paper; and he besought his young friend Timothy not to forget them. More knowledge to gain, more epistles to write! His conquering soul went marching on.

So we end our glance at the Epistles. There remains the last book in the Bible, the book of Revelation. It is a much-abused book. The first thing necessary is to forget most that you have heard about it. It is not a program of coming events. It has in it nothing about the next presidential election in the United States, nor anything about the state of the world. Its chief character is Nero. Indeed, the book is so simple it is hard to make readers believe its true explanation.

Remember, first, that in the interval between the Old and the New Testaments apocalyptic literature became enormously popular. There was a flood of books with dragons and grotesque animals representing peoples or nations or events. The Jewish imagination reveled in this style, which is illustrated in a part of Daniel, a very late book of the Maccabæan period, and much more dramatically in Revelation. At one time it seemed that all other literature in the Christian Church might be drowned out by the flood of this florid material.

Just after Paul and Peter were killed, John, the apostle, was banished to the island of Patmos. He was not yet the aged apostle of love; he was a hot-headed "son of thunder," and he wanted to write letters of encouragement to the churches in Asia Minor, the principal ones being seven in number. The letters, molded on a common form but straightforward enough, are in the opening chapters of Revelation. But John wanted to say something else and to say it in a way that would not get the people who had the letters in their possession into trouble. So he adopted the popular cryptic form which makes up the balance of the book. It should be studied through an opera glass and not a microscope. There is no use asking what is the meaning of every hair on the tail of each fantastic beast; the colors are put on with a big brush. But the three ideas are plain as a pikestaff. These ideas are:

1. Do not be afraid of the persecutions that originate in Jerusalem. That city will soon be in trouble with Rome and not able to persecute Christians.

2. Do not be afraid of the emperor of the mighty city on the seven hills that now is ruling the world; that city has trouble of its own coming, and it is not far off.

3. Hold to your faith, for it will survive. Jesus Christ is

greater than Nero, and His religion will last longer than the Roman Government.

The author spelled out Nero's name in a cryptogram, making the number 666. He disguised thinly the main things that he had to say. A Roman official who picked it up would have thrown it aside, saying, "What's this wearisome stuff? I haven't time to bother with it." Whereas if John had put his meaning into plain Greek any man having it in his possession would have been beheaded, and too many good men were losing their heads as it was.

How amazingly his great dream came true! The Roman Empire fell, and the one power that could avail to save it not from the pagans but to the future through the pagans was not the political or judicial power of Rome or the culture of Athens. That which saved civilization when Jerusalem was destroyed and Rome sacked by the vandals was nothing more or less than the Church of Christ. Read Gibbon's *Decline and Fall of the Roman Empire* and you get, from a rather unsympathetic scholar of cold temperament, the narrative of how it all came about. Even he warms and kindles as he tells about it.

But first read the book of the Acts, the Epistles and even fanciful, cryptic, vehement Revelation.

chapter 5

Ten Great Men
of the Bible

TEN THOUSAND ministers of all religious denominations were asked to name the ten greatest men in the Bible. It was not intended that they include the name of Jesus Christ; His name would, of course, stand first in importance in any list. But this chapter is to treat of ten others.

Saint Paul, Moses, David: these three led almost all the lists. Following them, the vote is more evenly distributed. The total number of men named is sixty. Some of those who attracted the smallest number of votes also inspired the best reasons for inclusion. From this notable list, probably the most interesting poll ever made on Bible characters, we select the following names, not in the order of votes cast but in chronological arrangement:

1. Adam, the first man with conscience and a knowledge of moral responsibility.

2. Noah, the man on whom at one time hung the hope of civilization.

3. Abraham, prince of pioneers.

4. Joseph, political economist, man of vision and integrity.

5. Moses, lawgiver, creator of a nation, the man who so firmly linked the rules of society with its religious standards

that the laws of most countries of today show his influence.

6. David, shepherd, soldier, singer and king.

7. Jeremiah, most heroic of that heroic group, the prophets.

8. Judas Maccabæus, the rebuilder of a nation.

9. John the Baptist, the herald of the dawn.

10. Saint Paul, apostle, traveler, author and martyr.

The reason for selecting the larger number of names from the Old Testament is doubtless explained by the longer period which it covers. The New Testament narrative, from the beginning of the ministry of Jesus until the destruction of Jerusalem by Titus, is only about forty years, whereas the Old Testament traverses many centuries.

1. *ADAM*

As we have previously seen, the account in Genesis of the world's creation does not have to be seen as conflicting with science. Similarly, the Biblical record of the emergence of life need stir no controversy. The broad outlines are the same. In Genesis "the waters bring forth abundantly the moving creature that hath life," and the paleozoologist agrees that they did. The parallels continue. Both accounts agree that the lower forms of life were followed by the higher and that man came last.

It would be foolish to say that the brief first chapter of Genesis takes account of every branch of science devoted to studying the same events. Differences exist but few now see them as forever irreconcilable.

Thus—in the majestic view of Genesis or the still sketchy accounts of the sciences—we have on the earth a new being, different from any other. He had a brain overarched by a skull of noble curvature, a tiny reproduction of the blue curve of the sky. This marvelous arch gave him a sphere of vision unique in creation. The eagle could see farther in its flight; the ape was stronger and a better climber, but he, man—and he alone—could look forward and outward and up.

Genesis gives us his name, Adam, and his dwelling place, "a garden eastward in Eden."

> And out of the ground made the Lord God to grow every tree that is pleasant to the sight, and good for food; the tree of life also in the midst of the garden, and the tree of knowledge of good and evil. (Gen. 2:9)

We witness the creation of the first woman:

> And the Lord God caused a deep sleep to fall upon Adam, and he slept: and he took one of his ribs, and closed up the flesh instead thereof;
> And the rib, which the Lord God had taken from man, made he a woman, and brought her unto the man.
> And Adam said, This is now bone of my bones, and flesh of my flesh: she shall be called Woman, because she was taken out of Man.
> Therefore shall a man leave his father and his mother, and shall cleave unto his wife: and they shall be one flesh. (Gen. 2:21-24)

Of all the trees in the Garden they might eat the fruit except one only, the tree of the knowledge of good and evil. But lured on by the serpent, they did eat of the fruit of that. They were discovered and promptly punished. The tribe of the serpent bears forever the signs of his punishment:

> And the Lord God said unto the serpent, Because thou hast done this, thou art cursed above all cattle, and above every beast of the field; upon thy belly shalt thou go, and dust shalt thou eat all the days of thy life: (Gen. 3:14)

As for Adam and Eve, they were cast out of the Garden. The ground was cursed with weeds and thistles; hard work and the sweat of their brows was to be their portion until they should return to the dust from which they came. So the Lord

> drove out the man; and he placed at the east of the garden of Eden Cherubims, and a flaming sword which turned every way, to keep the way of the tree of life. (Gen. 3:24)

A million sermons have been preached about Adam, berating him for his lost innocence, bemoaning his fall. How many of those sermons have overlooked the most significant phase of the story! Adam was innocent in the Garden, in the same sense that the sheep were innocent, and the sheep are just as innocent now as they were then. But Adam in Eden had no *character*, and character is the one good thing which God alone does not create. It is a joint product.

Just what the sin was which is recorded under the symbol of the tree and its fruit we do not know. It is an admirable symbol. The birds in Eden pecked holes in the fruit of that tree, as of many others. No fruit-eating beasts held it in special regard. Adam's sin was something which was wrong for him but not wrong for beasts and birds, some act of unbridled lust or bloody revenge; and having done it, he knew instantly that it was wrong. He heard the judgment of God. Somehow, in this new green universe, remorse and repentance entered into the soul of a living creature; and character began.

"A being such as I should be capable of something better," he said to himself.

Why did he say it?

What made him say it?

How was it that he knew himself to be different from the beasts that perish? Why was he so sure that it was wrong for him and not for them to use his brief opportunity for all it was worth? What persuaded him that God cared?

No matter if the story in Genesis be regarded as an allegory summarizing in the experience of one man a process which worked itself out through generations or as a literal record. The views of individuals and churches vary. The central fact remains, that one day somebody stood out against a background of innocent and contented animalism and assumed the self-consciousness and reproach which go with a moral nature. To that somebody, that Adam, we owe a debt which we can never repay. He was earth's first great hero.

Adam in the Garden, fattening on the fruits that grew without labor, has had too much attention. We care little for that brief inglorious period in his existence. It could not last long. Let us rather remember the later Adam, contending with thorns and thistles, trying hard to govern the rising generation which perplexed him as it has perplexed succeeding fathers, the Adam who earned his bread with the sweat of his brow, the Adam whose elder son killed the younger, the Adam who courageously, uncomplainingly carried on and handed down to his descendants a nature capable of responding to law and duty. That Adam is the first in honor as well as in time. He and Eve sent down to us the qualities that lift us out of the dust from which they came and back to which we, like them, return.

2. *NOAH*

Times of comfort and peace have brief histories. It is only when changes threaten and disaster impends that history dips her pen and adjusts her far-sighted spectacles to discover the nobleman.

> And God saw that the wickedness of man was great in the earth, and that every imagination of the thoughts of his heart was only evil continually. (Gen. 6:5)
> And the Lord said, I will destroy man whom I have created from the face of the earth . . . (Gen. 6:7)

Carlyle said that no age need go down to destruction if only there arises a man who knows his times and can lead. Noah had one of these qualifications but not the other. He could not lead. He preached for one hundred and twenty years to an ever-diminishing congregation. At the last he had only his own family standing by him, and was lucky to be able to hold even them.

You can imagine the derisive comments of his neighbors. Forty days and nights of rain, indeed! It never had happened before, it never could happen. Noah was a crazy old fool. Thus they commented, misplacing his tools no doubt and laughing as he hunted for them; thinking up new ways to annoy him and new practical jokes to perpetrate. "How's the weather this morning, old fellow? Doesn't look much like rain to me. When's your flood coming anyway? Guess maybe it ain't never coming."

But it did come!

> In the six hundredth year of Noah's life, in the second month, the seventeenth day of the month, the same day were all the fountains of the great deep broken up, and the windows of heaven were opened.
>
> And the rain was upon the earth forty days and forty nights. (Gen. 7:11-12)
>
> And every living substance was destroyed . . . (Gen. 7:23)

It is an interesting question for every man to ask himself: "If I had been on the earth in the days of Noah, should I have been one of the survivors or one of the wise ones who knew it all? If I had been in Jerusalem in the days of Jesus, should I have been one of the few who saw truth, even in its rough peasant garb, or should I have stood with the respectable, well-fed majority, shouting, 'Away with this disturber! Crucify!'? If I had been in the colonies in the days of George

Washington, am I quite sure that I should have risked my property and future with an ill-fed, ill-conditioned army of rebels? Shouldn't I perhaps have considered the Tories a much more substantial, sane and respectable lot?"

Only a few have courage and vision to stand against the crowd; Noah had both in plentiful amounts.

> Thus did Noah; according to all that God commanded him, so did he. (Gen. 6:22)

A grand tribute to a man who stood firm and true when humanity as a whole went wrong. He did what God told him to do, and he was justified in the result.

And then?

If you or I had written the story, we should have pictured the serene old age of Noah, in his uniform as a retired admiral of the navy, introduced to the fast multiplying posterity of mankind as the man who saved the world. We should have provided for him a future worthy of his great achievement. The record shocks us:

> ... and [Noah] was drunken. (Gen. 9:21)

Drunk perhaps with his success. Drunk with pride when people told him how all his weather predictions had come true. Drunk with the praise which he had richly earned and could not wisely appreciate. Drunk also with wine.

A shameful scene as he lay in his tent. Ham peering in with mocking laughter, and the other sons doing their sorrowful duty—a scene worthy of the reproach which Whittier wrote of Daniel Webster after his Seventh of March speech:

> So fallen! so lost! the light withdrawn
> Which once he wore!

The glory of his gray hairs gone
  Forevermore!
. . . .
Then, pay the reverence of old days
  To his dead fame;
Walk backward, with averted gaze,
  And hide the shame!

Noah was drunken. The man who had saved the world did not continue in the work of its salvation. The new age that followed the flood had to find new leaders for its new problems. Yet as long as the rainbow overarches the storm cloud the world will remember the integrity and courage and obedience of Noah.

And God remembered Noah . . . (Gen. 8: 1)

Let us not forget him.

3. *ABRAHAM*

Most of the pioneers since the world began have lived and died and left no memory of their deeds. They blazed the trails which those who followed trod into paths, and by the time that these had become macadamized highways it was too late to find the record of them whose adventurous feet had first passed that way. Edward Everett Hale found himself profoundly moved by his contemplation of the nameless saints whose heroism we have inherited:

What was his name? I do not know his name;
I only know he heard God's voice and came,
Brought all he loved across the sea,
And came to work for God and me;
Felled the ungracious oak,
Dragged from the soil

With horrid toil
The thrice-gnarled root and stubborn rock,
With plenty piled the mountain side,
And then, at length, without memorial died.
No pealing trumpet thunders forth his fame;
He lived, he died: I do not know his name.

But a few of the heroic adventurers left authentic records that defy the effects of oblivion. Prince of the pioneers is Abraham. He lived, as his ancestors had lived, in the fertile valley of Mesopotamia, a great landowner and shepherd.

And Abram was very rich in cattle, in silver, and in gold. (Gen. 13:2)

Lot, his nephew, was also rich.

And the land was not able to bear them, that they might dwell together . . .
And there was a strife between the herdmen of Abram's cattle and the herdmen of Lot's cattle . . . (Gen. 13:6-7)

More pasture was needed for their flocks, and to their neighbors that was a sufficient explanation of their migration; just as many historians regard "economic pressure" as the whole explanation of the journey of the Pilgrim Fathers and of so many other important movements in history. But there is something in men which responds to an impulse other than the mere need for more food or the desire for wealth.

Now the Lord had said unto Abram, Get thee out of thy country, and from thy kindred, and from thy father's house, unto a land that I will shew thee: (Gen. 12:1)
. . . and he went out, not knowing whither he went. (Heb. 11:8)

In those two sentences, one from the Old Testament, the other from the New, you have the real story of Abraham's migration. He was already on the way when the message came to him. It is interesting that his father, Terah, had heard a similar message years before and had started but never arrived.

> And Terah took Abram his son . . . and they went forth . . . from Ur of the Chaldees, to go into the land of Canaan; and they came unto Haran, and dwelt there. (Gen. 11:31)

Ur of the Chaldees was a city where the worship of the moon was the supreme form of religion. Terah revolted against it and, on hearing the voice of the Lord, started to get away from the land of idolatry. But he got only as far as Haran, and though the worship of the moon was in full swing there also, he settled down. With the growing tolerance of age, the moon worship did not seem so bad as it had in the fresh idealism of youth.

> Terah, the father of Abraham . . . served other gods. (Josh. 24:2)

He was old and tired. Nothing appeared quite so important as it had. Why raise a fuss with the neighbors? Better accept things as they were and rest easy. So Terah compromised. But his life was not a total failure. At least he had started, and although he did not arrive, he made the journey easier for Abraham. Of how many other lives was his life typical— men who aspire to be pioneers and set out in youth to make the full journey but travel no farther than from Ur to Haran and end by worshiping the same old moon god? Fortunate are they when their sons carry on!

God changed the name of Abram to Abraham.

Neither shall thy name any more be called Abram, but thy name shall be Abraham; for a father of many nations have I made thee (Gen. 17:5)

He was given children when more than ninety years old, and he lived to be a hundred and seventy-five, "an old man and full of years." Among many elements which combined to make him great, one is particularly worthy of remembrance—he was the real head of his own household. God said:

Abraham shall surely become a great and mighty nation, and all the nations of the earth shall be blessed in him. (Gen. 18:18)

Why?

For I know him, that he will command his children and his household after him, and they shall keep the way of the Lord, to do justice and judgment . . . (Gen. 18:19)

If leaders were chosen in our day on the basis of their proved power to govern their own families justly, how many would qualify? Maybe that lack in modern men is one reason why there are not more Abrahams.

4. JOSEPH

And Joseph was brought down to Egypt; and Potiphar, an officer of Pharaoh, captain of the guard, an Egyptian, bought him of the hands of the Ishmeelites . . . (Gen. 39:1)

And Joseph found grace in his sight, and he served him: and he [Potiphar] made him overseer over his house, and all that he had . . . (Gen. 39:4)

And it came to pass after these things, that his master's wife cast her eyes upon Joseph; and she said, Lie with me. (Gen. 39:7)

. . . he . . . fled, and got him out. (Gen. 39:12)

The illicit love of Potiphar's wife, and her revenge when the young overseer refused to betray the trust of his master, is the most widely remembered episode in Joseph's career. It has been the theme of plays and novels, and the cynical writers of all ages have scoffed at the young man's scruples and by their scoffing condemned themselves. For the story of Joseph is perhaps the finest single story in the Old Testament.

His father's favorite, and therefore the scorn and envy of his brothers, he made trouble for himself by the strange wisdom of his dreams and by his "coat of many colors," his father's gift. "Behold this dreamer cometh," they sneered, and forthwith they cast him into a pit, and smearing his coat with the blood of a kid took it home to their sorrowing father with a lie.

A commonplace age is always suspicious of dreamers. But what continent was ever opened, what railway built, what great discovery made, without their help?

The dreamer may finally, as Shaemus O Sheel informs us, "ride God's battle-field in a flashing and golden car," but he treads a long hard path in the beginning. The Ishmaelites bought Joseph when his brothers removed him from the pit into which they had cast him, and he tramped beside their camels down the dusty trail into Egypt. By sheer brains and force of character he won his way into Potiphar's employ:

> And he [Potiphar] left all that he had in Joseph's hand; and he knew not ought he had, save the bread which he did eat. . . . (Gen. 39:6)

Joseph's life stretched out before him with fine promise when the passion of a woman intervened, and evil days descended. "Behold this dreamer cometh"; unlock the prison door and let it clang behind him.

Who remembered him in prison? Potiphar's wife, perhaps, with a sinister smile at his scruples. His guilty brothers, like enough, with a lessening prick of conscience until they almost persuaded themselves they had forgotten. But the people whom he had benefited did not remember him. The chief butler promised not to forget, but being released "forgat him."

Only God did not forget him, and his dreams, which had been the original cause of his trouble, were finally to bring him release and success. In a previous chapter we have recalled the famous dream of Pharaoh and how, by its interpretation, Joseph was able to organize the food supplies of Egypt so that the abundant harvests of seven years were stored away against the famine of the succeeding seven years. All other lands were desolate, including the land where his father and guilty brothers dwelt, and at length the brothers were forced to go to Egypt to buy corn; they opened negotiations with Egypt's great official.

> And Joseph knew his brethren, but they knew not him. (Gen. 42:8)

His hour of revenge had come. For several days he kept them guessing. He locked them up and after their release kept Simeon as a hostage until they should return and bring their little brother Benjamin with them. They promised, and started off. Imagine their surprise when they opened their sacks to find not merely the corn they had come to purchase but the money which they had given in payment. They hurried on to Jacob, their father, and told him how the governor had received them and of his demand that they should bring little Benjamin when they came again. How they went again to Joseph, still without recognizing him; how they were received and entertained at his palace; the trick he played upon them to test their love for little Benjamin and so stir up the memory of their different treatment of the other little brother whom they supposed they had killed—all this is set forth in a style as fascinating as any novel. And, indeed, Thomas Mann made the Joseph story into *four* novels.

> And they went up out of Egypt, and came into the land of Canaan unto Jacob their father,
> And told him, saying, Joseph is yet alive, and he is governor over all the land of Egypt. And Jacob's heart fainted, for he believed them not.
> And they told him all the words of Joseph, which he had said unto them: and when he saw the wagons which Joseph had sent to carry him, the spirit of Jacob their father revived:
> And Israel said, It is enough; Joseph my son is yet alive: I will go and see him before I die. (Gen. 45:25-28)

So came the people of Israel into Egypt, saved by Joseph, who had power enough to secure protection and provender for them, not only during his lifetime but for four centuries after his death.

> And the children of Israel were fruitful, and increased abundantly, and multiplied, and waxed exceeding mighty; and the land was filled with them.
> Now there arose up a new king over Egypt, which knew not Joseph. (Exod. 1:7-8)

A new king, a new crisis, a new hero to meet the crisis; the next great figure of the Old Testament, Moses. It was his part to take the children of Israel out of Egypt, as it had been the work of Joseph to save their lives by getting them in. And when the day of deliverance arrived, and they marched forth into freedom and the wilderness, the procession was led by the bones of Joseph.

> And Moses took the bones of Joseph with him: for he had straitly sworn the children of Israel, saying, God

will surely visit you [he was a dreamer, you see, to the end]; and ye shall carry up my bones away hence with you. (Exod. 13:19)

5. MOSES

A celebrated clergyman, in recounting the curious happenings of a long ministry, said that the strangest letter he ever received was as follows:

> Reverend Sir: I will be at your church next Sunday morning and will deposit one dollar in the collection box if you will preach a sermon on the following text: "Put forth thine hand, and take it by the tail."

Just why the letter writer should have picked out that particular verse, or why the story should have stayed in my mind, I do not know. But I looked up the passage, and from time to time I have amused myself by asking other clergymen if they knew where it occurs. The usual guess is that it has to do with the story of Balaam's ass or with Saint Paul, who was attacked by a serpent while gathering wood for a fire after his shipwreck. As a matter of fact, it is to be found in the early part of the record of Moses.

Reared as the grandson of an emperor, doted on by a royal foster mother, Moses, who might have had every luxury, preferred—like Abraham, like each of the prophets, like John the Baptist and Saint Paul—to be "not disobedient to the Heavenly vision." He was modest, as most men of genius are.

> And Moses said unto God, Who am I, that I should go unto Pharaoh, and that I should bring forth the children of Israel out of Egypt? (Exod. 3:11)
> But, behold, they will not believe me, nor hearken unto my voice: for they will say, The Lord hath not appeared unto thee.

And the Lord said unto him, What is that in thine hand? And he said, A rod.

And he said, Cast it on the ground. And he cast it on the ground, and it became a serpent; and Moses fled from before it.

And the Lord said unto Moses, Put forth thine hand, and take it by the tail. And he put forth his hand, and caught it, and it became a rod in his hand: (Exod. 4: 1-4)

That rod was to play a mighty part in the history of the next forty years. By it the plagues were brought upon the Egyptians in tragic succession until even the stubborn will of Pharaoh was broken; the Red Sea divided at its touch to let the children of Israel pass through; and in the wilderness, when water failed, the rock which it smote gave forth a crystal stream. Moses had need of its help and of all the encouragement and support that Aaron, his colleague, and the strong men of the twelve tribes could give, for these undisciplined former slaves whom he led into the wilderness were impatient, restless and addicted to grumbling at every opportunity. As lawgiver, military commander and executive, he transformed them into a self-governing people, and left a body of laws which have come down to our own day as the foundation of modern jurisprudence and civic sanitation.

There have been many leaders of powerful personality who failed because they could not gather strong men around them. Moses was not one of these. He realized clearly the necessity for first-class helpers. He needed the wise counsel of Jethro, who saw clearly that the combined duties of administrator and judge were too much for any one man and urged Moses to set up a group of associate judges.

And Moses' father in law said unto him, The thing that thou doest is not good.

Thou wilt surely wear away, both thou, and this people that is with thee: for this thing is too heavy for thee;

thou art not able to perform it thyself alone. (Exod.
18:17-18)

He needed the sword of Joshua. He needed the eloquence
and priestly help of Aaron.

And Moses said unto the Lord, O my Lord, I am not
eloquent . . . but I am slow of speech, and of a slow
tongue. . . . (Exod. 4:10)
And the anger of the Lord was kindled against Moses,
and he said, Is not Aaron the Levite thy brother? I know
that he can speak well. . . .
And thou shalt speak unto him, and put words in his
mouth . . .
And he shall be . . . to thee instead of a mouth, and
thou shalt be to him instead of God. (Exod. 4:14-16)

The special talent of each of these associates supplemented
Moses' own abilities; he was intelligent enough to know that
they required supplementing. But the great essentials—courage, idealism, vision, faith—he borrowed from no man. He had
them in abundance.

For forty years he carried the burden. One by one his contemporaries dropped away, leaving him an old man among a
nation of children. We catch a glimpse of the towering lonely
spirit in the one Psalm which long and venerable tradition
declares to have come from him. We have quoted before
from the Ninetieth Psalm:

Lord, thou hast been our dwelling place in all generations.
Before the mountains were brought forth, or ever thou
hadst formed the earth and the world, even from everlasting to everlasting, thou art God. (Psa. 90:1-2)
For a thousand years in thy sight are but as yesterday
when it is past, and as a watch in the night.
Thou carriest them away as with a flood; they are as a

sleep: in the morning they are like grass which groweth up.

In the morning it flourisheth, and groweth up; in the evening it is cut down, and withereth. (Psa. 90:4-6)

So teach us to number our days, that we may apply our hearts unto wisdom. (Psa. 90:12)

"The days of our years are threescore years and ten," said that Psalm, "and if by reason of strength they be fourscore years, yet is their strength labour and sorrow." His own years, however, were many more.

And Moses was an hundred and twenty years old when he died: his eye was not dim, nor his natural force abated. (Deut. 34:7)

He died without ever setting foot on the Promised Land, toward which he had kept his people pointed through the weary years. Like so many other men of vision he never quite realized his whole ideal. But his was the leadership in the formative years of the nation; his the joy of standing on the mountain with God and there receiving the moral law that was to make all the difference between his followers and the heathen whom they were to meet and overcome. His was the vision from Mount Nebo of the fertile land which his people would inherit but in which he himself would never dwell. The thousands of years between us have not obliterated the high significance of his work.

And there arose not a prophet since in Israel like unto Moses, whom the Lord knew face to face. (Deut. 34:10)

6. DAVID

As long as the nature of boys remains what it always has been, David will have a fresh army of admirers with each new generation, for he is the original of all Jack the Giant Killer stories and has been the hero of boyhood for three thousand years.

With the exception of Paul no human character occupies so large a place in the Bible; of none are we given so vivid and compelling a picture. The most minute traits and characteristics are set forth in such a way as to make certain that the portrait was drawn from life. What a portrait and what a life! A red-headed shepherd boy, tending his flocks and playing his tunes in the lonesome fields, he is sent up to the army at the critical moment when its forces are paralyzed by the menace of the giant Goliath. What the swords of the stoutest warriors have been powerless to accomplish, he achieves by a well-directed shot from his shepherd's sling and becomes immediately a national idol. Triumphantly he is carried to the court while the bands play and the pretty girls sing and dance.

> And the women answered one another as they played, and said, Saul hath slain his thousands, and David his ten thousands. (1 Sa. 18:7)

Small wonder that Michal, the king's daughter, loved him and became his wife; small wonder that Jonathan, the king's son, formed a friendship with him which is one of the most beautiful in all history. Small wonder either that the king himself was jealous and resentful.

> And Saul was very wroth, and the saying displeased him; and he said, They have ascribed unto David ten thousands, and to me they have ascribed but thousands: and what can he have more but the kingdom?
> And Saul eyed David from that day and forward. (1 Sa. 18:8-9)

The jealous eyes of Saul, who was in a place too big for him and finally went mad trying to fill it, drove David out of the court and into the wilderness. There soldiers of fortune rallied to him from various motives, and he built up a lusty young army which, to his credit, he kept well-disciplined and free from the grosser crimes of guerrilla warfare. Neither the king's forces nor his plots could prevail against the young man's destiny. Fate had picked him out for leadership, and Samuel the prophet had placed the seal of approval on his claims; he was made for the throne and to it in due course he came.

In a previous chapter we have referred to his conquests, his qualities as an administrator, the sin which forms the one black spot on his reputation—a sin, by the way, which was not so extraordinary in a king of that period and would perhaps have been forgotten but for the magnificent humility of his repentance, and the Psalms that are his eternal claim to remembrance. We know that his administration was notable for justice:

> And David reigned over all Israel; and David executed judgment and justice unto all his people. (2 Sa. 8:15)

We are told that he was always accessible:

> And when the woman of Tekoah spake to the king, she fell on her face to the ground, and did obeisance, and said, Help, O king.
> And the king said unto her, What aileth thee? And she answered, I am indeed a widow woman, and mine husband is dead. (2 Sa. 14:4-5)

We know that he solidified his kingdom and made it respected among the powerful nations of that part of the world.

Let us pass by, then, the record of his official life and touch on two incidents that reveal his heart. It was after one of the great battles with the Philistines when his little force was surrounded and cut off from all supplies, even water, that David, worn out and thirsty, thought of the clear pure water in his father's well which had cooled his lips in boyhood. His parched throat yearned for it.

> And David longed, and said, Oh that one would give me drink of the water of the well of Bethlehem, which is by the gate!
>
> And the three mighty men brake through the host of the Philistines, and drew water out of the well of Bethlehem, that was by the gate, and took it, and brought it to David: nevertheless he would not drink thereof, but poured it out unto the Lord.
>
> And he said, Be it far from me, O Lord, that I should do this: is not this the blood of the men that went in jeopardy of their lives? therefore he would not drink it. . . . (2 Sa. 23:15-17)

It is easy to understand why men worshiped a leader like that.

The other incident occurred in the campaign against his son Absalom, the boy whom he loved more than all the world and who repaid that love by organizing a revolt and attempting to seize the throne. David gave orders that the boy was under no circumstances to be killed; but the zeal of a professional soldier was not to be curbed by such an order, and word was brought to the king that Absalom was dead. The revolt was broken, his throne was safe, he could go back to the security of the palace, but it all meant nothing. The feelings of the monarch were swallowed up in the heartbreaking anguish of the father.

> O my son Absalom, my son, my son Absalom! would God I had died for thee, O Absalom, my son, my son! (2 Sa. 18:33)

Perhaps the most poignant cry in history from a father's heart.

The faults of David are set forth no less clearly than his virtues; we feel the reality of him in every line. Yet no catalogue of his shortcomings can hide his essential greatness. He was a genius in war, in administration and in literature. He reorganized a government that lasted more than four centuries as a single dynasty and which lived as an ideal through thirty centuries. His songs hurled Cromwell's men singing into the thick of the fight:

> Far below the Roundheads rode,
> And hummed their surly hymn.

It was David's hymn which they sang:

> Let God arise; let his enemies be scattered: let them also that hate him flee before him. (Psa. 68:1)

And the same songs have sent the centuries forward marching to the music of hope:

> The Lord is my light and my salvation; whom shall I fear? the Lord is the strength of my life; of whom shall I be afraid? (Psa. 27:1)

7. JEREMIAH

It is a terrible handicap to the memory of a man when a descriptive phrase or adjective attaches to his name, for people feel that they are thereby relieved from learning anything more about him. Thus "the patience of Job" has effectually cloaked the real significance of that heroic figure; "as meek as Moses" has distorted the grandeur of one of the really great leaders of history; and the adjective "doubting Thomas" has libeled the brave soul who cried, "Let us also go up with

him that we may die with him." Similarly, Jeremiah has
been labeled the "weeping prophet," and, though there is
hardly any Old Testament character about whom we have
more biographical material, this totally unworthy phrase
constitutes his entire biography for a majority of people.

He did weep, and good cause he had to do it. God laid on
him a tremendous burden. Once when he cried out because
he was carrying every bit that he possibly could, God's
answer to him was that the worst was yet to come.

> If thou hast run with the footmen, and they have
> wearied thee, then how canst thou contend with horses?
> and if in the land of peace, wherein thou trustedst, they
> wearied thee, then how wilt thou do in the swelling of
> Jordan? (Jer. 12:5)

Only a courageous spirit could stand a message like that.
Jeremiah was, on the whole, the bravest figure in the Old
Testament. He was the kind of man who would have enjoyed
a home, but it was denied him.

> The word of the Lord came also unto me, saying,
> Thou shalt not take thee a wife, neither shalt thou have
> sons or daughters in this place. (Jer. 16:1-2)

He was a priest, but he had little to do with the Temple.
He was a man of property, yet he encountered continuous
privation. A friend of kings, he was cast into prison for
reproving royalty. A stern patriot, he was under suspicion of
giving aid and comfort to the enemy and was compelled at
one period to take shelter with the enemy against the friends
whom he had vainly sought to save. A natural optimist, loving
people and desiring to be loved by them, he was forced to
utter truths which estranged him from all companionship and
left him a lonely outcast in a hostile land.

Woe is me, my mother, that thou hast borne me a man of strife and a man of contention to the whole earth! I have neither lent on usury, nor men have lent to me on usury; yet every one of them doth curse me. (Jer. 15:10)

Jeremiah was a countryman, born in the little town of Anathoth. When the call of God came to him to stand forth as a turbulent prophet instead of a quiet priest, it found him modest and reluctant.

Then said I, Ah, Lord God! behold, I cannot speak: for I am a child. (Jer. 1:6)

The king of the country was Josiah, who meant well and tried to bring about a revival of religion. Apparently Jeremiah correctly estimated the ineffectiveness of Josiah's character and realized that the improvement was merely superficial. At any rate, he did not ally himself with the reform movement, which died quickly after the king's death. From this time on, under the driveling king Jehoiakim, Jeremiah was a stormy voice, denouncing wickedness in the nation and folly at court, and prophesying that Nebuchadnezzar would surely conquer Jerusalem. He was imprisoned. When he had written out his sermons and prophecies and was reading them at court, the king took the roll, slashed it with a penknife and threw it into an open fire. Finally the prophet was compelled to flee with a little group of refugees into Egypt.

There the women of the company found a new fad in religion. When Jeremiah spoke to the men, saying, "Stop your wives from worshiping the moon," they bluntly refused.

Then all the men which knew that their wives had burned incense unto other gods . . . answered Jeremiah, saying,
As for the word that thou hast spoken unto us in the name of the Lord, we will not hearken unto thee.

But we will certainly do whatsoever thing goeth forth out of our own mouth, to burn incense unto the queen of heaven, and to pour out drink offerings unto her, as we have done . . . for then had we plenty of victuals, and were well, and saw no evil.

But since we left off to burn incense to the queen of heaven, and to pour out drink offerings unto her, we have wanted all things, and have been consumed by the sword and by the famine. (Jer. 44:15-18)

In other words, "The Lord doesn't look after us and the moon does: why should we stick to the Lord?" It was the question that Jeremiah himself had to face on almost every day of his lonely, persecuted life. His Gethsemane is in Chapter 20, verses 7 to 9: "O God! I did as you told me and you didn't stand by me!" He would have liked to abandon it, but the word of the Lord was "in mine heart as a burning fire shut up in my bones." He could not escape his destiny, even though it led him over a pathway of thorns and caused him at last, according to tradition, to be stoned to death.

Baruch, his secretary, made a second copy of his biography and sermons after the king had burned the first, and this, with other material which the hero-worshipers of later periods added, is the book of Jeremiah that has come down to us. Baruch was faithful but disorderly or else was so pressed for time that he could not finish his work. The book is badly jumbled, and only by following the lead of scholars can one know how to read it to get a clear picture. Yet even the most desultory reading reveals the majesty of the figure that stalks through its pages. No man ever spoke the truth at greater personal sacrifice. Jeremiah stood firm against the threat of the court and the anger of the crowd; noblest of all, he stood firm when God Himself seemed to have broken His promises and abandoned His messenger.

8. *JUDAS MACCABÆUS*

It is well that the list of names which our ballot brought forth should include some that are comparatively unfamiliar. For that reason, and because of his importance, as well as the inspiring character of his story, we are glad to find Judas Maccabæus well up in the list.

His record falls between the Old and the New Testaments and is told in detail in the books which were formerly printed as part of the Bible and called the Apocrypha. A part of sacred literature before Jesus, these books were regarded as valuable but having a different quality from those that made up the Old Testament itself. Some of them ought still to be printed as part of the Bible, and none deserves to be wholly ignored.

Alexander the Great had conquered the world at one of the easiest of all dates to remember, 333 B.C. His brilliant life ended while he was still a very young man. When he was asked, "To whom do you leave your kingdom?" he answered, "To the strongest." Each of his four generals thought he was strongest, but not one of them was strong enough to conquer the other three. In the division which followed, Palestine was for a considerable time under the domination of Ptolemy, who ruled Egypt. He caused the Old Testament to be translated into Greek, a most wise and beneficial proceeding, for ancient Hebrew was no longer a spoken language and most of the Jews who could read at all read Greek. So the "Septuagint," alleged to have been made by "seventy" scholars, became the Bible version mainly in use then and even in the time of Jesus.

In the subsequent redistributions of authority, Palestine passed under the domination of a Greco-Syrian dynasty, whose outstanding representative was Antiochus Epiphanes. He endeavored to unify his little empire by instituting a kind of emperor worship, or worship of the state; then he sought to superimpose this on all the forms that were dominant in his land, especially the worship of Jehovah in the Temple at Jerusalem.

Many thousands of Jews accepted this bastard form of idolatry, including most of the priests, whose salaries went on as before. But there was one aged priest, Mattathias, who revolted and withdrew from Jerusalem to his summer home at Modin, taking with him his five sons, Joannan, Simon, Judas, Eleazar and Jonathan. Even that retired country village was not secure from the invasion of the new paganism. To his horror, the old priest saw one of his summer neighbors rendering the detested worship, a priest of God leading him in the new idolatry. Full of wrath, the old man killed both the idolator and the priest, and he and his sons fled to the mountains. There they rallied a band of revolutionists and began a series of night raids on their enemies. They gathered strength till they were able to meet the armies of Antiochus in open battle, at first with no hope of winning but with a determination to die fighting for God and their country.

Never was a truly noble cause more valiantly defended. In 166 B.C., Mattathias died, but not until he had seen the struggle on the high road to success. He counseled his sons to make Simon their political leader and Judas their captain, and they did so.

What followed is brilliant indeed. In 164 B.C. Judas defeated the imperial armies and captured Jerusalem. The Temple was cleansed and rededicated, and the worship of God was re-established. Judas was killed in battle in 161 B.C. The five brothers carried on in succession, each one grasping the sword as it fell from the hand of his predecessor, the hilt yet warm and the blade still red. For more than thirty years they fought their fight well and succeeded in giving fresh life to the nation, establishing again a Jewish dynasty in Jerusalem and making it possible for Jesus to come to a people who still worshiped the God of Abraham.

9. *JOHN THE BAPTIST*

If one were to seek out the most unselfish hero of history, it would be difficult to find anyone more worthy than John the Baptist. He inaugurated a great movement which he might easily have utilized for his own purposes. Just how influential he was we can see from the account of Paul's visit to Ephesus a quarter of a century after the crucifixion of Jesus; he found there a little group of men who were still disciples of John and knew hardly anything about Jesus. We find the same situation existing in faraway Alexandria; and we know the potency of John's name from the fact that Jesus used it in the last week of His earthly life for His own protection. The priests, His hecklers and baiters, were silent when He spoke it, fearing the people, "for all held John as a prophet."

Go back to the very beginnings of the Gospel: how did it start? By the preaching of John.

The beginning of the gospel of Jesus Christ, the Son of God;
As it is written in the prophets, Behold, I send my messenger before thy face, which shall prepare thy way before thee.
The voice of one crying in the wilderness, Prepare ye the way of the Lord, make his paths straight. (Mark 1:1-3)

John made his camp by the banks of Jordan, clothing himself in skins and eating locusts and wild honey; there he began to announce the coming of the kingdom of Heaven and to call on men to depart from sin. How did he know that the kingdom of Heaven was at hand? Who told him to proclaim the dawn of a new day? In what hour of the day or night does the Voice come to such a man, shutting him out from the company of his fellows, setting him apart for a lonely but majestic task? We shall never know the fullness of this mystery, but we are assured that in every age God has "left not himself without witness." To some souls in each generation He has spoken, and He still speaks.

John's success was almost instantaneous. Crowds went out from the city to attend his meetings; he became a sort of fashion, attracting not only the leaders of the smart set but a number of thoughtful and important people so that even the Pharisees began to give him respectful attention. One day an impressive committee went down the long winding road from Jerusalem to the Jordan. After putting up at the most reputable tavern in the vicinity and removing the traces of their travel, they waited on John in solemn array and asked him to declare whether he was the Christ, and, if not, what honorable title they might confer upon him.

> And he confessed, and denied not; but confessed, I am not the Christ.
> And they asked him, What then? Art thou Elias? And he saith, I am not. Art thou that prophet? And he answered, No. (John 1:20-21)

He had his chance to claim the great place for himself and refused it. He was only a "voice crying in the wilderness," he said, the forerunner of a Greater One to follow. He saw his own disciples leave him to follow Jesus, and, unselfish as he was, we may be sure that it was not easy. The time came all too quickly when even his most loyal supporters recognized that his sun was being eclipsed. They resented it.

And they came unto John, and said unto him, Rabbi, he that was with thee beyond Jordan, to whom thou barest witness, behold, the same baptizeth, and all men come to him.

John answered and said . . .

Ye yourselves bear me witness, that I said, I am not the Christ, but that I am sent before him. (John 3:26-28)

He must increase, but I must decrease. (John 3:30)

Even he did not realize perhaps how fast his following would diminish nor how soon the authorities would think it safe to seize him without precipitating a popular uprising. Suddenly he found himself in the darkness of Herod's prison with no audience to listen to his eloquence, no contact with the outside world except through a handful of still-faithful disciples. These brought him disquieting news. Jesus, whom he had hailed as the Messiah, to whose upbuilding he had sacrificed every personal opportunity and interest—this Jesus was not acting the role of a prophet. He did not fast; He did not withdraw into the wilderness; He did not denounce men for carnal sins. On the contrary, He was feasting in the homes of publicans and proceeding happily from village to village, surrounded by laughing children and a nondescript mob of undesirables. What was He doing to bring in the kingdom? How could He carry on so cheerfully when His cousin and faithful forerunner was in the shadow of death? Was He after all the true Messiah, or had John been mistaken and made his sacrifices in vain?

Tortured by such doubts, he sent two of his disciples to demand an explanation. They clambered down the rocks below the prison of Machaerus by the Dead Sea and up the slope on the other side of the Jordan, to find Jesus surrounded by enthusiastic crowds. They immediately sought a private audience with Him and insisted on the truth.

Art thou he that should come, or do we look for another? (Matt. 11:3)

What could He answer? How could He explain to these sorrowing, reproachful messengers that their master's method was not and could not be His method? How could He make them understand that He was in truth fulfilling John's prophecy, though He remained in the happy presence of the crowd and refused to fast or denounce? He did the only thing possible; He pointed to the results, hoping that they would carry convincing testimony.

Go and shew John again those things which ye do hear and see:
The blind receive their sight, and the lame walk, the lepers are cleansed, and the deaf hear, the dead are raised up, and the poor have the gospel preached to them. (Matt. 11:4-5)

Did the answer satisfy John? Did he die with the inspiring assurance that his short life was in the noblest sense triumphant, that he had delivered his message and that it was true? Or were the agonies of doubt and discouragement his final portion?

We can never know. The end came very quickly. He lost his head because a dancing girl pleased a cowardly petty tyrant, and Jesus did not interfere to save him.

When Jesus heard of it, he departed thence by ship into a desert place apart . . . (Matt. 14:13)

He summoned no battalion of angels to save His friend even as, a few months later, He summoned none to save Himself. But we know what He thought of that friend:

Verily I say unto you, Among them that are born of women there hath not risen a greater than John the Baptist . . . (Matt. 11:11)

10. *SAINT PAUL*

In the lists of names in this series, the greatest number of votes went to Saint Paul. Practically every list included him. In our discussion of the book of Acts we learned the details of Paul's contribution to Christianity. Even if we repeat a few facts we should look again at the great apostle, consider again the magnitude of his service.

He was born in Tarsus, a university town in Asia Minor near the northeast corner of the Mediterranean. He knew something of classic literature and philosophy, but whether or not he attended the local college we do not know. He was sent by his parents—Jews of the strictest sect of the Pharisees, although his father was a freeborn Roman citizen—to be trained by the famous teacher of the Pharisees, Gamaliel, who was of the tribe of Benjamin, a Pharisee of the Pharisees.

We first meet him at the stoning of Stephen when he is "a young man named Saul." We last see him in prison, "Paul the aged," waiting for the sword of Nero. Unconquered by his imprisonment and peril, he towered triumphant over circumstance in the assurance that he had fought a good fight and kept the faith and finished his course.

His conversion must have followed within a few months after the stoning of Stephen. That ardent young friend of the Gentile element in the infant church left a greater successor than he could possibly have suspected in one of the men who voted for his execution. So complete is the autobiographical data in Paul's letters and so large the imprint which he left on the book of Acts that we can trace almost every step of his apostolic career. There is nowhere a more glorious record.

He was "not disobedient to the heavenly vision," says the story of his conversion. Starting to preach in a preliminary way at Damascus, he seems to have felt almost immediately the need for a quiet time when he could think things through and evolve his own message. As we know, he retired into Arabia, and we lose sight of him for three years.

> Neither went I up to Jerusalem to them which were apostles before me; but I went into Arabia, and returned again unto Damascus.
> Then after three years I went up to Jerusalem to see Peter, and abode with him fifteen days. (Gal. 1:17-18)

Almost by inadvertence he reveals the ambition which he cherished on that first visit to the capital city—that of having an honorable place in Jerusalem near the head of the apostolic group—and of his sorrowful discovery that he was *persona non grata* to the disciples and must seek a field of work afar. It must have been a heartbreaking disillusionment for him, but it was one of the greatest blessings that ever happened to the world. For if Christianity had stayed only in Jerusalem it would hardly have survived beyond the lives of the men who saw it start.

Paul made three notable missionary journeys beyond the borders of Palestine. The first one, with Barnabas, to Cyprus and into nearer Asia Minor was in or about the years 47-48. The second, which lasted three years, 49 to 52, carried him around the end of the Mediterranean to Asia Minor, from Troas to Europe, and includes also a year and a half in Corinth. The third journey began in the autumn of 52 and extended to 56 and included a long stay at Ephesus. He was arrested in Jerusalem in April, exactly nineteen hundred years ago, at the time of the Passover, that being his fifth visit to the city since his conversion a quarter of a century before. For two years he was in prison in Cæsarea; it took him nearly half a year to get to Rome—for he was shipwrecked on the island of Malta and stayed three months there—and he spent two years in prison in relative comfort at Rome. Afterward there was apparently a release followed by another and fatal imprisonment, of the loneliness of which we have a record:

> For I am now ready to be offered, and the time of my departure is at hand. (2 Tim. 4:6)

We know not only where he went and what he said; we have read earlier what he suffered, how he was beaten, stoned, shipwrecked and forced on dangerous and painful journeys.

What sort of man was he, who endured so much and triumphed so abundantly? He was nervous, aggressive, self-assertive, proud—a little man apparently, with weak eyes or some other physical infirmity.

> Ye know how through infirmity of the flesh I preached the gospel unto you at the first.
> And my temptation which was in my flesh ye despised not, nor rejected, but received me as an angel of God, even as Christ Jesus.
> . . . if it had been possible ye would have plucked out your own eyes, and have given them to me. (Gal. 4:13-15)

Less eloquent than Apollos, he admits frankly that his bodily presence was unimpressive and testifies to some "thorn in the flesh" that was a constant source of suffering and humiliation. He seems to have had little consciousness of natural beauty, for though he traveled through some of the finest scenery in the world, there is no reference to it in his letters and no figure of speech drawn from nature. He delighted in words of power, which recur in his letters again and again. Like Oliver Wendell Holmes, also a small man, he admired athletics, and his writings abound with references to games and contests, to fighting the good fight and to winning the prize. Unlike the John of Revelation, he was no hater of Rome; on the contrary, he glorified in his Roman citizenship and made use of it on more than one occasion to save himself from the unjust measures of local officers.

What would the message of Jesus have become without Paul's missionary journeys and organizing ability? We can only guess the answer, but this much we know—that after about 150 A.D. Christianity nearly ceased to convert Jews and has made no notable progress in that direction since. The church in Jerusalem began to dwindle and finally faded out. But the churches which Paul planted, and the enormous momentum which his tireless energy provoked, were carried forward until even the Imperial City itself was compelled to bow its proud head. Those who affirm that Paul created Christianity do him poor service, for we know how indignantly he would have denied it.

> . . . was Paul crucified for you? or were ye baptized in the name of Paul?
> I thank God that I baptized none of you, but Crispus and Gaius;
> Lest any should say that I had baptized in mine own name. (1 Cor. 1:13-15)

He did not create Christianity, but he was the one whose vision extended it far beyond the borders of its original home, and he interpreted it in world-wide terms. He would not be satisfied until he had seen Rome; after that he planned the journey which he was forever talking about, "my journey into Spain," but never made. Nero blotted out the life that had achieved so mightily and that still had in its unwearied spirit the desire for much more achievement. But the soul of the man went marching on. It carried into Spain and beyond; it leaped the Atlantic and encircled the globe.

chapter 6

Ten Famous Women

THE SAME letter which invited ten thousand preachers to name the ten greatest men in the Bible asked also for a list of ten famous women. Seventy-four names were listed; the following ten are selected from those with the largest number of votes. They are arranged not in the order of their popularity but in their chronological sequence.

1. Eve, "the mother of all living."
2. Ruth (who had the largest number of votes next to Mary, the mother of Jesus).
3. Hannah, the devoted mother.
4. The one woman whom the Bible calls great.
5. Esther, the beautiful queen.
6. Mary, the mother of Jesus (on all lists).
7. Mary of Magdala.
8. The Bethany sisters.
9. The woman of Samaria.
10. The widow who gave the mites.

1. EVE

Every ancient people has its own story of the creation of the first man and woman. It is only fair to Eve to remember that in almost every story the woman gets the worst of it. Her biographer was a man (Moses or another), and the story was written in the days when men made the rules and wrote the records in every department of life and literature.

Let us recall also, for the sake of those who insist on the "economic interpretation" of history, that it was not a question of low wages with Eve. And for those who think that sinful people are just as sinful as they know how to be, let it be remembered that it was not the loathsome aspects of temptation that made their appeal to her but those that were rather fine and high. It is not written that "when the woman saw the fruit, that it was unripe and hard and bitter and had a rotten spot in the side and a worm at the root, she desired it," but when

> the woman saw that the tree was good for food, and that it was pleasant to the eyes, and a tree to be desired to make one wise, she took of the fruit thereof, and did eat, and gave also unto her husband . . . (Gen. 3:6)

Bad as that incident was, there are four things to be said in palliation of Eve's offense: The fruit was good to eat—she had an eye to food values; it was pleasant to the sight—she had an aesthetic nature; it was to be desired to make one wise—she was intellectually alert; she gave to her husband—she was generous.

So much for the Eve whom everybody knows, the Eve of the Garden and the transgression. We shall not linger with her. The Eve we wish to know better is the girl with an unhappy memory and swift disillusionment, going forth with the young man she loved to make a home "east of Eden." The word "east" is interesting. The whole progress of the race has been from east to west, following the sun. In our own country, for instance, the growth of most states and cities has been westward. The pioneers settled on eastern boundaries, made their fortunes, and from there they were crowded westward by succeeding tides of immigrants. Eve's move was eastward

instead of westward, but in all other respects she was the
mother and patron saint of all those pioneer women who have
followed their husbands into the new unknown. On the
Mayflower, on horseback through Cumberland Gap to the
land beyond the Alleghenies and the Blue Ridge, in prairie
schooner to the great open spaces, they have traveled. Eve
was the first of these pioneer women, carrying in her heart
the haunting memory of the comforts that she continued to
speak of as "back home."

With her into that home "east of Eden" went the hope of
humanity. The honeymoon is over, and now living is hard
work. The toil, the danger, the quarrels, perhaps, as to
whether Adam or she was the more to blame—for who can
doubt that in some moments of fatigue and discouragement
such discussions did not intrude?—all these made up the very
human routine of her days. And the baby, Cain!

There in the backwoods is heard the lullaby of this primi-
tive Madonna, singing the song that all mothers have sung:

I have gotten a man
From the Lord. (Gen. 4:1)

She knows very well that the child is Adam's son, and she
knows Adam too well to suppose that any boy of his can be
an angel; but she also knows that this child, this miracle of
small hands that have so powerful a grip at one's hair and
heartstrings, is *more* than a son of Adam:

I have gotten a man
From the Lord.

That is the theme of all cradlesongs. Eve it was who set
the mothers of the world to singing. She did wrong, in that
apple affair. But as a result of it she and Adam were no longer pensioners; they were working to pay off the mortgage.

And weren't they happier, isn't the whole race happier, in this bustling and chaotic world than if they had stayed in Eden? I sometimes wonder how much Eve really regretted!

2. *RUTH*

Now it came to pass in the days when the judges ruled . . .

Reading those first words of the Book of Ruth you are tempted to skip to some other part of the Bible that gives promise of more pleasant reading. For the "days when the judges ruled" were terrible days, days of anarchy and bloodshed, of regression and reaction after a cruel war, of disorganization and unrestrained living. We ourselves have lived through such periods in two World Wars and their aftermaths. If the historian of the future were to confine his researches to the newspaper headlines of the last ten years, he would doubtless say, "These were times of cruelty, crime and moral breakdown." Yet we know that underneath the superficial currents recorded in the headlines flows the tranquil river of family life; that even in the stormiest and most depressing eras the great masses of common folk go quietly on, loving one another, sacrificing for one another, carrying forward their daily tasks in kindliness and cheer.

So it was "in the days when the judges ruled." The headlines, as set forth in the Book of Judges, tell only of battle and bloodshed, intrigue and demoralization. But Ruth gives a picture of the life of a single family and has preserved for all ages one of the most beautiful love stories in the world.

The story has only four chapters; you can read it in fifteen minutes. It starts with a good citizen named Elimelech, a resourceful man and a loving husband and father. Because a famine had visited his own country he migrated with his wife, Naomi—who, like Eve, was a pioneer wife—and his two boys,

Mählon and Chilion. The new land offered food enough, but its climate was somehow unkind to the visitors, for the father died and afterward the sons, leaving Naomi and two beautiful young daughters-in-law, Orpah and Ruth. Naomi's only hope was to return to her own country, but she urged the girls to stay behind among their friends and relatives, who would look after them and doubtless provide other husbands. Orpah consented. Ruth replied in those magnificent words that have been the inspiration of much poetry and music:

> Intreat me not to leave thee, or to return from following after thee: for whither thou goest, I will go; and where thou lodgest, I will lodge: thy people shall be my people, and thy God my God:
> Where thou diest, will I die, and there will I be buried: the Lord do so to me, and more also, if ought but death part thee and me. (Ruth 1:16-17)

So Naomi went back to Bethlehem, her old home town, and the news soon spread about that she had brought a lovely young widow with her. They were very poor. Ruth spent her days following the reapers in the fields, for it was the law of Moses that he who owned the field should never gather quite all the crop but must leave a little in the corners that the needy might come and glean. As Ruth gleaned, Boaz, the most desirable bachelor in Bethlehem, saw her, and the romance began, as Naomi, the shrewd old matchmaker, had hoped it would.

"In the days when the judges ruled" the statesmen and the generals had their troubles, but life was not so bad a thing for simple common folk.

Have you by any chance read the genealogy of Jesus as it is given in the first chapter of Matthew? The long list of unfamiliar names makes a dull-looking page, but if you look through it someday you will note an interesting fact. Mostly the names are those of men, *but there are four women.* Who are these four whose names will live forever as having passed down through their veins the blood of our Lord? A curious group.

First of all, Tamar, whose tragic story is in the thirty-eighth chapter of Genesis. Denied her lawful privilege of motherhood by the death of her husband and the failure of her husband's brother-in-law to do his duty, and by the lack of oversight and authority on the part of Judah, her father-in-law, she tricked Judah into becoming the father of her child. It was a bold and extraordinary course of action, but she took it unashamed and thus made sure that the tribe of Judah should not pass away.

Rahab the harlot is second. Bathsheba is third, that brilliant woman who abandoned Uriah the Hittite to become the favorite wife of David and the mother of Solomon.

These are the first three of the quartet; each has a tarnished reputation but is strong and self-reliant with courage to play her own part.

And the fourth ancestress of Jesus? She is Ruth, the maiden of Moab, who said, "Thy people shall be my people and thy God my God."

3. *HANNAH*

There has been in this twentieth century a great deal of conversation about the "new woman" who has broken the chains of tradition and conquered kingdoms that formerly were reserved to men. In one sense this talk is all true. More women are doing more different things today than ever in the past, but when you have listed *all* these very modern activities you are surprised to discover that in every single one of them there was some woman of the Bible who distinguished herself thousands of years ago.

Does the modern woman write poetry? So did Deborah. Does she lead armies? Deborah did so. Does she preach? Huldah and Miriam were prophetesses. Is she a business manager? So were Abigail and Priscilla. Does she manage her house scientifically, or does she prefer rather to study and learn? Martha could probably have given her points on housekeeping, and Mary had a mind that was the pleasure and inspiration of her Lord. Human nature has not changed very much, and if you know all the people in the Bible you know all the *kinds* of people there are or ever will be in the world.

Princesses and penitents, maidens and matrons of every variety, but the grandest of all are the mothers. They are on almost every page, from the mother of the sons of Noah, who gave the race its new start, to the mother of the sons of Zebedee, who petitioned that her boys might sit one on the right hand and the other on the left hand of the Master. Highest in the list of the women for whom votes were cast in our selection, greatest of all Bible mothers—excepting only Mary, the mother of Jesus—is an old-fashioned Old Testament woman named Hannah, who named her first son

Samuel, saying, Because I have asked him of the Lord. (1 Sa. 1:20)

Like the hero Samson, who was born a little earlier, Samuel was dedicated for a great work. While he was yet a little lad, Hannah sent him to school to Eli, the grand old priest of Shiloh.

And she said [to Eli] ... I am the woman that stood by thee here, praying ...
For this child I prayed; and the Lord hath given me my petition ...
Therefore also I have lent him to the Lord; as long as he liveth he shall be lent to the Lord. ... (1 Sa. 1:26-28)

So Samuel grew up, as Eli's own sons did not, with a hunger for knowledge and a devotion to duty which made him the strongest constructive force in his generation. Every year Hannah went up to Shiloh to visit him, and every year she made him a "little coat." There is something in those words that reaches down and grips your heartstrings. You can picture the year-long care and yearning affection that went into that little garment. She did not buy the cloth and sew it up; she sheared, washed and dyed the wool, and carded, spun and wove it. She had to guess at the size, and you can see her going about to all the women of the neighborhood who had sons a year older than her own son had been when she last had seen him. Then she measured her own absent boy with a mother's imagination and cut the cloth to that measurement. And every year the coat was larger. Her boy, her own Samuel, was growing up, strong and tall, and would be a great man someday.

It all came true. The son of such a mother could hardly fail to be great. Samson had won sporadic victories and failed through lack of moral purpose. Samuel became priest, circuit judge, president of the school of the prophets, and guide to those who led armies, and in each of these positions he was a dominant figure. He became a state builder and a kingmaker. He stood in the gap during the transition from semianarchy to settled government. He practically wrote the constitution for the permanent rulership of Israel in the day of its kings.

Now and then as he rode on his circuit—holding court, opening religious festivals, organizing movements for sanitation and better government—he passed through the hill country of Ephraim; and surely a little woman back in the crowd saw him presiding and directing, and said, "That is my boy up there." And when it came to pass, as it did, that people said of Saul or of David, "He never could have been so great a man but for Samuel," there was a woman whose heart gave a great leap.

For Samuel himself could never have been so great a man if it had not been for Hannah.

4. THE ONE WOMAN WHOM THE BIBLE CALLS GREAT

Ask a dozen Bible students, "Who is the one woman whom the Bible calls great?" and they would likely give a wide variety of answers. Was it Pharaoh's daughter, whose wit and courage saved the life of Moses? Was it the mighty Queen of Sheba, ruler of an empire? Was it the mother of Solomon, who made him king, or the mother of John the Baptist, who consecrated him to his splendid mission? None of these; none of the women of royal birth; none whose close relation to kings or apostles made their names famous for deeds of public renown. It was quite a different sort of woman altogether. Let us look a moment at the picture of her which is given in the fourth chapter of Second Kings.

First of all, she was domestic, a homemaker, living not in the city but in one of the northern villages. Her husband was a farmer, which meant that he had his house on the edge of town, as was the custom then. A main road ran near by, and important people used it. Solomon appears to have traveled there in his time. Perhaps it was there that he saw the pretty girl whom he desired for his harem, but whose heart remained true to her shepherd love, as we have seen the story in the Song of Solomon. She perhaps deserved to be called great, but it is not for her either that the Bible reserves its finest title.

The "great woman" had executive ability. In the early days of her married life she had no children, and that fact shadowed her life. But she did not complain. The narrative distinctly implies that she accepted the situation and made the best of it, giving herself to such activities as lightened the load of her husband. She was religious and she was hospitable. To these last two characteristics she owed the friendship that brought her the happiness which she desired above all else, and won for her the place of honor in the Bible records.

> And it fell on a day, that Elisha passed to Shunem, where was a great woman; and she constrained him to eat bread. And so it was, that as oft as he passed by, he turned in thither to eat bread.
>
> And she said unto her husband, Behold now, I perceive that this is an holy man of God, which passeth by us continually.
>
> Let us make a little chamber, I pray thee, on the wall; and let us set for him there a bed, and a table, and a stool, and a candlestick: and it shall be, when he cometh to us, that he shall turn in thither. (2 Ki. 4:8-10)

As to what happened afterward, the fulfillment of her long desire for a son, the growth of the boy, his illness and his miraculous recovery at the hand of the prophet Elisha—all these are written in the next thirty verses of the chapter. They are well worth reading, but what most concerns us has already been related. She was just a small-town woman who loved her husband and wanted motherhood more than anything else in the world; she baked good bread and kept a clean guest room. The Bible does not tell us her name, but of all the women whose biographies it records it speaks of her alone as "great." It is true that some translations substitute "wealthy" for "great." It does not much matter. Whatever her material possessions, they were not so valuable as the qualities of mind and heart, faith and courage she displays. The word "great" applies still.

5. *ESTHER*

Many eminent scholars tell us that the Book of Esther and the Book of Daniel are two splendid pieces of propaganda, written to lift the spirits of the Hebrews in their days of exile and spur them on to daring deeds. This fact detracts nothing from our pleasure in the two books. Both are thrilling narratives, and no figure is more lifelike than that of Esther, the favorite of the harem, who by her courage saved her people.

The story comes late in the Old Testament chronology, dealing with the period when there were numerous Jews in Mesopotamia, descendants of those who were carried away captive by Nebuchadnezzar in 586 B.C. A hundred years had passed and, while many Jews had returned to Palestine, others were settled in different parts of the big unwieldy Persian kingdom ruled over by Ahasuerus

> which reigned, from India even unto Ethiopia, over an hundred and seven and twenty provinces . . . (Esth. 1:1)

The Jews in his reign suffered no political disabilities, and one of them, Mordecai, had done the king a great service.

He was plotted against by a politician named Haman, who through misrepresentation caused the king to promulgate a decree of massacre against the Jews. It was at this crisis that Mordecai went to Esther, demanding

> that she should go in unto the king, to make supplication unto him, and to make request before him for her people. (Esth. 4:8)

She replied that no one was permitted to approach the king without being sent for by name and that the penalty of disobedience was death. In noble words Mordecai argued the case, and at length Esther was persuaded.

Go, gather together all the Jews that are present in Shushan [she replied], and fast ye for me, and neither eat nor drink three days, night or day: I also and my maidens will fast likewise; and so will I go in unto the king, which is not according to the law: and if I perish, I perish. (Esth. 4:16)

The third day came. Modestly but with firm step and head erect, she moved into the inner court where sat Ahasuerus on his mighty throne. There was an awful moment of suspense while the courtiers watched to see what would happen to this girl who had dared to break the law. But her beauty was irresistible. The king held out his scepter, the sign of royal recognition. Esther knelt and touched it, made her plea and won.

A new decree was promulgated; the Jews were restored to favor and began promptly to take advantage of their opportunities. In poetic justice Haman was hanged on the high gallows which he had built for Mordecai. As for Esther, her name became imperishably glorious, the Joan of Arc of the Old Testament, the woman who dared and triumphed when the men of the nation were at their wits' ends.

The finest passage in the whole book is Mordecai's ringing answer to Esther when she hesitated to approach the king, arguing that her feeble strength and abilities could not possibly prevail in such an emergency:

Then Mordecai commanded to answer Esther, Think not with thyself that thou shalt escape in the king's house, more than all the Jews.

For if thou altogether holdest thy peace at this time, then shall there enlargement and deliverance arise to the Jews from another place; but thou and thy father's house shall be destroyed: *and who knoweth whether thou art come to the kingdom for such a time as this?* (Esth. 4:13-14)

Those words have rung down the corridors of time as an undying challenge to the courage and faith of youth. "Let no faintheartedness turn you aside from the duty to which you are clearly called, no matter how hard that duty may be or how much apparently beyond your powers. If you fail, someone else will do the job and win the glory. 'Enlargement and deliverance will arise . . . from another place.' But you will have been untrue to your calling, for how do you know but what you were sent into the world for this special duty at this special time?"

. . . and who knoweth whether thou art come to the kingdom for such a time as this?

6. *MARY, THE MOTHER OF JESUS*

We who call ourselves Protestants have been almost rude in our attitude toward the mother of Jesus. What beauty of face and figure there must have been in her whose own blood nourished and whose own body bore Jesus of Nazareth! What elevation in the mind that could conceive and chant the Magnificat!

My soul doth magnify the Lord,
  And my spirit hath rejoiced in God my Saviour.
  For he hath regarded the low estate of his handmaiden: for, behold, from henceforth all generations shall call me blessed.
  For he that is mighty hath done to me great things; and holy is his name.
  And his mercy is on them that fear him from generation to generation. (Luke 1:46-50)

Finish the reading of that great hymn of praise as Luke records it in his first chapter. Look in your reference Bible at the little index letters sprinkled through the text and the

corresponding letters in the margin. Note that the beginning
of the Magnificat is reminiscent of Hannah's rejoicing over
the prospect of the birth of Samuel, and that almost every
phrase suggests a possible source in historic records. This
young woman, sixteen or seventeen perhaps, had read the
literature of her nation and had made it her own. Her mind
and spirit were richly stored. Reverence, gratitude, high
spirituality and great sympathy with the common lot of
humanity are in the Magnificat.

Motherhood is the most expensive of all earth's luxuries,
and being the mother of the Messiah was a costly privilege.
Think what it meant to Mary to have to go into Egypt and remain there while Joseph, resourceful and strong though he
was, struggled to support the family. How her heart must
have yearned for her home and girlhood friends! Think of the
bewildering problems and perplexities of having a Son grow
up with ambitions and a range of interest and knowledge
which she and Joseph could only dimly apprehend. She knew
in the utmost degree the wonder and the worry, the high
hope and the deep concern of all the mothers of geniuses.

And they [Mary and Joseph] understood not the saying which he [Jesus] spake unto them.
. . . but his mother kept all these sayings in her heart.
(Luke 2:50-51)

Doubtless the family had to practice self-denial so that
Jesus might have time to study. Doubtless she was often
disturbed by His dreamy absorption in ideas and His apparent lack of interest in what they should eat, what they should
drink and wherewithal they should be clothed, though after
Joseph's death He took up the burden of family support and
carried it nobly until the younger children were old enough
to stand alone. It was not merely as "the carpenter" that He
was known.

There were times when she was troubled about Him; times when she wondered whether He could be quite right in His mind; times, like that awful day of His visit to Nazareth, when her spirit must have been rent asunder by fear of the forces arrayed against Him and a tragic premonition of what these would finally accomplish against her beloved Son. Yet troubled, and even doubting, she did not surrender. Of those who stood firm at the end, a large proportion were women, and she leads them all. Hanging in agony upon the Cross, Jesus gave His last thought to her future safety and comfort.

> Now there stood by the cross of Jesus his mother . . .
> When Jesus therefore saw his mother, and the disciple standing by, whom he loved, he saith unto his mother, Woman, behold thy son!
> Then saith he to the disciple, Behold thy mother! And from that hour that disciple [John] took her unto his own home. (John 19:25-27)

We are not given the record of her later years, but they must have been beautiful in faith and self-sacrifice, for the devotion of those members of the early church grew constantly more tender and their reverence more exalted. Only a beautiful spirit could have inspired such adoration. She is nobler, beyond comparison, than any of the other women of the Bible, and the women on the whole stand higher in the splendor of their faith than the men. Not one unworthy woman appears in the tragedy of the crucifixion.

7. MARY OF MAGDALA

The name Mary was immensely popular in the time of Jesus because of the love of the Jewish people for Mariamne, the Jewish wife of Herod, who was murdered by him. Hence there are so many women in the New Testament named Mary that we sometimes find it difficult to keep track of them. Foremost, of course, is Mary the mother of Jesus. Next in order of her importance is Mary of Magdala. Of her early history we know nothing except that she suffered with some nervous or mental complaint.

> And it came to pass afterward, that he went throughout every city and village, preaching and shewing the glad tidings of the kingdom of God, and the twelve were with him.
> And certain women, which had been healed of evil spirits and infirmities, Mary called Magdalene, out of whom went seven devils, (Luke 8:1-2)

Just what the "seven devils" were we are not told. The phrase has been assumed to mean that Mary was immoral, and for this reason prostitutes are often called Magdalenes. We have no proof either for or against this assumption, just as there is no evidence that Mary was "the woman in the city, which was a sinner," who washed the feet of Jesus with precious ointment at the feast in the Pharisee's house. If Mary *was* this humble and tearful woman, then noble indeed was her repentance. But inasmuch as definite evidence against her is altogether lacking, the world has been less than generous in so easily passing judgment; certainly her subsequent career proved her to be one of the grandest characters in Bible history.

Magdala is a town of Galilee, situated not far from Capernaum and Bethsaida on the Galilean lake. There Mary spent her girlhood; there she suffered the mental calamity which befell her, and if with the clouded mind came also the clouded reputation, we need not wonder at that. Her faith in Jesus restored her reason, and her sins, whatever they were, were forgiven.

We know the names of a few of the women who followed

Jesus on that last journey from Galilee to Jerusalem and "ministered to him of their substance." Three of them were named Mary. Some apprehension or expectation of crisis, some woman's instinct caused them to leave their homes and be His companions in this last stage of His public work. They were in the pitiful little procession that followed along the Sorrowful Way, and they were present also at the crucifixion. Possibly if we knew all the truth we should find there were five instead of three, the other two being Mary of Bethany and Mary the mother of Mark, in whose home the Last Supper was held. We are confident it was this Mary who was hostess of our Lord and His disciples at the Last Supper— and whose large upper room became the habitual meeting place of the disciples—because, when Peter was released from prison and at once sought his fellow disciples, he went to the place where they were accustomed to gather and it was the house of Mary, the mother of Mark. Her name appears but seldom, but her hospitality gave the infant church a home. She and quite possibly Mary of Bethany were there in the sorrowful procession of the Cross. But we are not sure of the five. We know that there were three there, and Mary of Magdala was one of them.

"Crucified, dead and buried!" Terrible words. The apostolic group was stunned and paralyzed. How the eleven disciples spent the hours from nightfall of Friday till dawn of Sunday we do not know. But on Easter morning, "while it was yet dark," these women who had seen Jesus crucified came with spices to anoint His body. They did not know that Joseph of Arimathaea and Nicodemus had already performed that melancholy service and that Jesus had been buried with a hundred-weight of spices, a prince's burial. They reached the tomb, wondering who would roll away the stone for them, and behold, it was already rolled away. And the angel said, "He is not here; He is risen." The others hurried back to tell the disciples, but Mary "stood without, weeping." She it was who first saw the Lord.

No wonder Renan, skeptic though he was, marveled at the faith which caused her to see that vision of a living Christ and to proclaim it. He had a skeptic's easy explanation, but he said that no sane person ever saw anything that gave to the world such comfort as the vision of love that the Magdalene beheld. Peter and John ran to the sepulchre and found the empty tomb; the whole city knew of it before night and wondered what had become of the body. But Mary's eyes first beheld Him, and her glad voice first told the incredulous disciples. In the power of her faith and the blessing of her good tidings only Mary the mother of Jesus deserves to stand before this other beautiful and devoted follower of Jesus, Mary of Magdala.

8. *THE BETHANY SISTERS*

They lived a little way out of Jerusalem in a sheltered suburban home which Jesus loved to visit for refreshment and rest. One of them, Martha, was the practical housekeeper; the other, Mary, had the soul of a dreamer and the eyes of faith. Down through the ages the sons and daughters of these two have come; the sons of Martha, careful for many things and good things at that; the sons of Mary, listening to the Word and treasuring it in their hearts.

Martha was not lacking in faith. Hers was one of the most beautiful of all confessions. Jesus asked her if she believed in a doctrine, and she said, "Yes, Lord; that is to say, I believe in you." As for the theology of it, she was bewildered. Her brother was dead; she did not see any way out of that sorrow, but she believed in Jesus, and He accepted that faith at its full value. Millions of people who are perplexed by the creeds ought to read the story of Martha and be comforted. She fretted once when she ought not to have done so, but when the test came she had a vital faith, even though she did not understand the creeds.

But Mary's was the inventive love that knew how to do the unusual thing and do it beautifully.

> Then Jesus six days before the passover came to Bethany, where Lazarus was which had been dead, whom he raised from the dead.
>
> There they made him a supper; and Martha served: but Lazarus was one of them that sat at the table with him.
>
> Then took Mary a pound of ointment of spikenard, very costly, and anointed the feet of Jesus, and wiped his feet with her hair: and the house was filled with the odour of the ointment.
>
> Then saith one of his disciples, Judas Iscariot, Simon's son, which should betray him,
>
> Why was not this ointment sold for three hundred pence, and given to the poor?
>
> This he said, not that he cared for the poor; but because he was a thief, and had the bag, and bare what was put therein.
>
> Then said Jesus, Let her alone: against the day of my burying hath she kept this.
>
> For the poor always ye have with you; but me ye have not always. (John 12:1-8)

Her love was prophetic. She had no inside knowledge of the plots to kill Jesus. She simply had apprehension of coming evil, and she knew that the time to do the beautiful thing is now, "against my burial." When Jesus was dead, no one of the disciples would have grudged the alabaster box, but He needed that fragrance while He lived.

Much of our extravagance at funerals is horrible, not because of the waste, for love demands an expression beyond the calculation of cold economy, but because it mocks the penuriousness of the years that have gone before. Mary knew that the time to be extravagant is when love can express itself in an appeal to life and not in a costly and useless libation after death. So she made her gift of three hundred pence, a year's wages for a workingman of those days, and Jesus said:

Verily I say unto you, Wheresoever this gospel shall be preached in the whole world, there shall also this, that this woman hath done, be told for a memorial of her. (Matt. 26:13)

He never said that of the deed of any man.

9. THE WOMAN OF SAMARIA

The whole community first to hear attentively the message of Jesus was neither Nazareth nor Jerusalem. The place of His youth cast Him out, and the city that should have enthroned Him sent Him to the Cross. The first city where Jesus was received and acknowledged was Sychar, a village in Samaria, close by Jacob's well.

It is historic ground. The two mountains of Ebal and Gerezim stand over against each other with a narrow valley between, and caravans and foot travelers go that way. In ancient times the patriarch, Jacob, dug a well there, and he and his family and flocks found refreshment. That well is still in existence. Upon its curb one day sat Jesus. It is the one spot on earth where we can locate to a square yard just where He sat or stood. He sat there, tired and thirsty.

A Samaritan woman came to draw water, and He asked her for a drink. It would seem a common enough courtesy, but it surprised her. It was true then that the "Jews have no dealings with the Samaritans."

Nothing in the life of Jesus is more impressive than His

enormous care for and sublime faith in the individual. Most reformers, impressed with the great responsibilities of their mission and the shortness of human life, have been busy, preoccupied, hard to get at. They have been "in conference," they have worked on schedule; you might see them perhaps for ten minutes a week from Wednesday, but you must see their secretaries first and make an appointment. We cannot be too often reminded that Jesus had only three short years in which to deliver His message and train a group of followers who would carry it on. From the hour when John the Baptist gave up his life in Herod's prison the shadow of the Cross fell dark across His path; He knew that the end was inevitable and could not possibly be far off. Yet He allowed Himself to be constantly interrupted, much to the impatience of the disciples and of Judas in particular. Little children flocked about Him, and the disciples tried to hold them off. He rebuked their efficient efforts to protect His time and conserve His strength.

> Suffer little children to come unto me, and forbid them not: for of such is the kingdom of God. (Luke 18:16)

He had time to attend feasts and social parties. On His last journey to Jerusalem—carrying as He did the burden and anxiety of the whole human race—He was not too busy to turn aside at the cry of a single blind beggar. And He did not hesitate, at that well in Samaria, to impart the most sublime truth of His whole ministry to an audience of one, a Samaritan woman. In an earlier chapter we have seen the care and understanding with which Jesus approached her, how He came at length to this:

> But the hour cometh, and now is, when the true worshippers shall worship the Father in spirit and in truth: for the Father seeketh such to worship him.

God is a spirit: and they that worship him must worship him in spirit and in truth. (John 4:23-24)

The Samaritan woman believed the message, the truth which He had never before spoken to anyone and was not to tell to His own disciples until some weeks afterward. He was the Christ, the Christ of the Samaritans as well as of the Jews, of all peoples everywhere, regardless of boundary, regardless of racial or religious traditions, transcending all barriers and all ritual and forms.

And upon this came his disciples, and marvelled that he talked with the woman: yet no man said, What seekest thou? or, Why talkest thou with her?
The woman then left her waterpot, and went her way into the city, and saith to the men,
Come, see a man, which told me all things that ever I did: is not this the Christ?
Then they went out of the city, and came unto him. (John 4:27-30)

Her neighbors, too, believed, first because of her testimony and then because their own hearts told them that He spoke the truth. Thus was the first community on earth evangelized with the Christian message. Who carried the message? A woman who had not been by any means what society terms a "good woman," but who was kind enough to befriend a stranger by giving Him a cup of water and who received from Him in turn, and passed on to others, a drink of the water of life.

10. *THE WIDOW WHO GAVE THE MITES*

Reckoning up the great givers of the world, the Carnegies with their libraries, the Rockefellers with their universities, the Smithsons and the Fords with their gifts of learning and research, the builders of hospitals, and the doers of great deeds of mercy, whose name stands as the one whose gift has produced more hard cash than any other? Without question it is the widow who gave the mites. As is usual where women play a part in the narrative, it is Luke who tells this story.

The scene took place on Tuesday in Holy Week, and rather late in the afternoon. It had been a day of controversy, and Jesus, wearied and rejected, was leaving the Temple. He and His disciples had been within the third court. The first was the court of the Gentiles, where any well-behaved person might go unhindered. The next was the court of the women, so called not because it was exclusively for women but because it was as far as women were permitted to go. The next was the inner court, the Court of Israel, as far as a layman could approach. Beyond that was the Holy Place, where only the priests had admission, and still beyond, the Holy of Holies, where the High Priest went once a year. Jesus and His disciples were all laymen; there was not a priest among them. They could go only as far as the inner court but not into the Holy Place, much less into the Holy of Holies. As they withdrew they passed through the court of the women. There were thirteen chests around the walls, with gold-plated trumpets into which contributions were dropped. The feasts brought many pious Jews from a distance, and this was the place where they made their offerings.

... many that were rich cast in much. (Mark 12:41)

There came a poor widow, slipping silently to a trumpet-throated receptacle near a corner, and cast in two copper coins so small in value that we have to reckon in mills to get an approach to an equivalent.

Obligation is commensurate with ability. From the throne of God down to mortal levels there is one rule—every moral being is under bond to do his best. God being perfect in goodness is no better than a good God ought to be. "Be ye therefore perfect, even as your Father in heaven is perfect" means no more nor no less than this, that God does His best and we ought to do ours. Christ's gift of Himself on the Cross was not more than Christ ought to have done. Luke asks "Ought not Christ to have suffered?" Certainly—if by so doing He could save the world. Even Christ did no more than the Son of God ought to have done. In some way we must do our best or we fall below God's measure and the measure of our own conscience. The poor widow gave her all.

And she has inspired millions and millions of people who, except for her, would have thought their gift too small or would have measured it by too unworthy a unit of devotion. If we were to reckon up the sums that have been given for charitable causes by reason of her gift, we should know that she was first among all philanthropists. We do not need to reduce the words of Jesus to cold arithmetical prose, but if we insist on that still it is true:

... this poor widow hath cast more in, than all they ...
(Mark 12:43)

chapter 7

How Did We Get the Bible?

WHILE THESE chapters were in preparation a surgeon of national reputation sent this request:

"Before you finish your story of *The Book*, please be sure to give us the answer to these questions:

"*How were the books of the Bible gathered into a collection and distinguished as a group by themselves? Who selected them and how do we know that the right ones were selected?*

"*By what means were these chosen books preserved and handed down? Who decided that they ought to be translated into modern languages and who did the translating?*"

Let us deal first with the Old Testament. It would be very pleasant if we could say that some one group of men, meeting in Jerusalem about 400 B.C., selected the books which we now have, and certified for all time that these and no others should be the Old Testament. But such is not the case. These books have exciting individual histories, but no story of how a single book was written is more fascinating than the story of how they came to form a great library in one volume.

The ancient Hebrews held many other books in high regard. Nearly thirty of them are referred to in the Old Testament. Twenty-four of these have been lost, though research may still turn them up. The story about the sun standing still for Joshua is quoted from an old book of war songs known as the Book of Jasher or the Book of the Just. David's "Song of the Bow" is also from the Book of Jasher, but except as it survives in these fragments the book has perished. So also has another old songbook, the Book of the Wars of the Lord, of which we have a fragment in Numbers 21:14. The books of Kings are largely compiled from more extended records, which sometimes are referred to by name:

> Now the rest of the acts of Jeroboam, and all that he did, and his might, how he warred, and how he recovered Damascus, and Hamath, which belonged to Judah, for Israel, are they not written in the book of the chronicles of the kings of Israel? (2 Ki. 14:28)

This does not refer to either of the books of Chronicles that we have, which are the final books of the Old Testament and were written long after the books of Kings; the citation is to a book which has been lost for centuries.

We see, then, that the Old Testament is the surviving portion of a much larger number of books. It does not comprise sacred as opposed to secular books, but is the whole body of ancient Hebrew literature now extant. Philo, an Alexandrian Jew who lived in the second century before the Christian era, gives a list of books of which all are known to us. In addition, we have seventeen not on Philo's list. Jesus, son of Sirach, who wrote in the second century B.C., closely parallels our list but does not stop with it. He recognizes the work of a contemporary, Simon, as worthy to be included and, what is rather remarkable, he thinks his own book good enough to be a part of the Bible. In the latter case his judgment is probably right. His book, Ecclesiasticus, is a noble and worthy religious poem, and we are poorer for having dropped it from our Bible with the rest of the Apocrypha. Josephus, the great Hebrew historian, does not name the books of the Old Testament, but he limits the period of their production to the end of the Persian rule and gives the number as twenty-two, the number of letters in the Hebrew alphabet. This was counting the five books of Moses as one, the twelve minor prophets as one, and making certain other combinations.

No two of these authorities precisely agreed, but two processes tended to fix the selection. First was the fact that Hebrew became a dead language four centuries before Christ, and was succeeded by Aramaic, another Semitic language. Jesus, we know, spoke Aramaic. The name for God which He taught, *Abba*—father—was Aramaic. His words on the cross, *Eli, Eli, lama sabachthani*, were Aramaic. He did not speak Hebrew, though He probably could read it. It was the language of the synagogue scrolls, and Luke tells us He could read those. But what He read was His nation's classic tongue and not His native speech. Parts of Daniel, a very late book, and one or two bits in the minor prophets are in Aramaic, but in general the Old Testament books that survived were in the old classic Hebrew. Those that bore a later stamp were received with suspicion, if at all.

The other factor which tended to fix a canon, or acknowledged body of books, was the translation of the Old Testament into Greek. According to tradition, a group of seventy Hebrew scholars was brought from Jerusalem by Ptolemy, King of Egypt. Their translation, called the Septuagint in honor of the seventy, was begun about two hundred and fifty years before Christ. The Old Testament of Paul and the early Christian Church was usually the Septuagint Greek Bible. It doubtless contained the body of sacred books which are known to us as the Apocrypha. These books are not now part of most versions of the Bible. Other books also once held sacred have not come down to us. The Apocalypse of Enoch is an example. Jude quotes it in the first chapter of his little epistle, the fourteenth verse.

Thus, while certain books from the ancient Hebrew had come to be accepted before the time of Jesus as entitled to special reverence, the fringes and margins of that collection were still open to dispute and were, in fact, disputed vigorously for two hundred years. For instance, a very early bishop of Sardis who made a journey to Palestine for the express purpose of learning, if he could, precisely what books the Jews accepted as canonical, omitted Esther, Ezra and Lamentations from his list. And the question of whether the two books, Ecclesiastes and the Song of Solomon, should be accounted sacred was not settled until the Council of Jamnia, about 90 A.D.

We may sum it all up by saying that the ancient books which were most used and gave most inspiration survived and, by being translated, secured a place for themselves in the canon. These include an out-and-out love song which has no religious motive; a book which does not mention the name of God, and another, Ecclesiastes, in which the pessimism of the unknown author contrasts with the sentiments of editors who added bits later. But the selection, made by the process of survival and on the basis of those books which were best beloved, is probably much finer than it would have been if a group of men, however devoted, had set themselves at any one time to assume the whole responsibility.

So much for the Old Testament. How were the New Testament books selected? Again by the process of use.

The first books, "read in churches" with the Old Testament selections, were apostolic letters, notably those of Paul, and including generally, though not invariably, the longer epistles of John, Peter and James. When the Gospels appeared, they were immediately used in like fashion, and at once assumed a place of priority, not because anyone in authority said it must be so but because they were so important and so interesting. For a good while there was no attempt to make complete collections. Few churches had all the New Testament books and many had other loved books, such as the Epistle of Clement and the Shepherd of Hermas.

When discussion began as to which books ought to be read regularly, there was immediate agreement on the most important ones, the four Gospels and the larger epistles. There was a good deal of doubt about Revelation and Second Peter and the two short epistles of the three from John. These seem to have been considered of less importance than other books. But gradually there came to be agreement, not generally by authority but by the test of usage. The youngest book in the New Testament was written about one hundred and fifty years after Jesus. Not for another two hundred and fifty years was the canon of the New Testament determined.

If anyone asks whether we know absolutely that every book in the Old and New Testaments is holy above all other books, the answer is, We do not. No one can say that Esther, which is in the Bible, is nobler than Ecclesiasticus, which has been dropped out; certainly it is not so religious or so sweet in its spirit. No one can say that the Epistle of Jude is more inspired than the Epistle of Clement. The mountain range of the Bible shades off into foothills, and we do not know just where the range begins or ends. But the range is there, towering magnificently above all other literature. Scholars may discuss its measurements and limits; the theologically minded may battle over its "inspiration." Let them argue. What the world needs is fewer folk to argue and a whole lot more to read.

We come now to the question: How were these chosen books preserved through the ages and passed down to us?

The need for Bibles grew constantly. For more than a thousand years copies were made by hand. Many were of great beauty, but no matter how scrupulous the copyists' care, errors crept in. Hence in making translations it became desirable to have as many of them for comparison as possible. The earliest manuscript copies that have survived to our time date from the fourth century after Christ, and the story of one of them, the Sinaitic, will illustrate the vicissitudes through which they have passed.

On a spring day in 1844 a German scholar, Lobegott Friedrich Konstantin von Tischendorf, arrived at St. Catherine's, a monastery of the Greek Church on the Sinaitic peninsula. His name, Lobegott, "Praise God," had been given to him by his mother who, having a presentiment that her child would be born blind, cried out with joy when she discovered that his eyes were all right. "*Lobegott!*" she exclaimed. His two eyes needed to be very keen, for his business as a scholar was to search for and examine old manuscript Bibles. On this particular trip he had been through the libraries of Alexandria and Cairo, as well as the convents of the Greek and Armenian churches, without success. His visit to St. Catherine's monastery was in the nature of a last hope, for it was known that a rich library had been preserved there through the ages, though it now was curiously unappreciated.

Lobegott was given free access to the library, but he did not at first discover anything of value. In the evening, however, a strange thing occurred. There was sent up to his room as kindling for the fire a basket containing some leaves of an old manuscript. He examined them. To his amazement he found a number of bits of the Old Testament in Greek. The monks took quick note of his cry of astonishment. Two similar lots of leaves had already been burned, but the monks, when they heard Lobegott's exclamation, immediately became as interested as he in the portions that remained. With great difficulty Lobegott secured permission to take back to Leipzig forty-seven leaves. They proved to be part of one of the oldest Greek manuscripts of the Old Testament in existence.

Immediately the eager scholar set to work through an influential friend to secure the rest of the volume, but the monks had learned its value and would not give it up. In 1853, when he was welcomed back to the convent, he could not find a trace of the lost parchment. In 1859 he returned for a third time, having now the authority of the Czar of Russia, for the convent was Greek and the Czar was the head of the Greek Church. Many valuable manuscripts were placed in his hands, some of which he had not seen on either of his previous visits; yet the chief treasure had disappeared as completely as if the earth had swallowed it up. Sorrowfully he prepared to depart. On his last evening he walked with the steward of the convent in the garden and then was invited to his room for refreshment. As they sat together at the table, the steward said casually, "I, too, have a Septuagint," and took down a parcel wrapped in red cloth.

Imagine the almost delirious joy of Lobegott when he saw not only the Old Testament pages he had glimpsed in 1844, but the New Testament complete! It was one of the most thrilling moments in the history of patient, scientific research, and a vital moment to the whole Christian world, for it gave us one of the oldest, finest and most accurate of all Biblical manuscripts. Until 1933 this so-called Sinaitic was in the library of Petrograd, the chief literary treasure of the Greek Church; then it was sold to the British museum.

There are only a few of these extremely old manuscripts, and the three most precious of them are the Sinaitic, the Vatican at Rome, and the Alexandrine, presented to Charles I of England in 1628 and placed in the British Museum upon its establishment in 1750. It is interesting that of the three finest Bible records one is in the possession of Protestants, one of

Roman Catholics and one of the Greek Church. Each sect is most generous in permitting the use of its treasure by scholars of all Christian communions, while taking the utmost care to preserve it.

There are, of course, thousands of fragments of the Bible or parts of it of more or less value. Among these are certain "palimpsests," or manuscripts, which later fell into the hands of those who wanted the parchment for other purposes and erased the Bible text and wrote other books instead. Chemical processes have been used to restore the Bible text, and in some instances valuable readings have been discovered.

This recital of the way in which manuscripts have been found brings us to the mention of a class of men of whom the average layman knows very little, and most of that little is wrong. These are the Biblical critics. "Criticizing the Bible!" What columns of rhetoric have been printed, what floods of oratory have been poured out by those who could not have told, to save their souls, what a Biblical critic is or what he does.

There are two kinds of Biblical critics: the lower or textual critics, and the higher or literary critics. The terms lower and higher do not mean that one group claims or is admitted to be more important than the other, much less that there is an assumption of arrogance on the part of those that are "higher." One kind of study simply follows and is built upon the other.

The lower critic is a man of technical skill in the deciphering of ancient texts and manuscripts. He has critical ability, that is, the ability to judge critically, for criticism is nothing more or less than the science of correct judgment. To most of us a manuscript of the fourteenth century might very well seem as ancient as one of the fourth. It could, for instance, be more soiled and show greater signs of age. But the critic does not look simply at the wear and strain. He is a judge of parchments, of methods of tanning skins, of kinds of ink, of styles of making letters. He distinguishes between "uncial" and "cursive" Greek; between "pointed" and "unpointed" Hebrew.

These lower critics are not widely known; they are not highly paid. Their work is a strain on the eyes and a tax on the mind, and they rather dread publicity, for as soon as one of them publishes a discovery which gets into the newspapers, some ignoramus who is unworthy to loose the latchets of his shoes raises a hue and cry. So mainly they bleed within their armor and are silent, but all the time their patient work is giving us a better and better knowledge of the Bible's exact meaning.

The other group of searchers are the literary or historical or higher critics. Who wrote these sacred books? Ezekiel claims to have written his own, and Baruch is thought to have been Jeremiah's scribe. We may infer that most of the books of the prophets were written by the men whose names they bear. But all the rest of the Old Testament is anonymous. People have rushed in to declare that certain books were written by certain men, but most such declarations are conjecture. The only way to find out who wrote a particular book, or at what time, is by a study of the book itself. For instance, when we read the first verses of Luke and find that they were written to a man named Theophilus, and then read the opening verses of Acts and find that they also are addressed to a man of the same name and that they refer to a "former treatise," we at once ask ourselves whether the two books were not written by the same man. It is a reasonable and proper question. In one way it makes no difference who wrote Luke and Acts, and if they were written by different men the fact is not of vast importance; yet both books are of more value to us when we find that the same man did write both and that the parts of Acts which use the pronoun "we" are parts telling of events that Luke himself saw.

So it is the function of the higher critics to find out as far as they can the date and authorship and relationships of the books, each to the other. These critics pay little attention to other treatises; their study is the Bible itself, and in the main they are a most reverent body of men. Perhaps a few of them grow cocksure, like young students of medicine in a dissecting room, and some of them make wrong guesses. But the only way to correct those bad guesses is by free discussion on the part of those who have special training and by application of common sense.

The Biblical critic to whom the world perhaps owes most is Jerome, who lived in the fourth century. By that time Latin had come to be the language of the Church, and there were Latin translations of the Bible, but poor ones, made from very faulty manuscripts. Jerome was an eminent scholar; to become still more proficient he went to Palestine and lived for a long time in Bethlehem. Two good women, a mother and her daughter, went with him; the mother, being a widow and possessed of wealth, furnished money and looked after his health. In spite of illness Jerome kept on. And so did the two women. Their care probably saved Jerome and enabled him to complete his great work. He took the oldest Hebrew and Greek manuscripts he could find and made himself a master of both languages. In years and years of lonely toil he made a new translation from Hebrew into Latin of part of the Old Testament; translated the Psalms from the Greek Septuagint, and revised the Old Latin Version of the Gospels. He called the completed work *Translatio Nova*, the new translation.

Was he thanked for his work? In the contrary, he was denounced for tampering with the word of God. His name was a reproach. But Jerome did not suffer in silence. He hit back at his critics, telling them exactly what they were. He called them "fools" and "stupids" and "ignoramuses" and "biped asses." To the end of his life he was cursed and denounced and called an atheist and a heretic. Meanwhile, by its sheer excellence his work kept gaining readers in every Western European country in every generation. By the thirteenth century it was being called the Vulgate, the popular. But not until the sixteenth century did complete vindication come—when the Council of Trent accepted his translation as authoritative. Today we say "Saint Jerome," but he was not called that while he was alive.

So the Bible passed into Latin. But we are most interested in how it was translated into English. There had been partial translations from the Latin from the time of the Venerable Bede and King Alfred, but the name of the great English pioneer translator is John Wiclif, who lived from 1324 to 1384. As a translation his work was of secondary value, for he, too, used the Latin and not the original tongues, but he put the Bible into the hands of the reading public of England, which was small but potent. He contributed much toward making the Bible what it is today, the Book of the common people. In England, as in all nations, the demand for Bibles increasingly exceeded the supply of patient copyists. The need to find a better, quicker way of making Bibles undoubtedly speeded the invention of printing.

More than a hundred and fifty years after Wiclif came William Tyndale, who undertook a translation of the New Testament from the original Greek. People were horror-stricken by the impiety of the idea. He had to flee to Hamburg, and never again set foot on his native shore. Against fierce opposition he continued his work. Tyndale determined to "make every plow-boy in England know the New Testament." His Book, printed by Caxton, had to be smuggled into

England and it was read by stealth. With such asinine drivel as the following, written by the pious Friar Buckingham, its circulation was obstructed:

Where Scriptures saith, "No man that layeth his hand to the plow and looketh back is fit for the kingdom of God"; will not the plowman when he readeth these words be apt forthwith to cease from his plow, and then where will be the sowing and the harvest? Likewise also whereas the baker readeth, "A little leaven leaveneth the whole lump," will he not be forthwith too sparing in the use of leaven, to the great injury of our health? And so also when the simple man reads the words, "If thine eye offend thee, pluck it out and cast it from thee," incontinent he will pluck out his eyes, and so the whole realm will be full of blind men, to the great decay of the nation and the manifest loss of the king's grace. And thus by reading of the holy Scriptures will the whole realm come into confusion.

Tyndale himself was treacherously dealt with and arrested, and lay for eighteen months in Antwerp for no crime other than that of giving to the people a truer version of the Scriptures. On October 6, 1536, he was strangled and his body was burned. Thus have Christian folk welcomed the better and more accurate translations of the Book which teaches kindness, tolerance, forbearance and the open mind; thus do they still denounce those men of learning who would lessen their precious and sedulously guarded ignorance.

King James I of England and VI of Scotland saw that he could not prevent the reading of the Bible by the people, and he determined to get credit for what his scholars told him was much needed, a reliable translation into good English, for all the previous versions had been made under conditions that rendered exact scholarly treatment impossible. So he appointed a group of scholars—High Churchmen and Puritans and those who were of no ecclesiastical party—to make a new version. Some of them had special skill in Hebrew and Greek; some were able to bring help from their knowledge of translations in the Italian, German, French and Spanish. Fifty-four men, of whom forty-seven have been identified, contributed. After four years of work they gave to the world that classic, that "well of pure English, undefiled," the King James Version. The magnitude of the achievement is more awesome when you learn that this version is 773,693 words long!

Perhaps no version in the English language will ever equal in rhythmic beauty that of the King James Version of 1611, but it is right that other versions and even new translations should be made. Each of these makes a contribution toward our better knowledge of the original. In 1885 the Revised Version was made by a joint commission of English and American scholars. Reference will be made in the next chapter to the wide interest in and influence of this scholarly version. It was agreed that the American members of the commission should issue no version of their own for fourteen years. In 1901 appeared the American Standard Revised Bible. Other and worthy versions continue to appear, as those of Moffatt, Goodspeed and the Riverside Bible translated by Professor William G. Ballantine. Latest of all is the Revised Standard Version; the New Testament was published in 1946, the Old Testament following in 1952. Probably no one of these will entirely supersede the King James Version, but each has its value for comparison. While no important doctrine has at any time depended on any of these translations, it is proper that the very best and most scholarly minds should be engaged—as they are—in the effort to secure the nearest possible approach to a perfect text and perfect translation of the Bible into English. The two critical sciences which deal with Bible study are said, with reason, to have called forth the most severe discipline to which the human mind has ever been subjected in critical study.

There may be readers of these pages who expected an affirmation that God in some supernatural way showed men just which books to select, dictating through all the ages the exact language of the original and teaching how to translate it free from error. It is a pity to disappoint them, but that is not the way it happened. The Bible rose to the place it now occupies because it deserved to rise to that place, and not because God sent anybody to prove its divine authority. Its answer to men's spiritual needs made it what it is. Like the blacksmith's anvil that had worn out a hundred hammers and still stood firm, it has outworn the attacks of ten thousand enemies. What is more significant, it has lived in spite of the folly of its defenders.

chapter 8

The Influence of
the Book

THE LONGEST telegraphic message that ever had
gone over the wires up to that time was sent from New York
to Chicago on May 20, 1881. Its 180,000 words were addressed to the *Chicago Times*, and the *Tribune* had a message
almost as long. The following morning both papers carried
in newsprint the four Gospels and the book of Acts. The
Times had Romans also. The next day both printed the rest
of the New Testament from copies sent by mail. Both proclaimed that they had performed the greatest journalistic
achievement of all time. They were right. Typesetting machinery was not yet in use. The *Tribune* employed ninety-
two compositors and five correctors, and completed the work
of taking, transcribing, correcting and setting up the text in
twelve hours.

On the same day this Revised Version of the New Testament was put on sale simultaneously in New York and
London. In New York 33,000 copies were sold locally and at
retail in twenty-four hours. Two million copies were sold in
Oxford and Cambridge before the edition was off the press. In
the United States, from May 20 until the end of the year
1881, thirty huge editions, mounting into millions of copies,

were sold. Nothing comparable had ever before occurred in publishing history.

Yet the power of the Bible to capture public imagination was demonstrated almost as impressively in our time. In the first three years following completion of the entire Revised Standard Edition more than three million copies were sold. Of course the King James Version is a best seller every year— and has been for centuries.

A few more figures give you some idea of the world popularity of the Bible. The American Bible Society *in a single year* issued 11,394,200 copies. Since 1816 the Society has published about 400,000,000 copies—*four hundred million!*

The New Testament, as we have seen, contains four short biographies of Jesus, each including some material not in any of the others. It has often been asked, "Since we have four, why not more?" Several of the apostles are supposed to have journeyed far and to have made converts in distant places. There is nothing inherently improbable in the thought that one or more of them may have written for his own converts in a distant region a little sketch of Jesus as he remembered Him. Such a sketch, though it probably would repeat much the four Gospels contain, might also give us a few more authentic incidents, perhaps one or two parables, or possibly a report of some discourse with Jesus hitherto unknown. It has been conjectured that such books were in actual existence.

Suppose that such a book, a new Gospel by Thomas or Andrew, were to be found in a far corner of Asia or Africa, and that some scholar of a reputation as well-established as that of Tischendorf, the discoverer of the Sinaitic manuscript, were to see it and pronounce it genuine. Suppose the authorities of the library or convent where it was found should say that scholars were free to examine and photograph and translate it, but that it must not be removed. What would happen?

The newspapers of New York and London, of Paris and Berlin, to say nothing of the universities in those and other countries, would charter planes to rush scholars and photographers to that place; they would run telegraphic lines and establish radio stations at the top of Mount Ararat or in the heart of the Sahara Desert. As fast as the book could be photographed and translated, it would be printed on the front page of every newspaper in the world and broadcast from the principal radio and television stations. It would appear in book form almost overnight, and would outsell all the current best sellers.

The author claims no gift of prophecy, but it may be noted that the sentences above (substantially unchanged from those written for the first version of this book) describe without too much inaccuracy and only a little exaggeration the excitement attending the finding of the Dead Sea Scrolls. And that discovery is nothing comparable to a new, authenticated Gospel.

In the eighteenth century that vitriolic genius, Voltaire, spoke of the Bible as a short-lived book:

> The Scripture was his jest-book, whence he drew
> Bon mots to gall the Christian and the Jew.

He said that within a hundred years it would pass from common use. Not many people read Voltaire today, but his house has since been used as a warehouse by a Bible society.

Thomas Paine, a much-abused man, said some good things which ought to be remembered to his credit, but in closing the first part of his *Age of Reason* he left this foolish summary of what he thought he had accomplished:

> I have now gone through the Bible, as a man would go through a wood with an ax, and felled trees. Here they lie, and the priests may replant them, but they will never make them grow.

Desperate efforts have been made to replant Paine's writings and give them again the influence which they were supposed once to have had. But if the Bible sells one single copy less for anything that Paine ever wrote about or against it, the sales reports do not show it.

If a modern American author writes a book which has a moderately good sale in this country, and a London publisher takes over an edition and sells it in England, the author thinks well of his effort. If his book is translated into German or French or Spanish or Italian or Russian or Scandinavian, he has reason to be proud. He is not likely to do more than this, and he may well congratulate himself if his novel or textbook or scientific treatise appears in a half-dozen tongues. But the Bible is extant in full, from the first verse of Genesis to the end of Revelation, in almost two hundred languages. In many other languages and dialects an entire translation is not yet possible. New alphabets had to be made; fonts of type had to be cast; difficult sounds had to be classified; grammars and dictionaries had to be prepared, so as yet in many dialects and mixed languages only the New Testament and some portions of the Old are printed. But altogether the languages and dialects in which the Bible, either in whole or in substantial part, is in the hands of the people number about 1,100, with a billion possible readers.

How difficult this rendering of the Scriptures into strange tongues has been may be illustrated by some of the odd printings in our language. We have the Breeches Bible, in which the aprons of Adam and Eve are thus translated; the Treacle Bible in which "Is there no balm in Gilead?" is translated "Is there no treacle (or molasses) in Gilead?"; the Bug Bible, with an infelicitous rendering of "creeping things," and the Wicked Bible, with the important word "not" omitted from the Seventh Commandment. If, with the finest scholarship and the utmost care, such lapses have occurred in our own tongue, imagine the obstacles to a clear understanding of the Gospel message among peoples where the language itself has to be reduced to writing by the missionaries before the work of translation can begin.

The man who invented the term "agnostic" was Thomas H. Huxley, the scientist. He did not deny, he merely did not profess to know. As in the early Christian centuries there were certain sects that professed knowledge and called themselves "Gnostics," he, admitting ignorance, called himself an "Agnostic." He was a member of the London school board, and the question was raised concerning the use of the Bible in the schools. It was generally supposed that he would oppose it. In *The Contemporary Review* for December 1871 he said:

I have always been strongly in favor of secular education, in the sense of education without theology, but I must confess I have been no less seriously perplexed to know by what practical measures the religious feeling, which is the essential basis of conduct, was to be kept up in the present utterly chaotic state of opinion on these matters without the use of the Bible. The pagan moralists lack life and color, and even the noble Stoic, Marcus Antonius, is too high and refined for an ordinary child.

Take the Bible as a whole, make the severest deductions which fair criticism can dictate for shortcomings and positive errors, as a sensible lay teacher would do if left to himself, all that is not desirable for children to occupy themselves with, and there still remains in this old literature a vast residuum of moral beauty and grandeur. And then consider the great historical fact, that for three centuries this book has been woven into the life of all that is best and noblest in English history; that it has become the national epic of Britain, and is familiar to noble and simple from John o' Groat's House to Land's End, as Dante and Tasso were once to the Italians; that it is written in the noblest and purest English, and abounds in exquisite beauties of a merely literary form;

and finally, that it forbids the veriest hind who never left
his village to be ignorant of the existence of other
countries and other civilizations, stretching back to the
furthest limits of the oldest nations in the world.

By the study of what other book could children be so
much humanized, and made to feel that each figure in
that vast historical procession fills, like themselves, but
a momentary space in the interval between two eternities,
and earns the blessings or the curses of all times, according to its efforts to do good and hate evil, even as they
also are earning their payment for their work?

Professor Huxley did not stand alone in this opinion. James
Anthony Froude, never accused of prejudice in favor of
orthodoxy, said:

The Bible, thoroughly known, is a literature in itself—
the rarest and richest in all departments of thought and
imagination which exists.

Said Frederic Harrison, an exponent of the religion of
Positivism:

The English Bible is the true school of English literature. It possesses every quality of our language in its
highest form. The book which begot English prose is still
its supreme type.

Lord Macaulay wrote:

The English Bible—a book which, if everything else in
our language should perish, would alone show the whole
extent of its power and beauty.

And Charles Dickens, writing to his son:

I put a New Testament among your books for the
very same reason and with the very same hopes that made

me write an easy account of it when you were a little child—because it is the best book that ever was or ever will be in the world, and because it teaches you the best lessons by which any human creature who tries to be truthful and faithful can possibly be guided.

So we might discuss the Book in its influence on literature and on law; in its contribution to the spread of the English language; in its inspiration of philanthropies, for, as Lecky said in *A History of European Morals,* it has "covered the globe with countless institutions of mercy, absolutely unknown to the pagan world." Volumes have been written, and will be, on every phase on this subject, but we do not need them. The monuments to the Book are all about us; every department of modern civilized life bears the record of its influence.

We could fill pages with more and more eloquent praise. Yet perhaps a few words written by Robert Louis Stevenson are enough. Try their truth when you next open the Bible.

I believe it would startle and move anyone if they could make a certain effort of imagination and read it freshly like a Book . . .